The History of Dress Series
Late Gothic Europe, 1400-1500

The History of Dress Series

General Editor: Dr. Aileen Ribeiro Head of the Department of The History of Dress, Courtauld Institute, University of London

Late Gothic Europe, 1400-1500

Margaret Scott

Mills & Boon Limited
London, Sydney Toronto

Humanities Press,
New Jersey

To my parents Charles
and Jean Finnie Scott,
for their unfailing help
and encouragement in
my every undertaking.

This edition first published in Great Britain in 1980
by Mills & Boon Ltd 15–16 Brooks Mews,
London W1.

ISBN 0 263 06429 8

and in the USA by
Humanities Press Inc.
Atlantic Highlands, New Jersey 07716

ISBN 0 391 02148 6

Designed by Mushroom Production · London

Map and diagrams drawn by Charles Rush

Filmset in Great Britain by
BAS Printers Limited, Over Wallop, Hants

Printed in Hong Kong for
the Publishers Mills & Boon Ltd
15–16 Brooks Mews, London W1.

Contents

List of Illustrations

Introduction

That this book has included the word 'Gothic' in its title, rather than simply stating the years which form its subject, is a reflection of how I wish to persuade the reader to approach the study of dress in northern Europe in the fifteenth century. Dress is the most immediate and silent form of expression for prevailing moods in a society, and consequently the most difficult to understand afterwards. So immediate is this reaction that to remark on it at all has the unfortunate air of a truism, but few of the 'sociologists' of dress, in talking of the effects of wars and economic crises on dress in our own century, have tried to examine how dress will react to external pressures *within* the formulae it has already set for itself. This is the point at which we run headlong into the problem of re-assembling the aesthetic values of five centuries ago. Because of either the reticence or the philistinism of fifteenth-century writers, we have few indications of how professional and amateur responded to artefacts in their private collections or in their parish churches. At best, we perform an academic exercize, taking many works to pieces and re-assembling them under various cross-references.

1,2. Information about dress can be found in unexpected places: these small figures support the moulding above a door in the house built by Jacques Coeur, financier of Charles VII, between 1443 and 1454 in Bourges, Central France.

That there was an intensely felt and overall aesthetic value governing the buildings in which people lived and the clothes in which they dressed, cannot be denied, and it is perhaps one of the periods in history when all areas of design were most closely linked. It would therefore be reasonable to expect to find some evidence that the same people were responsible for creating different artefacts in different media, but although craftsmen were often able to contribute to more than their one main skill, there is no direct evidence that painters had a greater role than tailors in the creation of 'fashion'. Perhaps the links between artisans subtly and unseen produced this coherent approach to design, and tailors themselves would have been unable to say whence came the ideas for the clothes they made.

The combination of this close linking of artisans and this lack of what, for want of a better expression, we shall have to think of as 'journalism' on the subject of design in the fifteenth century, means that anyone approaching the visual aspects of that century's civilization, is necessarily at the mercy of art historians:

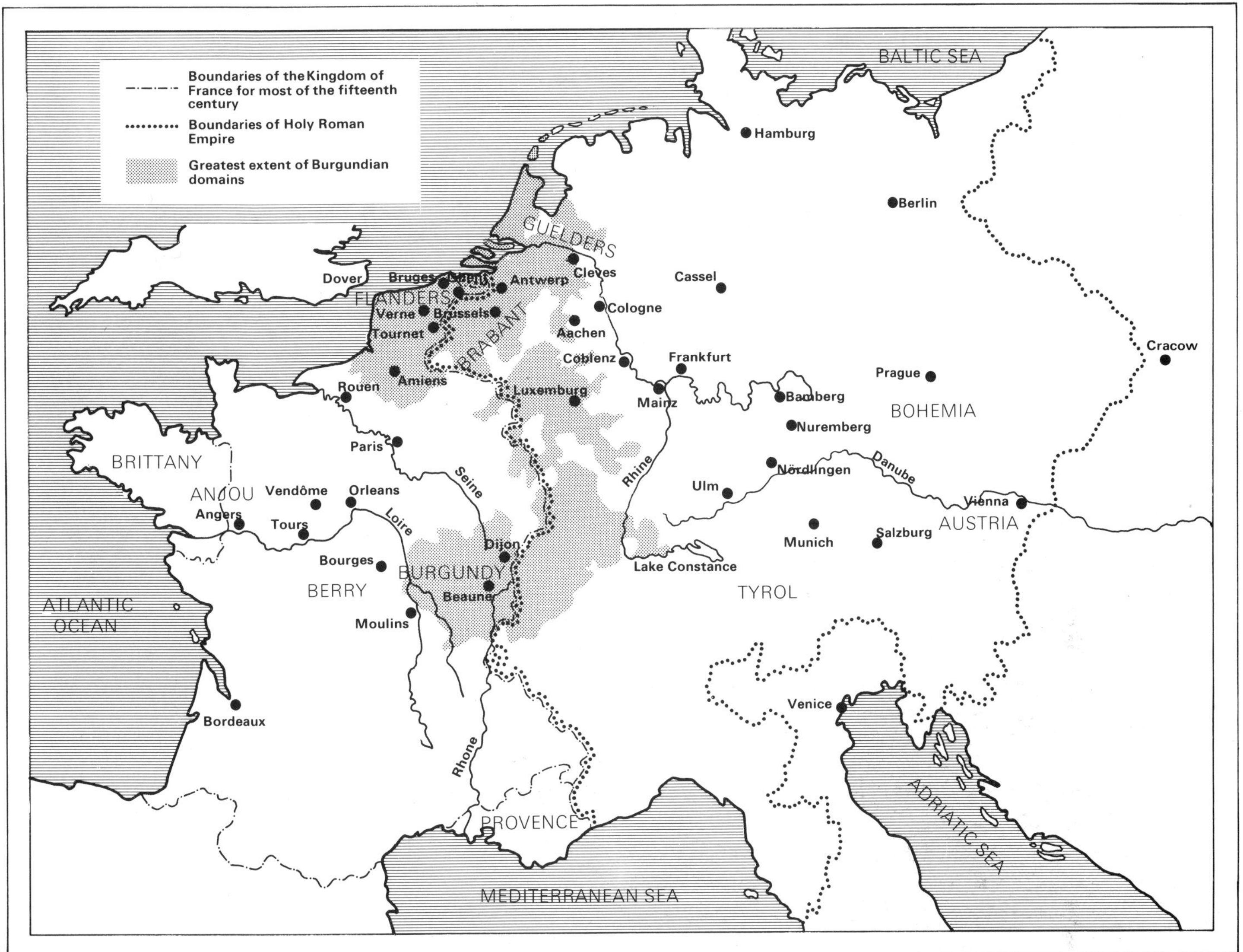

they provide us with essential dates from which to work outwards in our examination of dress, and it would be foolish and arrogant not to accord their efforts the place due to them in a study of the dress of the fifteenth century, hence what may seem to those interested only in the dress, too much art-historical information. This reliance on the art historian also means that virtually nothing can be said about dress in the British Isles which will have anything more than a parochial interest, as few of the painters or sculptors working there were of the standard of the Netherlands, France or Germany, and little solid study has been undertaken of the artefacts of this country in the fifteenth century. In addition, dress in the 'two kingdoms' was usually considered strange and old-fashioned by visiting foreigners, and there is little point in examining something so removed from the mainstream of fashionable developments.

In writing this book, I have attempted to weld together contemporary visual information with such documentary evidence as there is, mainly the wardrobe accounts of the French royal family and the Dukes of Burgundy, although there is a sharp

3. LEFT: Chances to observe the structure of dress are rare, but in this detail from 'The Martyrdom of St Hippolytus', probably painted by Dirk Bouts *c.* 1470, the saint's coat and hat have been thrown on to the ground, allowing us to see the V-shaped seam where the standing collar is attached, and the pleating at the top of the sleeves.

ABOVE: Map showing France, the lands of the Dukes of Burgundy and the Holy Roman Empire.

4. The most usual places to find depictions of how garments were put on or taken off are in illuminated manuscripts, where the illustrations often tell stories in some detail, but unfortunately these sources are usually kept in fairly inaccessible libraries. Here the Wavrin Master in his *Histoire de Girart de Nevers* (Brussels, Bibliothèque Royale, ms. 9631, f. 11) shows us the heroine unlacing her underdress as she prepares to take a bath, while her disloyal servant bores a hole in the wall to allow the villain to spy on her.

decline in the amount of readily available material in the second half of the century, which is inevitably reflected in the book: a thorough analysis of the unpublished wardrobe accounts of the period would require many years' careful study. In dealing with the documentary evidence for dress, I decided to keep, where necessary, to the original French names for garments, particularly when no adequate translation is available: the highly individual question of the spelling of words in the fifteenth century means that often the same word is spelt differently by the same writer on the same page, and I have tended to keep to the spelling of the original, simply because it is the original spelling. The accents which we are so accustomed to seeing in modern French did not exist, and although many of those who have published wardrobe accounts have added the accents, I have not done so when quoting from original documents, again because they were not present in the original.

Another, similar problem involves the translation of the names of individuals: English usage is quite happily inconsistent, translating a name but leaving a title in French, or vice versa. Finally, I decided to translate the most important names only, with the exception of Jean de Berry, who seems to have become firmly struck with that appellation in recent years, probably as a result of Millard Meiss's studies of the duke.

Finally, to all who love dress of any period: do not simply read books on the subject, but go to galleries and museums to see what your own eyes can tell you about hooks and eyes, buttonhole stitching and how the body is forced to behave inside its clothes. If this book stops groups of ladies who are being ushered round the National Gallery in London from being told that Giovanna Arnolfini is pregnant, then it will have achieved something.

1 The Lilies, the Leopards and the Lion: an historical background

The political history of France and the Netherlands in the fifteenth century is complex and unknown to most people. Because of its profound effect on the artists of the period, and hence on the visual sources, it must be outlined, albeit with a bias towards explaining the particular problems of a dress historian. Professional historians are asked to bear with what may strike them as too simple an account, while the uninitiated are asked to give some consideration to the pages which follow.

In 1356 Philip, the fourth and youngest son of John II of France, saved his father's life in battle, an action which earned him the nickname of '*le hardi*' (the Bold) and, in 1363, the Dukedom of Burgundy in eastern France. France had been at war since 1337 with Edward III of England, who was seeking the throne of France for himself, and the French king, by his generosity to Philip, was unwittingly laying the foundation of another power which would come to rival that of France itself. The death of the Count of Flanders in 1384 meant that his lands, in the north-east of France, passed to his daughter Margaret who was Philip's wife. Philip was thus ruler of a broken stretch of lands to the north and east of France, although he continued, like most of the aristocracy, to haunt Paris and the French court. Thereafter, the Dukes of Burgundy built up their lands and titles in these border areas by a judicious mixture of marriages and intimidation of relatives unfortunate enough to hold lands which the dukes thought they might acquire with advantage.

Charles VI of France (1380–1422) suffered from increasingly incapacitating bouts of insanity from 1392, and his uncles Philip and Jean, duc de Berry, acted increasingly on his behalf, with the help or interference of the king's brother Louis, Duke of Orléans. On Philip's death in 1404 his son John the Fearless inherited his father's titles but not, to his bitter annoyance, his father's position of power at court. His chief grudge was against his flamboyant and, reputedly, depraved cousin Louis of Orléans, a grudge which reached such proportions that in 1407 he arranged Louis' assassination, defending his action on the grounds of justifiable

5. One of many versions of a standard portrait of John the Fearless, Duke of Burgundy, 1404–19, in a bag-shaped hood and shoulder cape. This version belongs to the Louvre, Paris.

tyrannicide. This plea was accepted while he and his men were in Paris in force, but after they left, the queen, Isabella of Bavaria, and the Duchess of Orléans managed to have the verdict reversed. Theirs was a curious alliance, in that Louis was rumoured to have been the queen's lover, both women were foreigners who never gained the love and respect of the French people, and both had inherited a family feud.

An inventory[1] of the duchess's wardrobe in 1408, the year of her death, reveals a number of clothes in the style of her homeland, some recently acquired, which implies that even in matters of dress she refused to become French, while the queen had a German tailor called Hans.[2] To egg on the Orléans faction, the duchess seems to have made a point of appearing, with her retinue all in black, whenever she had the opportunity: it certainly impressed whoever gave this information to the chronicler Enguerran de Monstrelet.[3] The fighting between the two sides, frightening and disturbing as it was to the Parisians, had as yet no serious effect on the city's economic and artistic life.

In the winter of 1414–15 the Orléanists won a notable victory when John the Fearless was at last declared to be an enemy of the king and guilty of high treason. John was forced to abandon France for his northern lands, where the control of the king was replaced, very ineffectually, by the German Emperor. Free from king and emperor, John could act as he pleased, although at this time the only course open to him was to countenance and half-heartedly support the inroads of the English into France. In October 1415 the French were so badly defeated at Agincourt that in the following year John recognized the validity of the claim of Henry v of England to the French throne. However, in 1419, his treachery was fittingly rewarded. At a meeting on a bridge at Montereau with the sixteen-year-old Dauphin, whom he had rejected as his future monarch, John was, in his turn, assassinated, probably with the Dauphin's acquiescence, if not active connivance. The new duke, Philip the Good was, not unnaturally, forced into an even closer alliance with the English.

In 1420 Charles vi disinherited the Dauphin, ostensibly for his part in the murder, and recognized Henry v of England as his rightful heir, giving him Catherine of France as his wife. Henry was thus Charles's son-in-law and adopted son. Two years later, first Henry, then Charles, died, leaving a baby, Henry vi, as ruler of both kingdoms. To cement the Anglo-Burgundian alliance the young king's uncle, John, Duke of Bedford, the Regent, married Philip's sister Anne. About the same time, Philip deprived another sister, Margaret, of her dower lands, because her husband had taken the bizarre step of joining the Dauphin in his increasingly fruitless attacks on the English from his 'kingdom' in the unoccupied Loire valley. The effect which Joan of Arc had on the Dauphin's war effort from 1428 onwards is too well known to be detailed here, but it is perhaps less well known that

6. Jean de Berry sets out on a journey in the company of splendidly attired courtiers, including a young man to the right in a pink gown lined with white. The night sky has been stylized into swirling patterns of lights in this scene which was added to Berry's *Petites Heures*, *c.* 1412, by the Limbourg brothers. (Paris, Bibliothèque Nationale, ms. lat. 18014, f. 288v.)

when she was captured, it was Philip the Good who handed her over to the English and her death in the flames at Rouen three years later. Joan had attempted to re-unite Philip and the Dauphin, for the good of France, and it is therefore ironic that four years after Joan's death and twelve years after confiscating his sister Margaret's lands because of her husband's support for the Dauphin, Philip defected from the English cause and pledged his loyalty to Charles VII, by the grace of God, King of France, the same Dauphin who had also murdered John the Fearless. The alliance with England had not been happy, despite the importance of Philip's Flemish subjects of imports of English wool for their extensive weaving trade, and the death of Philip's sister Anne, Duchess of Bedford, in 1432, weakened the link with the English cause. Philip's change of allegiance and the death of the Duke of Bedford happened in the same year, 1435: in 1436 these events resulted in the expulsion of the English from Paris, after ten years of mastery.

Philip's return to the fold was only superficial. For years he had been free of allegiance of the French crown, and the German emperor had extensive territories enough to worry about (see map), without troubling to oversee too carefully what was being done in the west. (However, in 1416 the Emperor Sigismund had travelled as far as England in his attempts to speak to all the protagonists and persuade them to make peace.)

The Grand Duke of the Occident, as the Duke of Burgundy came to be known, had now at his disposal the wealthy cloth-weaving, agricultural and trading provinces on the edge of the North Sea, to which merchants from the north and south of Europe flocked as to a crossroads. With the wealth which these ventures engendered, the ruler and his subjects could afford to patronize the greatest artists in the land or entice others from their previous employers in the war-torn south.

Until *c.* 1420, Paris had been in the position of artistic patronage which Flanders was about to assume. For decades it had been the home of many workshops of painters, mainly book illustrators, whose long and proud history had seen the production of the most sophisticated examples of Gothic painting in existence and had counted many royal personages among their distinguished clientele. Bonne de Luxembourg (died 1349) had treasured the books they produced and passed on her love of them to her son Jean, duc de Berry (1340–1416), the most noted and omnivorous, but discerning, collector of his day. His inventories[4] reveal a dazzling collection of ever more splendid prayerbooks, precious stones, real and fake antique jewellery, gold-patterned velvets and everywhere the motifs of his favourite animals, lions, bears and swans, of which he kept live examples for his own amusement. Those who wished to placate his not overly charitable nature tended to present him with treasures for his collection, like the gold collar of little white enamelled bears

and rosettes with diamonds in them, which was given to him as a New Year's present in 1410.[5] Some of Berry's enthusiasm for fine objects seems to have been communicated to his nephew John the Fearless of Burgundy, as the two men continued to exchange illuminated manuscripts even after the murder of Louis of Orléans. (Berry had to take a position in the Orléans faction, as his son-in-law, Bernard d'Armagnac, was one of their leaders, whence their more usual title of 'Armagnacs'.)

With Berry's death, and those of his great painters, the de Limbourg brothers, in 1416, French painters lost one of their most discerning patrons and three of their most inventive colleagues. The rest of the decade, being taken up with repelling the English and controlling the outbreaks of civil warfare, presents a far-from-cohesive picture of artistic patronage, although some of the great workshops, like that of the Bedford Master, kept on working. The takeover of most of north and central France by the English in the 1420s does not seem to have impressed the capital's painters, most of whom seem to have drifted out of the English-occupied zone to new and more peaceful centres in the unoccupied west and south-east, either following the nobility into exile in the 'kingdom of Bourges' along the unoccupied Loire valley or, in the case of Netherlanders, perhaps returning whence they came, to reinforce already existing but possibly rather feeble workshops.

As the English were noted more for their vices, like excessive eating, drinking and swearing, than for their interest in anything as effete as 'culture', it is hardly surprising that artists looked round for other employers. (Joan of Arc's soldiers, who were forbidden to swear, nicknamed their English opponents the 'godons', from their habit of saying 'God damn'; in 1475, as part of an attempt to bribe Edward IV not to invade France, Louis XI gave Edward and his army the run of the city of Amiens and its taverns for three days, at Louis' expense. Later Louis' closest adviser, Philippe de Commynes, found English soldiers wandering drunkenly through the town or snoring off their excesses—a spectacle still pointed out to visiting friends by the inhabitants of French Channel ports on summer weekends.) The Regent, John, Duke of Bedford, ordered books from the workshop whose master is now called after him (the 'Bedford Master')[6] but otherwise more exciting developments were taking place elsewhere.

One of the prime targets for artists seeking a patron to replace Jean de Berry must have been the energetic and forceful Yolande of Aragon, wife of Duke Louis II of Anjou, titular King of Naples and Sicily. Yolande bought Jean de Berry's *Belles Heures*[7] after his death and patronized an associate of the Bedford and Boucicaut Masters, known as the 'Rohan Master'. In 1413 the ten-year-old Charles (later VII of France) was betrothed to Yolande's daughter, Marie of Anjou, and soon came to rely more on Yolande than his own mother. One of Yolande's sons was René, later to inherit his father's titles and become known as another seeker after things refined and rare, much like Jean de Berry. Later, as Dauphin, Charles lived in the area of Bourges and Tours, whence came Jean Fouquet (*c.* 1420–*c.* 1481), the first important French painter after the dispersal of the Parisian ateliers. Clearly, the existence, albeit a peripatetic one, of the court in that area would have attracted some painters to seek a living there, as would have the mere presence of Yolande and René. In later years René built up his own circle of artists, like the Master of René of Anjou and Nicolas Froment, in Anjou and Provence. However, the damage had already been done to a tradition of continuous centralized artistic activity, and the philistine son of Charles VII, Louis XI, did little to encourage artists or designers. The few artists of any eminence in France in the later fifteenth century were Netherlanders, or Frenchmen who had been trained in Netherlandish traditions. Some of the descendants of the glittering courtiers who had swarmed into Paris at the start of the century had been attracted to the more stylish court set up by Philip the Good, and with the shift in the centre of artistic output, the focus for fashionable dress probably swung north with the painters and the courtiers.

7. Catherine of Cleves, from her Book of Hours, *c.* 1430, in the vaguely Teutonic dress of the Northern Netherlands. (New York, Pierpont Morgan Library, M995, f. Iv.)

The culture of the court of Philip the Good is often called Franco-Burgundian, because the language of that court was French and Philip insisted he was not an independent prince, just the first peer of France. His father too had insisted that this was the case, on one occasion embarrassing his daughter-in-law, Michelle of France, by kneeling before her as his sovereign's daughter, who therefore out-ranked him. However, dress in the kingdom of France and the domains of the house of Burgundy does not display the uniformity which the epithet 'Franco-Burgundian' might seem to imply. It is chiefly in the dress of women that the differences lie, differences which become more marked as one progresses further north and east, towards the areas open to influences from Germany, where even men's dress takes on a different, occasionally bizarre, form. The rulers of Guelders and Cleves spent much of their time with Philip's court and therefore must have been quite aware of what constituted fashionable dress there. However, the products of the workshops of the Utrecht area around 1430 show ladies in dress which would have been considered old-fashioned by their counterparts further south. One of these ladies (illus. 7) was Catherine of Cleves, the niece of Philip the Good, and wife of Arnold, Duke of Guelders. One can only assume that when these rather far-flung aristocrats came to Philip's court they dressed in accordance with the fashions prevailing there, and that when they returned home, they 'went native' in their dress. It is inconceivable that any of these beings, whose wardrobe accounts reveal an inordinate degree of self-

8. OVERLEAF: A Fishing Party at the Court of Holland, regarded as showing the young Jacqueline of Bavaria standing fishing in the company of her mother, the older woman in the left foreground, and her father, Count William, the man on the right holding the baton. Other figures have been tentatively identified as including Jacqueline's four husbands. The extravagance of the gowns' trains and sleeves mark the wearers as aristocrats. This drawing may record a wall-painting produced late in her lifetime. (Paris, Louvre, Cabinet des dessins.)

absorption in matters of dress, would have paid any artist who had painted them in the kind of attire with which they would not have cared to be associated, and the pictures of Catherine, being in her Book of Hours, would most certainly have had to meet with her or her father's approval.

Thus even in some aristocratic dress native tendencies may well have been conflicting with those of the 'hot house' varieties produced at the ducal court. This conflict is true too of the languages of the Netherlands. French was the language of the duke and his civil servants and any native Flemish speaker who hoped to better his lot in life had to learn French to enable him to move from the one world to the other; no native French speaker seems to have felt the need to learn Flemish to enable *him* to move in the two worlds. (This linguistic dichotomy resulted, in the last century, in Flemish-speaking soldiers in the Belgian army having to obey commands in French from French-speaking officers, and in this century, in the centre of Brussels being nominally bilingual, although anyone who has tried to ask for directions on buses there, in French, knows how determined people can be to speak Flemish only, and vice versa.)

Further north Catherine of Cleves had her Book of Hours written in Dutch (or Flemish or Netherlandish, however one cares to define the language at this date) and the House of Bavaria, which had ruled Holland for several generations, published all their decrees in Dutch, despite their close links with the Dukes of Burgundy. The last princess of the House of Bavaria in Holland, Jacqueline (died 1436), was the daughter of William VI of Holland and Margaret of Burgundy, the sister of John the Fearless; through four marriages she had experienced life at the courts of France, Burgundy, and England and in provincial Holland. Apart from being a knight errant's ideal of a damsel in distress, with her battles against Philip the Good for her inheritance, Jacqueline provides an ideal example of how the Netherlandish nobility could live in several worlds. Her background was Dutch/Burgundian and she lived in France, Brabant, England and Holland. The cultural backgrounds of many of Philip's courtiers were probably as hybrid as Jacqueline's, and yet few of them showed any desire to be anything other than Burgundians, however each of them interpreted that idea.

Until Philip the Good's move to the north, there had been no such thing as a fully developed artistic circle round the Dukes of Burgundy as there had been in Paris, although Philip's father and grandfather had encouraged some artistic activity in Dijon in the shape of the sculptures and paintings for the family burial place at the Chartreuse de Champmol, a Carthusian monastery then just outside Dijon. Its remains today lie within the town, in the grounds of a psychiatric hospital. There one can still see the well in what was once the monastery's cloister, surmounted by extremely impressive and naturalistic figures of Old Testament prophets, over whom there used to be a carved Crucifixion, the work of the Dutch sculptor Claus Sluter between 1395 and *c.* 1404. Philip the Bold also commissioned massive statues of himself and his duchess, with their patron saints, for the doorway of the monastery church. In 1410 John the Fearless completed his father's tomb, which had been worked on from 1385 by various sculptors including, latterly, Claus Sluter and his nephew Claus de Werve. Painted and carved altarpieces were commissioned from Melchior Broederlam and Jacques de Baerze, but despite the extreme beauty and sophistication of all these works, they were conceived of simply as items to the greater glory of the House of Burgundy, in their home territories. They were not yet part of the trappings of the everyday life of the still Paris-based Dukes of Burgundy. It was not until the virtually independent power of the third Duke, Philip the Good, became clearly established in the north that a completely new centre of patronage and artistic activity could be built up around Brussels and Bruges.

9. The Birth of the Baptist, one of the later, Eyckian additions to Jean de Berry's *Très Belles Heures de Notre Dame*, made after the book had left Berry's hands and been split up. The Eyckian feeling of this scene is typified by carefully included details like the hinges on the cabinet, the whiskers on the cat which has just finished licking out a bowl, and the way in which the bed curtains loop between their supporting rings and then fall in smoothly undulating folds. (Turin, Museo Civico.)

There is little surviving evidence of the nature of the artistic activity which had existed in this area before the transfer of the seat of Burgundian power: panel painters had been working in Tournai in Flanders (e.g. Robert Campin, active from 1406, died 1444), and in Holland Jan van Eyck had been in the service of John, Count of Holland, from 1422 until John's death in 1425. It has been claimed and denied that during, or even before, these years Jan van Eyck worked on some of the unfinished pages of one of Jean de Berry's manuscripts, the *Très Belles Heures de Notre Dame*.[8] In 1425 Van Eyck went south and into the service of Philip the Good, who seems to have valued him very highly, not simply as a painter, but as a man of considerable discretion who could be entrusted with delicate diplomatic missions. The first date on a work by Van Eyck is as late as 1432 ('The Adoration of the Lamb' in St Bavo's Cathedral, Ghent) and the temptation to ascribe unsigned and undated works to his 'missing years' is obvious.

Until *c.* 1430, most of the artistic remains of importance to us are illuminated books, which can have a better survival rate than panel paintings or figure sculpture, simply because they could be locked away safely for years in cupboards in private dwellings: the paintings and sculptures were far more usually on display in public places like churches where they could suffer the vandalism of the casual visitor or the invading army, or the iconoclasm of the Reformation or the French Revolution. Documentary sources however are fairly widespread, as the disposal of every penny from royal and noble households was carefully recorded by the pedantic civil servants within them, and family records were important as indications of entitlement to objects or lands.

While France was making a successful, but disastrously expensive attempt to drive the English northwards to the

Channel, Philip the Good and his people grew wealthier and more self-satisfied; according to Philippe de Commynes, who defected from the service of Philip's son Charles to that of Louis XI of France, this self-satisfaction was largely responsible for the downfall of the power of the Netherlanders, who forgot that they owed everything to the benevolence of God. He criticized '*les despenses et habillemens et d'hommes et de femmes*' and their extravagant banquets; he was shocked by the bathing parties and other great festivities at which riotous and shameless women were present.[9]

The society of Philip's court was very much male-dominated, as his third wife Isabella of Portugal was far more interested in the splendours of the next world than in those of this. Philip's numerous mistresses kept themselves out of public attention, and although their roles were known at the time, they never exerted much political influence, and not one is mentioned by the chroniclers as being flamboyant or a leader of fashion. The inventors of all the bizarre female headdresses worn at Philip's court in the middle years of the century must remain unknown; the inventor of new shock tactics in dress at the court of Charles VII was his mistress, the notorious Agnès Sorel. The queen, Marie of Anjou, was a domesticated creature, who quietly and contentedly brought up her numerous children in the safety and tranquillity of the Loire castles, refusing to concern herself with power or the pleasures of life at court. As was the Duchess of Burgundy, she was deeply religious, and dressed in black. The matriarchal nature of her mother, Yolande of Aragon, passed her by completely, but reappeared in her niece, Margaret of Anjou, daughter of King René of Anjou and wife of the feeble-minded Henry VI of England. Ironically, it was at her brother's court that her rival Agnès seems to have attracted Charles's attention when she was an attendant of René's wife. In 1444 Agnès was an attendant of the queen and officially known as 'la dame de Beauté', a pun on 'the lady of beauty', Beauté being also the name of a castle given to her by the king. The Burgundian chronicler Georges Chastellain denounced the extravagance and indecency of her dress, as well as the way in which decent women were encouraged to follow her shameless example.[10] Charles was forty-one and Agnès about twenty-two; she was, in addition to being part of the cliché of older man falling for a much younger woman, the first of the royal mistresses who were to wield power in politics and taste in France, before her early death in 1450.

The king's lapse into some pleasure-seeking is understandable as for the first time since his youth he had the upper hand in the Anglo-French conflict: Paris had fallen to his forces in 1436 and by 1453 the English were driven back to Calais which they continued to hold well into the next century. France was devastated by the war, but France was *his* at last, and the main threat from the north-east, the Duke of Burgundy, was at least nominally on good terms with him. However, the years of constant warfare across the kingdom had left few men the chance of becoming painters of great skill, or of finding suitable patrons, as everyone who could bear arms was drafted into the army. Although Jean Fouquet and his assistants produced portraits and illuminated manuscripts, their work did not extend beyond the court circle, and Fouquet stands as an isolated outcrop of artistic activity at this period, working at Tours from 1448 until his death over thirty years later.

With the defeat of the English and the return of peace, more peaceful arts could have grown up again, with proper encouragement, but Charles died in 1461 and was succeeded by his remarkably philistine son, Louis XI. Louis exhibited a great lack of interest in his dress, which was felt by his contemporaries to be most unbecoming to a king, who ought to know how to dress to impress those around him: the king's preference for shabby clothes seems almost like an affectation when it is set beside the tastes of his courtiers. Louis' life was one of ceaseless physical and mental activity riding round his kingdom and weaving snares for the unwary rulers of neighbouring countries, whence his nickname of 'the Universal Spider'. He made a virtue of meanness, which should perhaps be called 'thrift' since it was meant as a good point, and his second wife, Charlotte of Savoy, was as self-effacing, domesticated and unexciting as his mother had been. Neither the king nor the queen wanted to be trendsetters, and after the death of a son in 1472, Louis was frightened into vowing never to touch another woman apart from his wife 'who was not at all one of those women in whom one could take great pleasure, but she was a good lady'.[11]

Louis shocked contemporary opinion by ordering that his tomb effigy show him clad, not in robes of state, but in his old hunting clothes, with his favourite dog sitting beside him. When the English threatened to invade France again in 1475, Louis took what, to his contemporaries, must have seemed the coward's way out: instead of arming the whole country and allowing more pointless battles to flatten the crops in the countryside, he bought Edward IV off with a great deal of money and annual pensions to the English nobility. The English chose to regard this money as tribute, but Louis must have been aware that he could stop paying these bribes whenever he felt France was strong enough to withstand whatever an English army might do to it. When Louis died in 1483, France was stronger than she had been since the beginning of the century, although still something of a cultural desert. Louis's lasting contribution to France was the recovery of many territories from the semi-independent magnates who held them: when Charles the Bold of Burgundy was killed in 1477, leaving only an heiress, Louis speedily removed the duchy and title from her control, on the grounds that they had been entailed to heirs male; René of Anjou was persuaded to leave Provence to

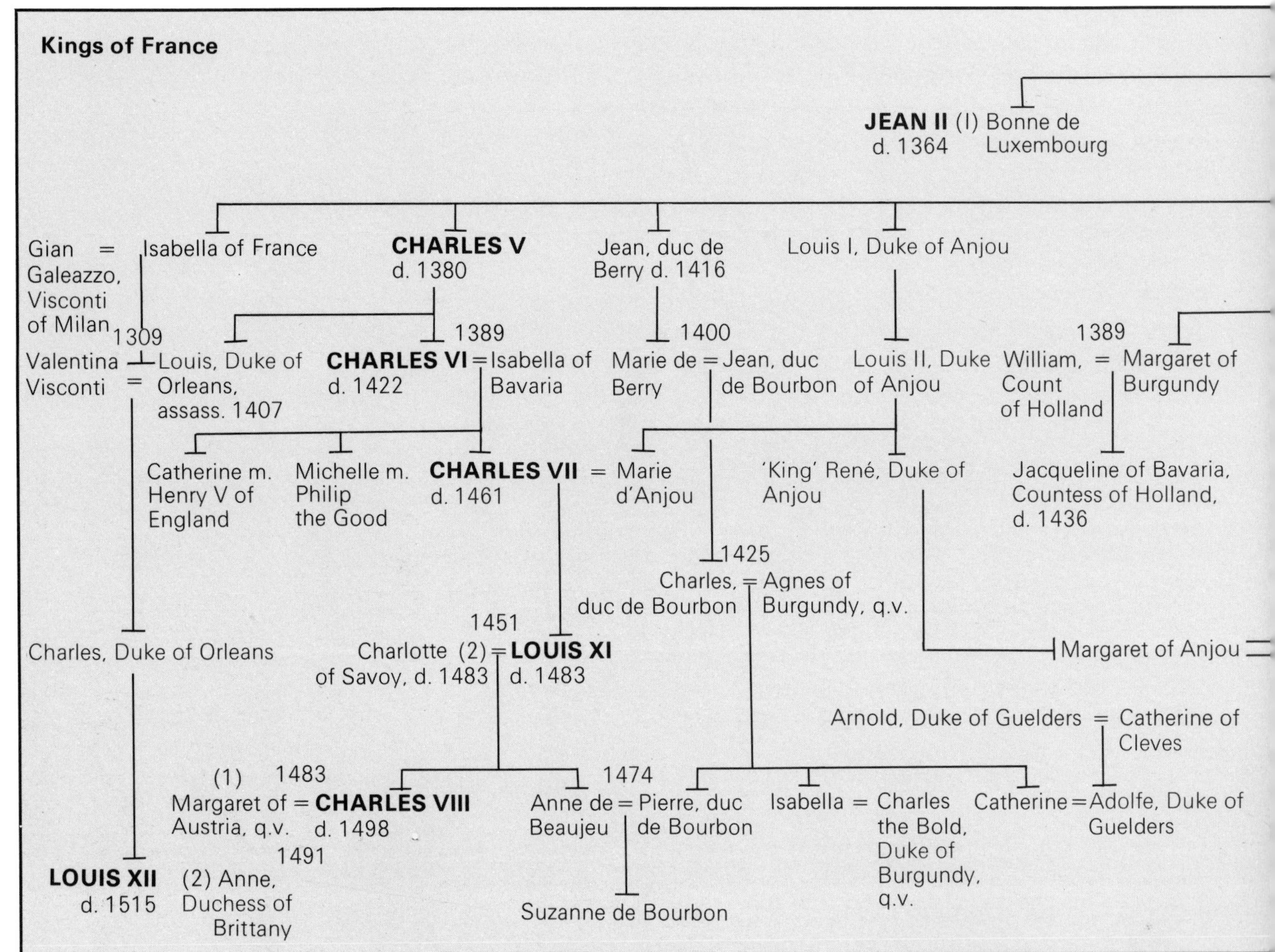

his childless nephew, on whose death the land would pass to the French crown, which it did in 1481; Louis' wearing-down of the Duke of Brittany ensured that the duchy would revert to the crown, which it did in 1491 when the heiress married Louis' son, Charles VIII.

However, in Anjou and Provence, Louis' uncle, René of Anjou, had kept a glittering court, at which he had held fantastic tournaments in the 1440s, and in the 1450s had written several allegorical works. The tournaments called for the most splendid accoutrements which the tailors and the painters could devise, as well as the most exotic textiles which merchants could import from the Middle East, while the literary exercizes called for illustration by a highly skilled painter, at one time thought to have been René himself. Certainly, René's lifelong devotion to aesthetics may lend support to this idea, but the painter, whoever he was, is now usually called 'the Master of René of Anjou'. Where this painter came from is unknown, but the solidity of his figures is as French as Fouquet's (see p. 48).

Thus the work of artists in France in the second and third

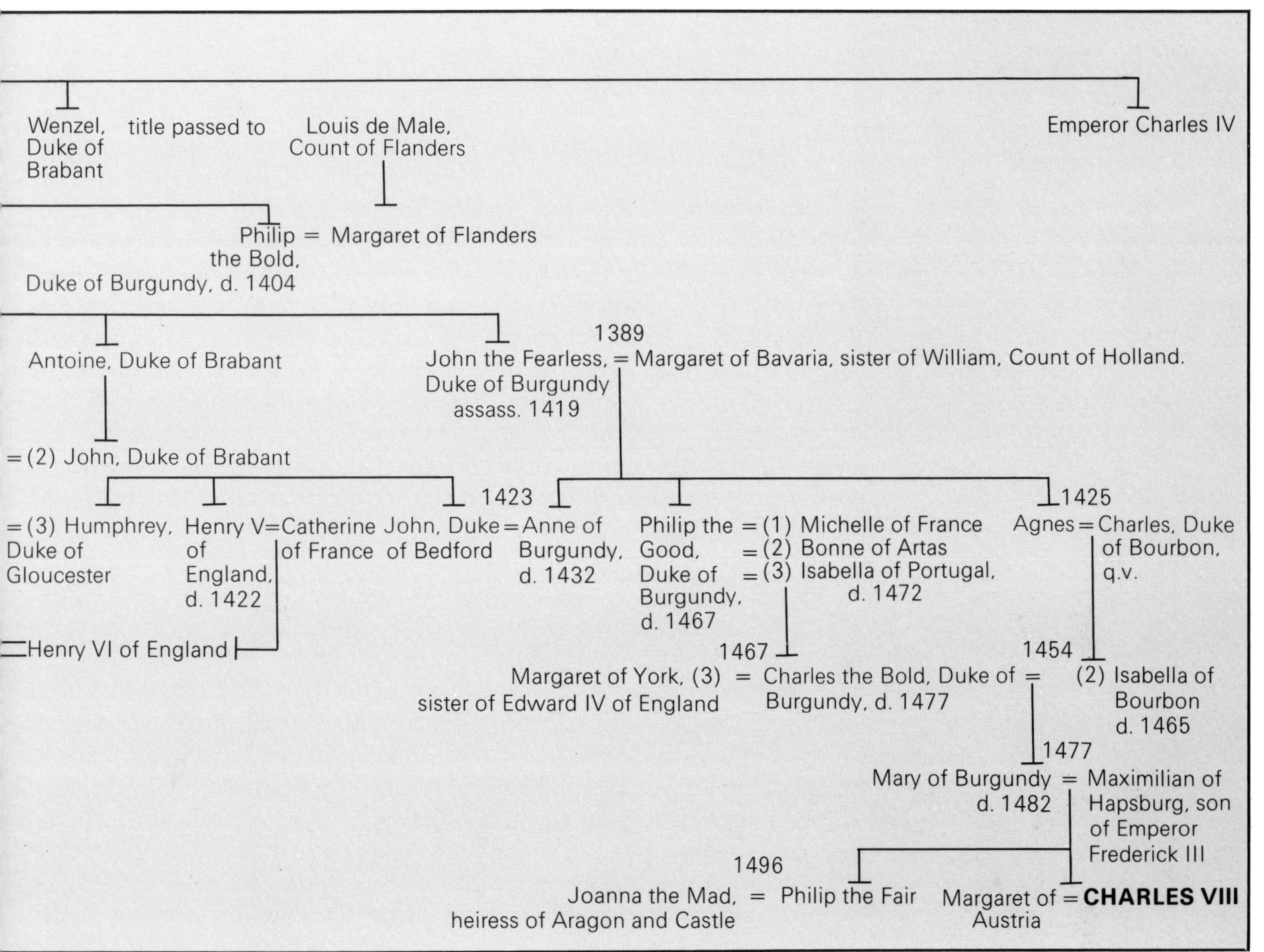

quarters of the fifteenth century is quite clearly based in the provinces, not in Paris, which must have hindered greatly the development of a coherent national style, since there was no central point at which they could meet regularly to exchange ideas. The René Master must have known Fouquet, as the Angevin court lived mainly at Angers and Saumur until 1471, when it moved to Provence. These two may have been the only French-trained masters of any consequence in France at this time, as other painters were certainly not immune to a high degree of Flemish influence.

The picture one builds up of French art after the fall of Paris in 1426 is of a patchy network of artists, setting up probably limited workshops in the few places which seemed likely to offer enlightened patronage, and it is consequently very difficult to trace every stage in the development of a fashion in dress, be it aristocratic and therefore national, or middle class and possibly more local.

Not until the end of the century does the history of the Netherlands become as troubled as France's. After making his

10. ABOVE: Philip the Good, Duke of Burgundy (1419–67) at prayer, from his Breviary, *c.* 1460, in one of the many black gowns which he wears in depictions and his wardrobe accounts. (Brussels, Bibliothèque Royale, ms. 9511, f. 398.)

11. RIGHT: Maria Portinari, an Italian living in Bruges and wearing Flemish dress, painted *c.* 1473, aged about seventeen, by Hans Memlinc. (New York, Metropolitan Museum of Art.)

peace with Charles VII, Philip somehow managed to keep as friends his ex-allies in England. His subjects in Ghent and Lille depended on the importation of high-quality wool from England and Scotland to make into the prized woollen cloths which merchants came to buy every year from far and wide. Peace with France automatically guaranteed friendly relations with Scotland, and it was as well to maintain them because of the valued trade with Edinburgh merchants. Trade with Scotland was typical of that carried out in Bruges with poorer countries in northern Europe: the Scots brought valuable furs, wool, salted fish and freshwater pearls, which they sold for cargoes of silks, spices and the occasional work of art. Looking for these furs and locally woven cloths would come Italian merchants, who had the silks and brocades which could not be produced in the North because the climate did not appeal to the silk worm. The position of Flanders, on the crossroads of the North, at the eastern end of the English Channel on the continental side, made it an obvious place to set up an international marketplace, and it is hardly surprising that the people did as Commynes said they did, and grew smug.

The duke had to be much more careful of the feelings of his subjects than he might have cared to be, although he was not particularly fond of the English: when he upset the citizens of Ghent in 1453, he had to face a revolt, which he succeeded in quelling, only to be presented shortly afterwards with a book, specially commissioned by the town, in which were listed all the privileges of the city, granted by his predecessors (see illus. 84). (Years later, in 1488, his grandson-in-law, the Emperor Maximilian, was imprisoned by the outraged citizens of Bruges, and had no real means of punishing them when he was finally released.) There had been a sizeable community of Italian merchants living in Paris before the English occupation, and later Bruges was to be home to several of them, along with representatives of the Medici bank, who acted as cashiers and providers of travellers' cheques for anyone journeying through and beyond Flanders. Although Philip's portraits suggest a haughty, self-willed man, his subjects were grateful enough to regard him as 'good', which his reign undoubtedly was for their prosperity.

Nor was trade the only thing which flourished under the good duke. Within a few miles of each other, towns supported great artists and their workshops, in a way in which the whole of France was incapable. Jan van Eyck settled in Bruges, where he died in 1441; his traditions were carried on by his quirky but unimaginative successor, Petrus Christus, who died in 1472–3. Hans Memlinc came from north-western Germany to settle in Bruges, and although his placid works seem to belong in the quiet canal-threaded town which Bruges is today, out of the tourist season, it is much more difficult to imagine them in the bustling trading port it was in the fifteenth century, and to which it

12. A fashionably sway-backed Philip the Good, surrounded by his hour-glass shaped courtiers, receives a copy of *Le débat sur l'honneur*, from the kneeling translator, Jean Miélot, probably shortly after 1450.

approximates still in the summer. The docility of Memlinc's art continued in the work of the Dutch-born Gerard David (died 1523), almost as though the art of Bruges was losing its vitality as the city lost its, when the silting-up of the port and of the attitudes of the inhabitants to outsiders slowly pushed traders northwards to Middleburg and Vere, outside Antwerp, where a ferociously and tastelessly Italianizing–Gothicizing theatrical form of painting was growing up to meet the demands of clients whose appreciation of art was doubtless as recent as their acquisition of money; the clothes painted by these 'Antwerp Mannerists' are as structureless as the people wearing them.

Although Philip's existence was almost as peripatetic as that of the French kings, his artists were able to maintain fixed residences and not suffer artistically because of it, mainly due to the compactness of the Burgundian territories. What happened in the duchy proper is less encouraging, as Dijon was still regarded as the ducal family's mausoleum. Almost the only time a Burgundian chronicler mentions Dijon is when someone has to be buried there. There was too much to be seen and done in the international atmosphere of Flanders. Because Flemish painting, with its luminosity, was greatly admired in Italy at the middle of the century, works were produced for export to Italian patrons, like the 'Sforza Triptych'. probably from the studio of Rogier van der Weyden, in Brussels.[12] Among the resident Italians who patronized the local artists were the Medici bank manager, Tommaso Portinari and his wife, Maria Baroncelli. Memlinc painted them shortly after their marriage in 1470, when Maria was fourteen;[13] he next painted them *c.* 1473 (illus. 11 of Maria). However, when they wanted something really impressive to send back to Florence, they turned to Hugo van der Goes, who produced the massive altarpiece, still in Florence, known as 'the Portinari Altarpiece'.

Great prestige was bestowed internationally on Netherlandish painting, and although the duties of most town painters were fairly humble, Brussels had managed to persuade Rogier van der Weyden to become its town painter by 1436, a post he occupied until his death in 1464, when he was accorded the privilege of a burial *within* the church of Sainte-Gudule (now the Cathédrale-St Michel). He painted portraits of the members of the ducal court, including lost originals of the duke and duchess, but his attachment to the court was not as personal as had been Van Eyck's. When he died, he was succeeded by a number of now anonymous disciples, including the Master of the Legend of St Barbara and the Master of the Legend of St Catherine, who must have had access to his files of preparatory drawings to have been able to produce the 'Melbourne Triptych' of *c.* 1490, which is crammed full of 'historical' portraits, as living and dead members of the ducal family watch 'The Miracle at Cana' or 'The Miracle of the Loaves and Fishes'.[14] (The study of history painting at this

Colour Plate **1.** In this scene the Limbourg brothers most nearly approach an accurate record of the prevalence of black in fashionable dress. The small boy on the left is probably wearing livery colours cleverly incorporated as dagging on his sleeves.

13. Before an assembly of Roman worthies in various aspects of exotic dress, the heroine and her anxious father stand with her two fashionably dressed noble suitors, as both young men argue their claims to the young lady's hand. (Brussels, Bibliothèque Royale, ms. 9278–80, f. 16.)

date and the sources available is fascinating in its own right.)

Although many fifteenth-century panel paintings are very small, having been designed for private houses or private chapels, they are crammed full of minute details, an approach which painters like Dieric Bouts and Hugo van der Goes happily retained when working on panels as large as Bouts's 'Justice' panels (3.23 metres high).

Such an attitude should have been conducive to the production of very fine manuscript illuminations, but unfortunately this is generally not so. A book may contain a good first miniature which is followed by indifferently executed scenes, betraying the existence of a highly organized workshop-and-retailer network, where a customer could get quality according to what he was prepared to pay. A book of the sustained quality of

Colour Plate **2.** Petrus Christus painted this scene in a goldsmith's shop in 1449. It is possible that the brown damask-patterned belt in the foreground had been brought in by a customer to have a buckle and tag made for it, not unlike those worn by Rogier's young lady (colour illustration 10).

14. One of many versions of a standard portrait of Charles the Bold, Duke of Burgundy (1467–77) in a figured velvet gown, from an original probably produced in the studio of Rogier van der Weyden. (Berlin-Dahlem.)

La fleur des histoires is rare (illus. 97): far more typical is *Le débat sur l'honneur* (illus. 12 and 13), where the first scene, of Philip the Good's court, for all its posturings, conveys admirably the eccentricities of current fashion, only to be followed by more mediocre pages in which less acutely observed fashionable dress is mixed up with all the usual signs for foreigners or the past, such as beards, strange hats, turbans, and short-sleeved gowns. In the 1460s the monotonous flashiness of the shop run by Loyset Liédet lends credence to Commynes' remarks about the overspending of the period: too much money was chasing too little taste. Into this overpoweringly superficial world came the Master of Mary of Burgundy, who gave back to Netherlandish manuscript painting the delicacy and delight in observation of plants and animals which it had been losing. Suddenly, apparently real flowers strew the edges of pages, with a dragonfly perched momentarily on them, so delicate that the flowers can be seen through its wings. Some may argue that *trompe l'oeil* painting in any form is in bad taste, but the Mary Master painted out of a true delight in everything he saw in a real garden, not the conventionalized garden which manuscript borders had become. He pointed the way to another generation of book illustrators, working between Ghent and Bruges, presumably on a highly organized and specialist basis, but with the introduction of printing presses all over Europe the demand for such elaborate prayer books fell away, as the less wealthy could buy books with printed texts in which only the odd illustration was added, or in which the illustrations were printed and coloured afterwards by hand or left plain. Illuminated books continued to be produced for the wealthy, but their very costliness compared to printed books tended to make them more luxurious than ever, as if to justify their cost—a rationale which leads only into a vicious circle.

The effect of the death of Philip the Good in 1467 is almost like a cliché, as the glory of the Burgundian court was really his achievement, and thereafter everything declined. His heir, Charles '*le téméraire*', translated into English, not as 'the Rash' as it should be, but incorrectly as 'the Bold', was a deeply devout, sober and very approachable man, who showed unfortunately increasing signs of mental instability towards the end of his life. His deeply pious and ascetic nature was probably inherited from his mother: neither of them enjoyed being surrounded by Philip's horde of illegitimate children, and Charles's refusal to behave as his father had done caused a great deal of disapproval and surprise among his contemporaries, who thought that princes *ought* to be promiscuous. In fact, only the need to secure the goodwill of England against France, which the new duke refused to acknowledge as his homeland, persuaded Charles to marry Margaret of York, the sister of Edward IV. After the wedding the couple lived separate existences, and rarely met. Margaret encouraged William Caxton, then resident in Bruges, in setting

up a printing press, commissioned many devotional works and applied herself to the well-being of her step-daughter; Charles got on with dreaming dreams of grandeur, through military conquest. He was quite unable to deal with the complexities of the mind of Louis XI of France, who preferred peace to war and the persuasion of money to that of brute force. As the marriage of Charles and Margaret was childless, and seemed likely to remain so, Louis began working out means of marrying the heiress Mary to a Frenchman.

In 1472, as Charles's instability grew, Philippe de Commynes fled to the service of Louis XI, never explaining the circumstances of his change of allegiance. Whatever Commynes' reasons, Charles was not a safe person to be around if one wanted to die in one's bed, as Commynes did, and not on some far-off battlefield deep with snow, as Charles did.

The person Charles admired most was Alexander the Great, whose father had also been called Philippe: taking this almost as an omen, he managed, between 1467 and 1477, to annexe enough territory to hem France in from the Channel to the Swiss border. Louis' concern for France was understandable, and his glee was almost fiendish when he heard of the death of Charles in battle in January 1477 (1476, old style): going to war was a summer pastime, and to invade Switzerland in the winter was an act of folly, not courage, making the French epithet for the last great Duke of Burgundy far more apposite than its English mistranslation.

The speed with which Louis annexed the duchy of Burgundy made it essential that a husband be found for the twenty-year-old heiress, who proved very difficult to please. The citizens of Ghent, thinking to assert themselves once more by taking advantage of her helplessness, tried to marry her off to the Duke of Guelders, once they had extorted further privileges for the town; the Dowager Margaret of York suggested that Mary marry her brother George, Duke of Clarence, but an English prince was not good enough. Finally Mary decided on the son of the Emperor Frederick III, Maximilian of Hapsburg, to whom her father had already betrothed her. Had Maximilian been a younger son, this marriage would not have had the consequences which it was to have for the Low Countries in the sixteenth century, but Maximilian was the emperor's heir, and any children of the marriage would inherit the lands of both parents. Maximilian had the military force to control his wife's subjects, but not the wit to gain their respect. It was fortunate for him that when Mary was killed in a hunting accident in 1482, Margaret of York was still on hand to undertake the upbringing of their two children, Philip the Fair and Margaret of Austria, to whose interests she was as devoted as she had been to Mary's.

In 1496 Philip the Fair married Joanna, the daughter and, ultimately, the heiress of Isabella of Castile and Ferdinand of

Aragon, providing for their son, the Emperor Charles v, the vast Hapsburg empire which controlled Spain, the Netherlands and what now constitutes Germany and Austria. When the Reformation took hold in the Netherlands in the sixteenth century, its supporters were bound to be in conflict with rulers in whose souls Roman Catholicism was as deeply entrenched as it was in Spain and Austria. Initially, Mary's inheritance had been secured to her by her marriage to Maximilian, but ultimately that marriage caused the political annihilation of her lands, at a time when their artistic heritage too was facing the threat of obliteration by ill-digested influences from the south of Europe.

A survey such as this can be baffling in its complexities, but it should enable the reader to see what the difficulties are in trying to assemble a continuous run of visual material and why gaps occur in the record. Written evidence exists at every point, but without its visual counterpart it makes tantalizing and unsatisfactory reading. However, the two forms of material welded together should and often do provide proof of what may otherwise only be suspected of being the explanation of a type or aspect of dress in a painting or a text. The greatest difficulty is groping one's way through periods of darkness where artists may have worked, although they have left virtually nothing behind them. The bizarre mixture of aesthetic splendour and personal cruelty against which the early years of the century were enacted in Paris produced some of the most delicate and beautifully illustrated books, most of whose creators appear suddenly, as if out of black holes on the edges of France, and then vanish almost as mysteriously. Where was there available training good enough to make Van Eyck a great prize for the Duke of Burgundy, and why is there virtually nothing before him?

Some of these points have been explained above, as the shifting of artists with the shifting of power and patronage: the English rule made Paris unattractive to painters who fled elsewhere, and those who chose to try their luck in Flanders probably came off best. Once artists could get a living in the Netherlands, it becomes much easier to build up a coherent picture of artistic training and tradition, concentrated as it was in a very small area.

However, the resilience of the two areas, France and the Netherlands, was quite different. As France became politically more powerful, the Netherlands as an independent entity ceased to exist. The art of both areas suffered in varying degrees from the inroads of alien, Italian art, the worst artists probably suffering most because they understood least the underlying concepts. French sources remain patchy for the first quarter of the sixteenth century, although the Netherlands continued to produce valuable and detailed sources of dress history, in the works of Quentin Metsys, Jan Gossaert and Hieronymus Bosch, as well as many anonymous masters.

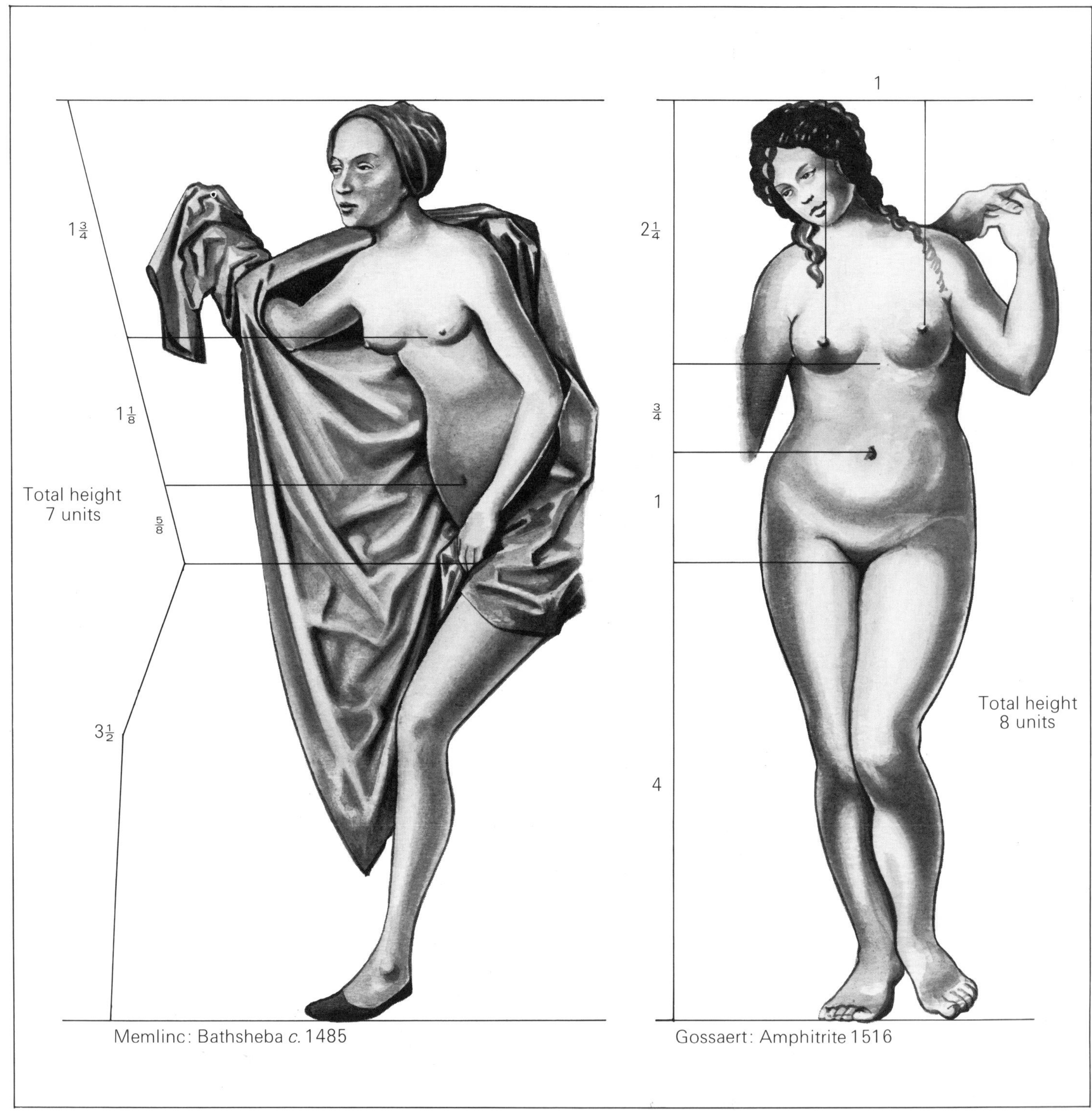

Memlinc: Bathsheba *c.* 1485

Gossaert: Amphitrite 1516

2 The Gothic Nude

To understand why people of any period look as they do *in* their clothes, one must first understand what they look like, or thought they ought to look like, *under* their clothes. If we look at our ancestors of five centuries ago, we receive a considerable shock, as human anatomy seems to have altered far faster than the laws of evolution would allow under normal conditions. Between us and the fifteenth century lie five hundred years of an artistic tradition for depicting the human body, particularly the unclad human body, which is based on the Italian Renaissance idea of human anatomy, which in its turn is dependent on the ideals evolved in Greece in the fifth and fourth centuries B.C.

Since the Renaissance, most artists have accepted these ideals of muscular, broad-shouldered men and full-breasted women with discernible waistlines and short, full hips: only minor alterations were imposed on these ideals by the whims of passing fashions. In addition, most post-Renaissance depictions of nude females have had an erotic purpose, no matter how intellectualized the artist may have made them by presenting them as classical heroines or allegorical figures, and we today can recognize that purpose. However, a survey of visual sources in fifteenth-century northern Europe presents us with a different concept of the human body, particularly of the female body, a concept so different that it is difficult to believe the evidence of documentary sources that this, to us, alien female form was actually considered highly desirable.

Although few of us would be able to give the mathematical proportions worked out for areas of the body in relation to each other by classical or classicizing (Renaissance) artists, most of us would instinctively recognize a marked departure from them. If we use the length of the human head as a measurement, we would expect to see men whose total height equals about eight head lengths, legs four heads, shoulders about two and a half heads wide and pelvises almost one and a half heads wide. Women would likewise have legs half their total height, with the use this time of the space between the breasts as a secondary measurement; this should also be the distance from the lower breast to the navel and from the navel to the thighs. Instead, we tend to find men whose height corresponds more or less to those canons, except that the legs gradually seem to take up more of the height, until in Memlinc's 'Martyrdom of St Sebastian' in the Louvre (*c.* 1490)[1] the saint's legs are actually four and a half times the length of the head. The shoulders of well-bred men are never more than one and three quarter heads wide until the very end of the century; the pelvis is usually slightly narrower than one and a half heads wide: in other words, it conforms better to modern standards. In addition, the bones within male and female bodies are usually depicted as very fine, with just enough flesh covering them to stop them from looking like near-skeletons, and this helps the artist greatly in his portrayal of slender, ethereal creatures. Virtually the only men who have heavy muscles are coarse, ill-bred louts, like the shaggy scowling executioner in the 'Martyrdom of St Denis' of 1416 by Henri Bellechose and his sadistically cheerful counterpart in the mid-century 'Retable of St George'.[2] (Public executioners, though essential figures, were nonetheless social outcasts, expected to live outside the towns they served, and as such could clearly not be expected to possess any refinements of person or personality.)

Women present a more radical departure from the classical format, in that their legs often seem to be less than half their total height. The distortion of the female body is aided by the elongation of the space between the lower breasts and the navel to twice the classical norm, as well as the placing of the breasts themselves very high up on the rib cage, towards the arm socket, and the omission of a definite waistline, in favour of a long swelling stomach: as Kenneth Clark said, 'By some strange interaction of flesh and spirit this long curve of the stomach has become the means by which the body has achieved the ogival rhythm of late Gothic architecture.'[3]

Almost the only literary description of male beauty occurs in a poem written by the French poetess, Christine de Pisan, 'Le livre du dit de Poissy'. In it, Christine describes a journey she made in April 1400 with some friends to see her daughter in the convent at Poissy, and on the journey the travellers entertained themselves with discussions about love. One of the young women tells of the knight she fell in love with seven years previously and with whom she had two happy years before he left for, and failed to return from, a campaign to help the King of Hungary against the Turks. This paragon was not yet twenty-four years old, tall and straight, with broad shoulders, long powerful arms and long straight hands, low hips and strong lean legs (with no veins!). His face sounds, by our standards, somewhat effeminate—he had hardly begun to shave his small round chin, his lips were red but not too full and his mouth small ('*n'ot pas jusqu'aux oreilles bouche grande*'); his nose was straight, with a long point; and his eyes, which did most damage to the lady's heart, were well-spaced, brown, laughing and gentle under long arched eyebrows and brownish curly hair.[4] Otherwise, a man's moral qualities were of far greater importance in making him attractive, or so most writers would have the reader believe.

Descriptions of ideal women are much more common, and tend to follow a somewhat monotonous pattern. Christine's heroines are usually blonde with well-spaced grey eyes; the Poissy poem mentions a girl with this conventional beauty with, in addition, little ears and '*grossete*' mouth, a white, round bosom, long thin arms, long fingers, long thin body, low hips, hollow back, round soft stomach, thin legs and little feet.[5] This picture is from the very beginning of the century, but the late fourteenth century poet, Eustache Deschamps, produced several poems which give a clearer picture of the type of ideal female beauty which evolved *c.* 1380 and which was to dominate the north of Europe throughout the fifteenth century. A compilation of the attractions of his heroines gives a standard of a young girl, aged about fifteen, with skin as white as the fleur-de-lis and rosy dimpled cheeks, fair hair, like fine gold, high forehead, little eyebrows, grey or green eyes, straight nose, round chin, red lips and compact white teeth. All this is set on top of high-set bosom, long arms, slender back, narrow waist, '*bon cul de Paris*' and little round feet.[6] An ugly woman is described as being as fat and round as an apple and as dark as an owl;[7] the dislike of dark colouring is repeated in a poem where he declares himself to be ugly, partly because he is short and fat, partly because he has black hair and could be mistaken for a Moor (his nickname was 'Morel', the Moor).[8]

With this information as a starting point we can now consider how closely the visual evidence matches the literary ideal. Male nudes are less widespread in art than female nudes and tend to be restricted to figures of Adam, the Souls at the Last Judgement, Christ and various Christian martyrs; Christ's emaciated body is perhaps an unreliable source of visual information, as its appearance may be influenced by the artist's desire to convey asceticism and physical suffering, but Adam and the Souls are much more likely to be representative of the ideal form as, respectively, the founder of the human race and the mass of humanity. Female nudes are somewhat more widely represented, as Eve, the Souls at the Last Judgement, and in occasional scenes of voyeurism, of Susanna and the Elders, of David and Bathsheba, both of which have the sanction of Scriptural authority to make them respectable subjects for depiction, and the more overt scenes of ladies in their baths being spied on by young men. Even 'respectable' painters like Jan van Eyck and Rogier van der Weyden seem to have produced paintings of this type, although they are now lost.[9] One final word of warning is required. Perhaps nowhere is it easier to be misled by the minutely detailed and almost photographic technique employed

15. The God of Love brings his children to the aged poet Guillaume de Machaut, who leans eagerly but somewhat arthritically out of his study to welcome them. Both the God and Machaut wear draped clothing over the half-tailored sleeves of *c.* 1370.

by Van Eyck and his successors than in the depiction of human beings. This technique can persuade us that what we see in a painting is a completely objective view of reality, simply recorded by the painter and presented for our enjoyment. In fact, in the depiction of human beings, clad or not, few artists can escape completely from the aesthetic ideals of their time, to present us

16. A fashionably dressed procession from Jean de Berry's *Très Belles Heures de Notre Dame*, *c.* 1380.

with recognizably living people. Holbein managed it in his portraits, but Goya, while knowing one thing about anatomy, is confused into expressing another by transferring the effect of the high-waisted dress of his 'Clothed Maja' on to the body of his 'Naked Maja'. Instead, most artists conform more or less closely to purely contemporary canons, presenting us with a highly *subjective* view of reality. Thus, faced with the depiction of the young (probably teenage) Giovanna Arnolfini (illus. 59) in what is presumably meant to record a 'perfect marriage', Van Eyck presents us with a lady whose demureness and passiveness match those of his young, idealized Virgins: when he portrayed his own wife (illus. 64) we can see behind the bland insipidity imposed by the contemporary fashion for eyebrow-less (and hence, expressionless) female faces, to a not-so-young, but very determined woman.

Let us now turn to a more detailed examination of the visual evidence. The female ideal of high-set bosom and protruding stomach seems to have become important *c.* 1380, when the most serious problems in dressmaking had been solved, those problems being the cutting of garments to fit tightly without wrinkling and the setting of sleeves into curved armholes. The two phenomena must be connected, as must the curious stance of curved spine with head thrust forward which appears very clearly in early fifteenth-century figures of Eve.

From the 1370s comes a scene (illus. 15) of the God of Love presenting his children to the poet Guillaume de Machaut:[10] Love's son wears a hip-length doublet which fits badly around the top of his arm, as do the dresses of the two girls. Both sexes have lumpy chests, which make them look like badly stuffed teddy bears, and the girls in their wide-necked dresses stand as upright as their brother. Their hair is plaited at the sides of their heads, but it does not hide their faces.

By about 1380 things were beginning to change: the *Très Belles Heures de Notre Dame*, begun *c.* 1380 for Jean, duc de Berry,[11] contains some scenes where human anatomy seems to have altered considerably, mainly because of the external demands of a new type of dress. The men have longer toes, slightly flatter chests and shorter doublets, all of which are minor alterations beside those which have taken place in the women (illus. 16): female heads jut forward under deep-brimmed hoods which conceal the face completely from the side, and the spine has developed a curve as the stomach is thrust forward, the shoulder blades out and the bust tucked in. The cause of this sudden deformity would appear to be the newest and ultimately favourite weapon in the female wardrobe—the plunging neckline. Now the previously wide neckline has also lowered to reveal for the first time to a startled male population, the female bosom with a minimum of covering. The poet Eustache Deschamps denounced this fashion, as it drove many men to think about rape; older women sewed two bags into the front of their undershirts, into which they put their sagging breasts before lacing themselves up tightly, and each verse ends with a cry which reflects how torturous the whole process must have seemed '*Dame, aiez pité de tettine!*'[12] Even at the end of his life (*c.* 1406) Deschamps was still denouncing wide necklines, which, he said, married women used to make other men want them.[13]

The wearing of such open necklines must have caused women *c.* 1380 considerable discomfort, possibly more mental than physical; after all, clothes may actually be positioned quite securely on the body (and the tightness of the bodices in illustration 16 would presumably have ensured that) but strangeness of attire can make the wearer feel awkward and uncomfortable. Doubtless women feared that the new wide *and* low necklines would reveal even more than they were intended to, and consequently adopted a stance which would minimize the danger. The thrust-back shoulder blades would have given two extra points over which to stretch and catch the neckline, while this action of itself would inevitably cause the bust to look smaller as the chest appeared concave between the points of the shoulders. Hunched shoulders lead easily to a curved spine, which tends to lead to the protruding of the pelvis. Add to this the likelihood of most women of childbearing age being pregnant every year, with the effect of constant pregnancies on their figures, and we have a possible explanation of the basis in reality from which evolved the fifteenth-century ideal female figure: aesthetic ideals have always been hampered by the resistance of reality.

All women seem to have been expected to display a pronounced 'pregnant' stomach, regardless of their marital status. The girls who represent the zodiacal sign Virgo in calendar miniatures, such as in the Duke of Berry's *Belles Heures* (by 1409) and his *Très Riches Heures* (by 1416) and the virgin-martyr St Catherine in the former manuscript, seen almost nude on folios 17 and 17v, all conform to the type described by Deschamps and Christine de Pisan, even to their blonde and somewhat insipid prettiness.[14] The desirability of that type is shown by two scenes in the *Belles Heures* involving temptresses: on f. 186 two girls lounge elegantly before the hermit-saint Jerome, causing the saint to turn from the church before which he kneels and from his prayers, and on f. 191 a beautiful woman sent to seduce a Christian youth crawls languidly over him as he bites off his tongue and spits it in her bland face (illus. 39). Similarly, no-one could have understood Adam's willingness to be led astray by Eve, had she not been worth the threatened punishment, and the Eve in illustration 17 stands before God, head thrust forward, spine curved, with long hips and a somewhat pregnant stomach over short legs.[15] How little her figure differs from that of a woman on the point of giving birth can be seen by comparing it to that of Pamphila in labour of *c.* 1412,[16] and how completely female one artist felt the whole outline to be, together with its swaying hips and drapery, can be seen in the *Livre des merveilles du monde*, which John the Fearless of Burgundy gave to Jean de Berry in 1413 as a New Year's present. This book told of the adventures of Marco Polo, his father and his uncle; in Chaldea they came across men dressed as women, and women dressed as men. The painter simply transplanted female heads on to the trousered, pot-bellied figures with upright bearing he usually reserved for Oriental males in the manuscript, and bearded male heads on to sway-backed bodies with swollen stomachs in long, close-fitting dresses (illus. 18).[17]

This form continues unchanged into the 1430s; the virgin saints in the Van Eyck brothers' 'Altarpiece of the Adoration of the Lamb' in Ghent, finished in 1432, lurch out from behind some foliage,[18] and Jan van Eyck's Giovanna Arnolfini in 1434 shows the swollen stomach exaggerated by the fur-lined skirt of her gown which she holds in loose folds over her body. Much nonsense was talked about this lady and what she and her husband had possibly been doing six months before they eventually got round to marriage, by art historians in the nineteenth century, who were too blind to make use of the rest of the evidence under their noses. Eve in the Ghent 'Altarpiece'[19] shows very clearly what her companions would have looked like without their best dresses and what Giovanna Arnolfini looked like two years later under her elaborate green gown (illus. 59).

During this period men have fairly solid, if slender, torsoes, and rather too elegantly slim legs, as in the *Très Riches Heures* Adam (illus. 17). On the whole, fashion for men from *c.* 1400 allowed them to cover their legs to mid-calf or floor level, and the

pronounced vertical folds on their slightly high-waisted gowns would help to create an illusion of length of leg without the use of very long toes on their shoes, as had been the fashion *c.* 1390 and as was to become the fashion again in the 1450s and 1460s. The neck was elongated in both sexes by the simple expedient of moving the hair line up the back of the head and shaving the head to half way up. Otherwise, male anatomy is not remarkable in this period.

Around 1440 it is possible to detect a slight change in the stance, and hence the outline, of women. The neck is no longer thrust forward quite so abruptly and the shoulders are sometimes drawn back instead of being hunched forward. The bashful upward glance of Giovanna Arnolfini is replaced by a more direct gaze as the head is thrown back, although the spinal column does not achieve an unbroken diagonal. Van der Weyden's 'Triptych of the Last Judgement' at Beaune,[20] painted between 1443 and 1451, contains men with emaciated arms and legs, and women so slender, apart from their vast middles, that all are helpless as they fall into the pit of Hell and drag others with them as they attempt to grab hold of anything to prevent their descent: their matchstick bodies are quite without power. Fairly untypically, not one of the Resurrected wears anything to indicate his or her rank on earth: all the more poignantly, they go to Heaven or Hell without any comfort or protection from familiar objects. The lack of devils to torment the Damned adds to the horror of their

17. LEFT: The Limbourg brothers depicted the Garden of Eden as a walled garden set round an extremely large Gothic fountain, and entered by a Gothic gateway. After Eve has yielded to the persuasiveness of a golden-haired serpent resembling herself, she and Adam are driven forth by a flaming red and gold angel into a barren landscape of hills and sea.

18. ABOVE: The inhabitants of Chaldea as Marco Polo encountered them and as they were depicted by one Parisian illustrator, who had never seen trousered women in his life.

being sucked, completely defenceless, into eternal torment through their own inner evil. On the other hand, this same slightness of form makes the Blessed seem ascetic and ethereal enough to be fitting inhabitants of the Heavenly Kingdom. The original psychological impact of this depiction, where only the impassive St Michael, weigher of souls, is splendidly clad, must have been beyond our 'enlightened' comprehension. However, this diminishing of the bulk of the male body and its apparent lengthening must not be confused with an actual lengthening of it from its eight head-lengths formula. There is a useful contemporary parallel in the scene of the presentation of Jean Wauquelin's *Les chroniques de Hainaut* to the Duke of Burgundy, after 1446 (illus. 74), where men's gowns are beginning to rise to just above knee level to expose what were probably meant to be elegantly slender legs, which were artifically lengthened by the wearing of shoes or boots with pointed toes. Now that women's anatomy is slightly less bizarre, the urge to distort seems to have turned its attention to men.

Netherlandish artists seem to have fallen prey more readily to this obsession for underfed male bodies than French artists did, as witness the scene of the trial of the duc d'Alençon in Vendôme, painted in or shortly after 1458 by Jean Fouquet (illus. 91), and the many scenes painted in the 1460s by the Master of René of Anjou. The trial scene is figured with men who conform to the fashion for short gowns and long pointed toes, but remain fairly solid and stocky in spite of the visual trickery of fashion. The Master of René of Anjou produces even stockier figures, who stomp their way very determinedly and prosaically across the landscape, quite at odds with the elegant world of myth which they inhabit. However, there is an advantage to be gained from these figures in that they bring the world of myth and allegory nearer to reality than any over-refined ideal characters could have done.

The Netherlanders continued to play with altered human anatomy, particularly in manuscript painting, which seems to have demanded more and less realism at the same time than did many panel paintings: more in that most manuscript pictures involved complex scenes set indoors or out-of-doors where even the most elaborately hatted lady could be reduced to a manageable size against her surroundings, and her attire depicted as it was every day, which a portrait painter, in mainly half-length portraits, could not always do; less in that manuscript paintings often served the purpose of enlivening otherwise fairly dull romances and histories, into which it would have been legitimate to introduce exaggeration towards the fashionable ideal in the depiction of their heroic characters. Most secular manuscripts are fundamentally nothing more than very costly, very classy strip cartoon books, and the rationale of the illustrators of such phenomena does not seem to have altered much in five centuries.

The vastly underrated and under-employed Master of

Colour Plate **3.** The Master of 1456, portrait of an unknown man. Concentrating on the head and shoulders reinforced the 'uphill and downdale' outline of men's dress of the 1450s created by high-standing sleeve heads and collars.

Wavrin was the most economical of the manuscript illustrators, producing pen and wash drawings which caught the essence of the fashions of the 1460s, without getting trapped into the over-elaboration of many of the works produced by a favourite illustrator of the Burgundian court, Loyset Liédet. Liédet too manages, underneath the superficial glamour of his work, to convey the aims of the fashion-conscious in these years, with ladies of too-high foreheads and men of too-long and too-slender legs and feet.

In panel painting these exaggerations in male anatomy can be matched with Dieric Bouts' 'Damned' in Lille, (possibly of 1468) where, against a sky lit to an eerie green and gold sunset by the fires of Hell, the pale bodies of the lost are flung to an eternal night of torment by grinning black and red devils, who, long before the evolution of the concept, clearly derive considerable job satisfaction from their tasks.[21] Commissioned from the same painter in 1468 and delivered by 1473 is the scene of 'The Ordeal by Fire' from the 'Justice of the Emperor Otto' panels (illus. 115). There, elegant men, of impossibly slender and elongated limbs stand around the Emperor's throne; if the Emperor himself were to stand up, his head would go through the roof. (The abnormally wide shoulders of the men do not derive, as yet, from any change in the ideal of the body underneath.) The attenuation of the legs could be aided by the spiky forms of Northern armour, as in Memlinc's St Michael in the 'Danzig Altarpiece' (by 1473), where the armour-clad warrior saint stands on a small rock, over whose edge the long-pointed toes hang down.[22]

Had the attenuation of only the lower half of the male body continued a few years longer, artists would have been in danger of producing figures whose ability to hold themselves upright would have been in grave doubt. Generally, in the 1470s there was a tendency in male dress away from the top-heavy bulk of pleated and padded shoulders and sleeves, to a smoother, narrower vertical line, from which most of the bulk of the old gowns disappeared. The initial result of the loss of the wide-shouldered look was to produce some very tall figures indeed, as in Engelbert of Nassau's copy of Quintus Curtius's *Historia Alexandri Magni* (illus. 110) and in a drawing of a presentation scene now in Washington DC.[23] It is perhaps significant that both of these works are Netherlandish, in view of the remarks made above about the greater realism of French art at this date, and Memlinc's almost mannerist elongation of vertical forms, particularly in his 'St Sebastian' of *c.* 1480. Left to his own devices to produce the face of a holy or historical person, Memlinc would usually fall back on his preferred facial type with its long thin nose, as witness countless Madonnas and saints. Apparently, before painting Martin van Nieuwenhove's real face (illus. 131), Memlinc 'blocked in' his head in accordance with his own ideal, complete with long thin nose.

Colour Plate **4.** In his wings for the 'Bladelin Triptych', apart from using the more obvious extravagances of jewels and cloth-of-gold, Rogier has dressed one courtier in violet, a fairly unusual colour when worn over other garments of yellow shot with pink. Shot colouring was also unusual in the fifteenth century.

19. The Last Judgement of more 'Italianate' men and women as depicted by the Master of the Joseph Sequence, *c.* 1500.

After this brief period (perhaps less than ten years) of extreme attenuation in dress and skeleton, first the outer, clothed appearance and then the actual structure of the male body change rapidly. From *c.* 1480 onwards, gown lapels grow wider and sleeves grow bulkier and looser, until men's gowns seem to be several sizes too large for them. Martin van Nieuwenhove is perhaps thought of as having a Gothic type of body beneath his clothes, but one cannot be so sure of the appearance, a few years later, of the so-called 'Charles VIII' (illus. 144) where the gown sleeves twist in a confusing tangle round his arms, while the gown is in danger of slipping off because of its size and uncontrolled bulk.

The effect of this outward squareness on the concept of the body underneath can be gauged by comparing these men with the Resurrected in the 'Last Judgment Triptych' by the Master of the Joseph Sequence (formerly called the Master of the Abbey of Affligem), painted sometime during the married life (1496–1506) of Philip the Fair and Joanna the Mad (illus. 19).[24] There the men are much more heavily built than Van der Weyden's or Bouts' Resurrected, and even Philip, who appears in a wing of the altarpiece, seems, under his cloak and armour, to be a little more solid than he might have appeared ten or fifteen years earlier. (Joanna and the women will be considered later.) By the time Jan Gossaert came to paint 'Neptune and Amphitrite' in 1516,[25] the classical canon of more heavily built, muscular men was quite acceptable to artists who had visited Italy to see for themselves the messages of Italian Renaissance art. Memlinc and his followers had known of Italian ideas only at second hand, and the results of their attempts to introduce them into their own work are usually fairly horrendous, as swags of plant life and *putti* intervene unhappily across the tops of classical columns in otherwise Northern surroundings, inhabited by northerners clad in Gothic taste (e.g. Memlinc's 'Resurrection' in the Louvre, where a Gothic Christ steps forth from the tomb under an Italianate framework very similar to that beneath which a donor kneels before the Virgin, in Vienna.[26])

In twenty years the ideal male figure had changed from Gothic to classicizing, but the corresponding change in the female ideal took longer to effect. Memlinc painted 'Bathsheba', emerging from her bath, *c.* 1480 (illus. 20):[27] although she still conforms to the Gothic ideal, the stomach is slightly less pronounced and the rib cage, where it joins the stomach, gives a hint of acceptance of the waist's natural level. This is matched by the way in which her attendant's dress seems to continue, unbroken by the line of a high-set belt, towards the natural waistline. Both women correspond to Memlinc's long-nosed ideal. (King David was not the only person who enjoyed looking at naked ladies: J. Huizinga in *The Waning of the Middle Ages* cites several examples of processions which featured nude women under the guise of

classical goddesses, who were clearly the highlight of these events.[28] How naked these ladies really were is open to conjecture, not so much because of their modesty as because of the relative inclemency of Northern weather.)

Women became as emaciated as men in the 1470s, but whereas men began to 'square off' in the 1480s, women remained confined in very close-fitting clothes into the 1490s and early 1500s. In her portraits from the 1470s Maria Portinari seems flat-chested (illus. 11), as do the donatrices of the 'St Hippolytus Triptych' (illus. 124) and the 'Donne Triptych' (illus. 123), as well as the female saints in the latter. The nude Eve in the Vienna triptych[29] has almost no bosom at all. Both portraits of Barbara van Vlaenderbergh (see p. 190) reinforce the impression, as though women's clothes were flattening what little bust fashion had previously allowed them. Certainly, neither Memlinc's Eve nor Bathsheba could be described as a large lady compared with even Van Eyck's Eve.

The compression of the female torso continued into the 1490s: good comparisons of the bulk of men and the slenderness of women can be seen, in France, in the portraits of Pierre de Bourbon and his wife Anne de Beaujeu, *c.* 1493 (illus. 141 and 142) and, in Flanders, of Jan de Sedano and his wife (illus. 133 and 134). The replacement of the spiky V-neck by a squarer neck in the later 90s undoubtedly helped the change in women's dress, but very few women looked as square as men even by 1510: Joanna the Mad retains the Gothic stomach but also acquires a bust again, and the resurrected women in her altarpiece are also more Gothic than the men. The donatrices in David's 'Baptism of Christ Triptych' (*c.* 1507)[30] look heavier and more matronly than the women of the 1490s, but it is not until nearer 1525 that women suddenly become very busty, as in Bernard van Orley's depiction of the women of the Haneton family, who have at last matched their menfolk in bulkiness of body and attire.[31] (Gossaert's 'Amphitrite' of 1516 is also more 'classical' in build, although her breasts are still rather high-set.) This very sudden filling-out of the female body leads one to suspect that the very flat chests in the 1470s, 1480s and 1490s were no more natural than their almost overnight growth in the 1520s.

What prompted all these changes, and why were there varying speeds of their adoption by men and women? We have seen that the most likely explanation for the curious female form of hunched shoulders and protruding stomach was the adoption of a new and uncomfortable form of dress: that this ideal remained in favour for so long, despite its patent unnaturalness, is an indication that it matched some already prevailing aesthetic notion in other areas of art and design, not necessarily, as Kenneth Clark seems to imply (see p. 40), that it was created by that aesthetic mood. The form was not simply an acceptance of the destructive effect of several pregnancies on a woman's figure,

20. Bathsheba steps from her bath into slippers and a linen robe offered by her servant, but not before King David has glimpsed her and decided to send her husband, Uriah the Hittite, to his death. King David was painted in the sixteenth century, but the subject must have been intelligible to most contemporary viewers without this addition, as it was one of the few chances for an artist to paint 'respectable' scenes of naked ladies. Bathsheba's bathrobe is gathered at the back into a straight collar and her servant's underdress has a gathered and probably detachable hem.

21. LEFT: This unknown couple were painted by the Master of the Embroidered Foliage, probably *c.* 1495. The man's dress is quite bulky, while the woman's still seems to have been poured very smoothly round her torso and her upper arms.

22. Marie d'Harcourt, the childless Duchess of Guelders, depicted wishfully as Mary the Annunciate in her Book of Hours *c.* 1415, epitomizes the triangular shape of the fashionable Gothic female as her gown and figure splay outwards from a narrow upper torso. The gown sleeves trail over on to the margin of the page.

as nothing in the nude, apart from the stomach, was allowed to sag or grow fat at the same time. That it was not prompted by a desire even to *suggest* fecundity is shown by its uses on countless virgin saints. It seems to have been accepted because it bore some relation to Gothic ideals of attenuation from a solid base, and doubtless women who were pregnant nearly every year were grateful for the camouflage which fashion provided as their figures sagged behind tightly laced bodices (compare Deschamps' remarks on older women and tight lacing on p. 44).

If one considers the female body as being basically pear-shaped or, more politely, an isosceles triangle resting on its base (the hips) with the head as its apex, one has to consider the male body as a similar triangle, reversed, with its base being the shoulders and the hips its apex, which can even be extended to the toes. Today's popular concept of Gothic architecture probably owes more to the ideas of Victorian designers of local churches and to the cinema than to appreciation of original buildings, but the cinema in particular has the merit that it, like a good cartoonist, has caught the essence of Gothic's love of the ambiguously defined outline, with its clusters of pointed turrets, of varying sizes, peppering towering castles set on jagged outcrops of rock. Perhaps only vampires ever inhabited such castles, but these fantasy buildings, although Gothick rather than Gothic, help to explain what was done to that most unyielding of building materials, the human body, in an attempt to Gothicize everything.

The unambiguous verticals and horizontals and consequent right angles of classical and classicizing architecture were totally opposed to indigenous Northern taste in the fifteenth century, and it was only by gradual exposure to Italian ideals that the North could assimilate them. Men changed from wearing highly Gothic dress in the late 1460s to much squarer, more horizontal dress in one generation, but women's dress shows the continuing effect of Gothic elongation for the whole of the transition period in male dress. It is not difficult to find an explanation for this: as diplomats, traders, sailors or soldiers, men travelled further and more freely than women and were generally more receptive to new ideas because of their greater freedom. Although a few women were highly educated and noted patronesses of the arts, such as Margaret of York, Duchess of Burgundy from 1468, most were appallingly under-educated by today's standards, and were deliberately kept so by their families. When the Duke of Brittany enquired about his prospective daughter-in-law, Isabella Stewart of Scotland, he was delighted that she was not particularly bright, remarking that all a wife need know was the difference between her husband's shirt and his doublet; Isabella's more intellectual sister Margaret, Dauphine of France, infuriated her husband by sitting up all night writing poetry and discussing it with her friends. Satirists felt a dull wife was as much a curse as a clever one—what was a woman supposed to be, one may ask? Presumably women outside court circles had little contact with their foreign counterparts, and their enforced ignorance of matters outside their own concerns, with the conservatism this was likely to entail, is reason enough for their slowness to accept the new impulses from the South which were affecting the attitudes of their menfolk. This slowness in its turn forced their dress, and the ideal controlling it, to continue in the Gothic trend longer than did men's. When another type of female ideal was finally accepted by women, a complete generation of men had grown up viewing themselves and their buildings as increasingly rectangular or square shapes.

The final acceptance by women of all that this new approach to dress entailed meant that the Gothic mood had lost its hold on the imagination of northern Europe, and motifs from Gothic architecture and dress would be used only to evoke strangely splendid moments from the past, as in the 'Antwerp Adoration of the Magi', where clothes with slashed edges and Gothic ruins add to the mannerism of the whole scene.[32] Thus, an entire view of people and objects changed, and 'Gothic' was on the way to becoming 'Gothick'.

3 Moralizing and Manufacturing

In the history of dress, men have outdone women in the splendour of their dress, women have outdone men or both sexes have shared flamboyance or drabness. In the fifteenth century, the dress of the fashionable man was as flamboyant as that of the fashionable woman and it is therefore strange that the vast majority of attacks on the excesses of fashionable dressing were directed against women's attire. Eustache Deschamps did make one or two unkind remarks about men's dress, but these comments (p. 86) could pass unnoticed in his pursuit of one of the traditional themes of misogyny, the folly of *women's* dress. Men could hardly have suspected fashion of being an insidious capitalist plot to part silly women from their money as often as possible, as they may think it is today, but even 600 years ago, in Paris of all places, the average man seems to have thought that a self-effacing tidiness in women's dress was preferable to the latest extravagances of high fashion. Writing for the benefit of his daughters in 1371 and 1372, the Chevalier de La Tour Landry warned them against making themselves ridiculous by being too far ahead of fashion or adopting the dress of other countries. An example of the first fault is a girl who in 1372 had produced the most fantastic headdress her friends had ever seen, an '*attour a gibet*' (gibbet headdress), held up on long silver pins. This, the Chevalier felt, was carrying ingenuity too far. Guilty of the second fault was a lady from Guyenne, who objected to the fact that her cousin's wife in Brittany did not have such wide fur trimmings on her gowns as she herself wore: her cousin replied caustically that in that case he would make his wife wear her clothes inside out, showing the fur lining, so that they would appear to be completely of fur. The refinements of dress to which she referred were imported from England, and he disapproved very strongly of Englishwomen's dress ('*mais en Angleterre en a moult de blasmées, si comme l'on dist*': 'but in England there are many women who have been the subject of reproach, it is said').[1]

Apart from his protests about low necklines and tight lacing (see p. 44) Eustache Deschamps disapproved most of women's large headdresses, which made them look like stags, snails, owls or cats. He asked Juno to '*l'umble joli faictes renouveller*': 'bring

23. The last word in sinful dressing *c.* 1400—the Whore of Babylon in an Apocalypse manuscript, in a tightly fitting dress with wide neckline and trailing cuffs, and the type of hairstyle increasingly reserved for queens (which she was), worn with a crown. (Paris, Bibliothèque Nationale, ms. néerl. 3, f. 20.)

back the pretty modest headdress'.[2]

Writing between 1392 and 1394 the unknown citizen of Paris, called the *Ménagier de Paris*, suggested that his wife, who was only fifteen years old, should avoid new-fangled ideas in dress and too many or too few frivolities. She ought to be neat and orderly, ensuring before she left her room that her shirt collar did not appear over her dress collar. His ideal wife is such a paragon of demure sweetness and kindliness, with no will but his, that one begins to suspect that at this date men may have regarded fashion as a subversive influence in the lives of their womenfolk, leading a dutiful wife's thoughts away from ensuring the comfort of her lord and master. The Chevalier had rationalized his disapproval of fashion into disapproval of the sin of pride, concerning which he recounted a tale of what befell a knight's three wives after their deaths. The one who had committed adultery several times, but had confessed her faults every time, was to spend 100 years in Purgatory, while the one who had plucked her eyebrows and temples and painted her face to make herself pleasing to the world, was to spend 1,000 years in Purgatory, being stabbed daily by devils in every spot where she had plucked her forehead. The wife who had owned ten pairs of gowns, lined with the finest fur, was damned for eternity, because the cost of one of her gowns would have clad fifty poor people who were freezing in the winter. All this, however, does not mean that the Chevalier disapproved of smart dressing: by dressing in her best clothes to go to church, a woman would be honouring God, and to dress shabbily was an insult to him.[3]

Deschamps' 'Miroeur de mariage' presents a gloomy picture of wayward wives intent on deceiving their husbands with the help of immodest attire. The author of *Les Quinze Joyes de Mariage*, written presumably after 1396, and called blasphemously after the Seven Joys of the Virgin, had a very jaundiced view of women: a woman would nag day and night until her husband put himself in debt to buy her new clothes, to match her friends', at which point she would say sweetly that she had never meant him to go to such lengths.[4]

If men in the fourteenth and fifteenth centuries believed quite seriously that women were out to ensnare them by the frivolity of their dress, they were as mistaken as men have been since. It is quite obvious that one aspect of dress, the décolletage, was being used in a blatantly sexual way by some women, but low necklines are never mentioned as part of the keeping-up-with-the-Joneses practised by all the wicked women of poetry and prose. Women there are much more concerned with having the latest headdress, wide fur trimmings, a long train or expensive textiles, all at least as good as the woman next door's. Because one aspect of women's dress was so clearly aimed at getting, and holding, male attention, men flattered themselves into thinking that all the attendant monstrosities of fashion were also designed to interest them. Had that been the case, women would quickly have abandoned all the devices which attracted so much adverse comment: that they did not abandon them, suggests they were engaged in some sort of game among themselves. Male writers may even have observed enough to record women's remarks on dress in dialogue, but they did not take the time to ferret out the reasons behind them, psychoanalysis not being a mediaeval pastime.

If, however, men were genuinely concerned for the safety of women's souls, then all these moralizing attitudes would be very commendable. Unfortunately, the deep strain of misogyny inherent in mediaeval literature, which had as its extreme opposite the adoration of an untouchable goddess by a knight, reveals that men were generally more worried about their creature comforts, their purses and the safety of their own souls when faced by these wanton daughters of the first temptress, Eve. The most popular poem of the fourteenth and fifteenth centuries, the *Roman de la Rose*, held that every woman had her price, a view challenged by Christine de Pisan, with the support of Jean Gerson, the chancellor of the Sorbonne. The logical outcome of all the neurotic spiritualized love affairs advocated by the tenets of chivalry was a crop of tales of clever unfaithful wives who preferred sin to neurosis, like those told by Boccaccio in *The Decameron*, which was translated into French in 1414 and enjoyed great popularity throughout the century; the existence of competent businesswomen, recorded as members of craft guilds, shows just how far the meek ideal was from reality. Women's completely uncontrollable obsession with fashion may have been the last straw for many a husband or father, wondering if he was as firmly in control of his womenfolk as the church and the law told him he ought to be. But how else was an under-educated, well-to-do woman, whose home and children were looked after by servants, to spend her time?

After perusing these attacks on women's dress one would assume that at least men at this period were conforming to the standards of sobriety they expected of women, but wardrobe accounts reveal that this is hardly the case. John the Fearless spent vast sums of money on his and his attendants' clothes, as did his uncle, Jean de Berry, who was seventy-five when he died in 1416. The latter's sartorial arrangements were certainly not those of an elderly, conservative, gentleman. For the aristocrat, male or female, dress was the most immediate and telling way of indicating his or her wealth, position and, during the Burgundian-Armagnac fighting, political allegiance. Occasionally sumptuary laws were passed in vain attempts to keep the masses within their proper places, by restricting the amount of silk or precious furs or even fashionableness in their clothes. Thus, dress could be used, if the system worked, to indicate precisely where a person belonged in society, whose servant he was, and even what office or task he performed. Women, by their persistent pursuit of the ever-more expensive and fantastic in dress, repeatedly broke through these class-dress barriers, disrupting one manifestation of divine will as it had planned the hierarchy of fifteenth century life.

The rumblings and grumblings about other people's clothes continued throughout the century: sometimes they are silly, sometimes they are infuriatingly snobbish, particularly when the

24. The Death of Alexander the Great, as visualized *c.* 1450, with the mourning women at the foot of the bed in fashionable dress and the servant entering on the right, providing a good example of how dress was meant to separate the classes: the servant's dress would have been much more fashionable in the 1430s. (Paris, Bibliothèque Nationale, ms. fr. 9342, f. 210v.)

matter of the hierarchical use of dress was involved. In 1409 the master of the king's household was taken to his execution dressed in the full livery of his office, the implication being that he was not just an individual who had offended, but a royal servant: many of the charges against him were trumped up by John the Fearless to remove an opponent from the court, but it was true that the master had been arrogant enough to enter the Parlement de Paris without removing his hood, even in the presence of the king, an action which could be interpreted as *lèse-majesté*.[5]

Insufficiently grand dress offended Henry v of England when in 1420 the marshal of France, the seigneur de l'Isle-Adam, came to greet him, wearing a gown of rough white *gris* (a woollen cloth of any colour): the king asked coldly if that was the gown of a

25. A lady receives a suitor in her chamber. This shows the type of respectable dress to which Parisian prostitutes were aiming in the 1420s, with the turned-down fur collar on the gown and the metal-studded belt. From the poems of Christine de Pisan (late 1410s?), London, British Library, Harley ms. 4431, f. 56v.

marshal of France, to which he received the reply that the marshal was a rough traveller and the gown was the same as the body, as it had been made for the boat trip necessary to get to the king. No more was said about the incident, except by two chroniclers who seemed to find it worthy of mention as, presumably, a reflection of contemporary attitudes to the respect due to a monarch through the attire of those around him.[6]

Henry was construing this, probably rightly, as a gesture of insult, not as a mark of the marshal's humility: humility usually involved degradation imposed by the removal of the outer garments, such as happened in 1453 when over 2,000 burghers of Ghent were forced to ask pardon for their revolt against Philip the Good, without their hoods and barefoot, dressed in black. However, the councillors and aldermen suffered more, as they had to appear in only their shirts and drawers.[7] Similarly, the Church imposed penances to be performed, in public, in this latter state of 'undress', and the state often carried out public executions on half-dressed victims, among fully-clad spectators. Women were allowed to retain their kirtles, as witness the burning of the wicked Empress in Dirk Bouts' 'Justice of the Emperor Otto' (illus. 115).

While Parisian prostitutes were to be taken to court in 1422, 1425, 1426 and 1446 for dressing like respectable women, respectable women were taken to task by travelling preachers in 1428 and 1429 for the enormity of their headdresses. Also stepping beyond their proper places were Charles VII's mistresses Agnès Sorel in 1450 with her gown trains longer by a third than those of any other lady, her headdresses higher by a half, as well as her household more lavish than the queen's, and, later in 1461 her niece, and successor, and her attendants with their clothing as rich as that of queens, and their estate greater than a queen's. In 1465 a lawyer's daughter from Le Châtelet in Paris was engaged to an attendant of the seigneur de Saincte-Marie; she took up, not what befitted her own or her betrothed's rank, but what befitted his master's, '*habit de damoiselle et grant estate*'. This assumption of the dress of one's betters brings out the self-righteous snob in an anonymous chronicler of the new fashions of 1467, when the lower orders, '*les petites gens*', took to wearing silk and velvet doublets, '*chooses trop vaines et sans doute haineuses a Dieu*'.[8]

Divine authority was also invoked by Alain Chartier in his 'Miroir aux Dames' (which unfortunately lacks a date but may be of *c.* 1430)[9] to dissuade women from wearing, yet again, horned headdresses. If God had wanted Eve to have horns, he would have given them to her: instead they were given to the devil, as a mark of his pride and fall from heaven. Other women were running counter to the biblical injunction against the wearing of clothes of the opposite sex, by wearing '*bourreaulx*' (*bourrelets*), which he equates with men's hoods: presumably these were the more sensible items for outdoor wear shown in illustration 63, and it is harsh of Chartier, having complained of devil-like horned headdresses, to point out that by wearing these more rational alternatives to what he disliked, women were running the risk of damnation. In his view this risk was not worth the easing of passing mockery for being out of step with fashion.

Attitudes to the dress of others could have unfortunate consequences: in 1463 a meeting between Louis XI of France and the King of Castile ended in furious disagreement, which had been aggravated by the rude remarks of each group of courtiers about the dress of the other. The future Duke of Albuquerque appeared on a boat whose sail was made of cloth of gold, while he himself wore boots covered in precious stones. The French said, untruthfully, that he had rented the jewels and borrowed the cloth of gold from churches. The Castilian king was ugly and the French made fun of his clothes, which they did not like. The French king was as badly dressed as he could be, in short clothes made of poor cloth, and an eccentric hat with a leaden badge on it: the Castilians made fun of *his* attire, saying that he was dressed thus out of stinginess.[10]

However, the Burgundian court never struck anyone as shabby: even the blasé citizens of Paris, who were not in the habit of rushing into the streets to look at a few passing grandees, rushed out of their houses as Philip the Good passed through the streets in 1461. This same splendour caused ill feeling among the retinue of the Count Palatine during his visit to Brussels in 1467/8: his Germans spoke enviously of it, while the Burgundians took grave offence at the way in which the Germans threw their boots on to the rich bedcoverings, proving that they were less well-bred and resulting in a lessening of the respect for the Germans which the Burgundians had felt before they met.[11]

Dress clearly mattered far more deeply than we can easily comprehend: an almost unfathomable class-consciousness demanded that laws be passed to ensure that the outward appearance of the various classes kept everyone, visually, where they belonged. (The main value of these sumptuary laws lies not in their effectiveness, but in what they can tell of fashionable developments.) Shabbiness and splendour alike attracted adverse comments, while men seem to have felt themselves peculiarly immune to the blandishments of fashion, seeming to regard their own attire, no matter how lavish it may appear today, as generally being far more in accord with the dictates of good taste and sense than women's. But such has always been the male viewpoint, always more loudly expressed when men were almost alone in having the right and ability to express their views for posterity.

Now that we have examined the complaints aroused by fashionable dressing, it would only be fair to try to track down the instigators and methods of supply of the offending items: unfortunately, all the evidence of the inventors is negative, although there is plenty of evidence about the manufacturers. It is almost impossible to ascertain who was responsible for fashion, as the professional fashion designer was an unknown animal: what did exist were tailors who made up customers' own cloth into garments, or who sometimes made up full-size patterns for garments in cheaper materials, but in the proposed final colour, for the approval of a client; and painters, who were employed to devise fancy dress for entertainments. Thus, in 1403, five and a half ells of blue fustian (a cheap cloth) were used '*pour faire un patron a manches de houppellande*' for Isabella of Bavaria;[12] such a rare event would have been unnecessary if the sleeves had not been in need of the queen's approval, and she herself must have been uncertain how these, presumably new, sleeves would suit her, as normally clothes seem to have been made up without this intermediate stage, perhaps from already-existing pattern blocks made up for each customer, or from standard sized blocks. (As an accurate fit was not essential with the voluminous *houppelandes*, an approximate fit from standard-sized garments may have been sufficient, but the closely fitting *cotes hardies* and *pourpoints* would have required greater accuracy of cut, and may therefore have involved greater subtlety of pattern-making.) In the case of these new sleeves, perhaps the queen and tailor worked together to devise them: if the tailor thought them up, he would have needed the queen's approval before he could incorporate them into a garment, and if the queen had thought them up, she would have needed the tailor's help to realize her idea.

One can speculate about the involvement of artists, as they seem to have been particularly responsible for the designing, as well as the production of fancy dress, which fits in with that employed in paintings. In 1398 Colart de Laon, painter to Louis of Orléans, made several '*demis corps à grans manches*' (large-sleeved bolero jackets?) for the duke's squires, for a joust, and in 1400 he produced a jousting harness, i.e., designed a 'fancy dress' armour; in 1425 Philip the Good employed '*Hance de Constance, paintre . . . a faire patrons* [make designs, or full-scale patterns?] *et autres choses de son mestier*' to make clothes for a joust which Philip was planning to hold against Humphrey, Duke of Gloucester, the current husband of Jacqueline of Bavaria, in the dispute over her lands which Philip had illegally annexed. The joust never took place and Hance's trip to Paris to look for materials, as well as all his efforts, was in vain.

Perhaps the most significant of these painters' activities, and certainly one of the most elaborately documented, concerns Hue de Boulogne, Philip's painter, who in 1427–8 was paid forty-nine *livres* for having made '. . .*VII habis de drap de soye de pluiseurs coulleurs et estrange fachon, propices a danser la morisque. . . .*' ('seven outfits of silk cloth of several colours and of foreign type, suitable for dancing the *morisque*'—a primitive type of ballet involving figures in Moorish or middle-eastern dress). These outfits were flashy and theatrical, with little relation to true eastern dress, being decorated in the most fantastic manner with gold and silver leather, and 'Saracen' lettering with little whirls made to look like cloth of gold. The borders and the sleeves were enriched with gold tinsel of 'three double slashes', whatever that was, to look like gold fringing, and other, different trimmings. All the outfits had hoods, some with snakes as decoration, and long animal-like necks, all laden with clasps and the strongest 'shaking' gold (loosely attached leaves) which could be made. The outfits were completed by cloth hose with gold lacquered snakes' heads coming from above to bite the knees from which gushed drops, like blood, and other '*devises*', beards and '*estranges cheveux*', shoes and bells.[13]

A variety of examples of 'Saracen' dress, as visualized around 1415–20, can be seen in works attributed to Robert Campin, 'The Marriage of the Virgin' (illus. 26) and the 'Seilern Triptych' (illus. 27), both works rich in the exotic.[14] Examination of this almost contemporary visual evidence puts before us certain features which do not accord ill with the scanty documentary evidence. Tinselly gold borders for the *morisque* dancers, bells, beards and wild hair, with applied lettering and imitation cloth of gold all fit in well with the jewelled gold ribbons, trimmed borders, beards and longish hair, and Kufic (Arabic) lettering on gold stripes, on the figures in the 'Marriage of the Virgin', although the latter have little room left to add dagging to their attire. We need not look for a close parallel to the snakes on the *morisque* hoods and hose as they are simply a grotesque touch which would fit in with the mood which applied useless chains to the tunic of the 'Seilern Triptych' soldier. The link which clearly existed between the permanent and ephemeral depictions of 'Saracens', particularly as painters were called on to produce both representations, makes it clear that artists were felt to have some special understanding of and skill with one particular form of dress, and one could therefore hope for references to their being asked to produce designs for other types of clothing.

Unfortunately, such is not the case, and the evidence suggests that artists in producing exotic dress were working not from the depths of their imaginations, but from well-established patterns, perhaps by now kept among their own drawings for easy reference, but originally suggested by some academic or other who had more immediate access to sources of information, like books of travellers' tales.

At their most important, the plans for pictures were often worked out by eminent theologians who incorporated iconography so obscure that the artists could not have thought it up for themselves: one example of a theologian at work, which is particularly interesting for a dress historian, concerns the scheme devised by Jehan Germain, Bishop of Nevers (died 1460) for two tapestries, the one showing the Church and its defenders and the other showing sinners in their worldliness..[15]

26. Robert Campin's 'Marriage of the Virgin', which takes place, as did all mediaeval marriages, outside a church. This painting is rich in colouring and in types of exotic dress.

27. OVERLEAF: Campin's 'Seilern Triptych', in which the folds in the garments of the kneeling women in the central panel take on a sculptural feeling, reflecting Campin's recorded links with Tournai sculptors.

Naturally, fashionable dress appears only in the second scheme. The sinners read and listened to lewd songs and stories, the men flaunted their arms, thighs and 'rude bits' before the women, who in their turn showed off their breasts and necks, painted their faces, dressed themselves '*estroitement*' (in tight clothes) and elegantly to attract men, liked to be seen naked by men in public baths, and used herbs and witchcraft to keep men enslaved to them. As usual, women commit more sins than men in this list; it would have been interesting to be able to compare the finished product with the suggestions for features to be included.

A set of instructions with a far less moralistic tone but with greater explicitness concerning dress comes in the shape of a work written *c.* 1417 by Jean Lebègue, notary and secretary of the king and clerk of the *Chambre des comptes* (the Exchequer), as a guide to illuminators faced with the task of illustrating copies of Sallust's account of the conspiracy of Catiline in Rome (63 BC). Since copies of Sallust were in Latin, a language not necessarily understood by painters, Lebègue's book must have been very useful, as he gives a few words of the Latin, saying, 'Where it says . . . make a picture of . . .', and even describes the clothes of the people in the scene, as well as their actions and positions, which makes him particularly valuable to us. The text has fairly recently been published, along with illustrations taken from a manuscript which is clearly dependent on this instruction manual.[16] (Its information has been incorporated in the glossary.)

The need for theologians to work out complex iconographies is obvious, but the existence of a comparatively humble work such as Jean Lebègue's suggests that there was a need for such works, and that others must have existed: the incorporation of historical features like dagging, or fringing, into later fancy dress, whether in art or in masquerades, could thus be explained as the effect of the continuing use of instruction books, along with artists' own pattern books and observation of older paintings around them. Without such material to fall back on, Memlinc would have been unlikely to think up the heavy fringing which decorates the armhole of an attendant's jacket in the Granada 'Deposition' of *c.* 1475, or a very similar jacket worn by one of the soldiers in the Lübeck 'Crucifixion' of 1491.[17]

Eastern dress as depicted by artists probably also had an authentic source, no matter how warped it became by the understandable inability of some artists to comprehend fully their sources. The *Livre des merveilles du monde* shows this confusion very nicely (illus. 18). Marco Polo described what he saw, but the painter could translate the description only into terms with which he was familiar: thus we see, not a convincing depiction of men in long robes and women in trousers, but a laughable transposition of male heads on to female bodies, both of which fit in with the painter's already existing notions of what was suitable for each (see p. 45).

René of Anjou's accounts give the impression that the great connoisseur was not averse to incorporating foreign elements into his everyday life, as he owned, among other exotic things. Turkish knives, a Turkish hand basin, four Moorish bottles, thirteen pairs of Turkish pattens (over-shoes), and nine pairs of leather pattens in the Moorish fashion, of which three pairs were gilded, the others being '*ouvrez a la morisque*'. Some of this 'Arabic' equipment may have been made in Europe for festivities, but some of it must have been real, as no-one would have bothered to store and inventory the cheap, ephemeral things put together for masques. In 1448 was recorded a habit of '*drap de Turquie violet et rayé de rayes noires*' with great, wide sleeves, amongst the normal clothing issue for the king and his court. The colour combination of violet and black, even in stripes, fits in well with René's general preference for a grey/black colour range and may well have been for his own use. René also kept a Moor at his court, dressed in '*robes de sarazin*'.[18]

28. The donatrix from 'The Sforza Triptych', produced probably in the studio of Rogier van der Weyden for export to Italy. The woman's dress is not Netherlandish, nor is it Italian: rather, it is a toned-down version of 'foreign' dress, with its short sleeves worn over the split sleeves of men's doublets, and an arrangement of plaits and headband such as was to reappear on Van der Goes's 'Portinari' Magdalene, another 'foreigner'.

Jacques Coeur, treasurer of Charles VII, after a glamorous life trading across the Mediterranean and making too much money for his own good, was arrested in 1453 on various charges, including conspiring with the Saracens and poisoning Agnès Sorel. After his escape, his goods were inventoried and sold, including what must, with his trading connexions, have been genuinely Arabic outfits; two of these outfits were, again, striped and included '*tocques*' (turbans?).[19] In the next year, at the Burgundian Feast of the Pheasant, one of the entertainments included a giant in a long gown of striped green silk, wearing on his head '*une tresque* [torque] *à la guise des Sarrasins de Grenade*' (i.e., of the Moors of Granada in Spain), and leading an elephant on which sat Olivier de la Marche, dressed as a nun, symbolizing the Church and reciting a plea for her freedom from the Infidel.[20] (Western Christianity felt insecure after the fall of Constantinople to the Saracens the year before.) It is impossible to say how accurately this particular outfit matched genuine Saracen dress, but in a written account of it, it sounds, from its resemblance to Jacques Coeur's, as though it may have had some basis in reality.

A continuing tradition of incorporating various elements, such as fringing, stripes, beard and strange hats, in any mixture required, added the desired effect of the exotic to any scene remote in space and time, and historical, geographical and structural accuracy were not generally sought after, except by Hieronymous Bosch, many of whose attempts at International Gothic dress, while necessarily of his own time, do have a proper structure, suggesting that for the more intelligent painter, making clothes 'work' was an interesting and rewarding exercize, whether carried out only in two dimensions or in three, before being committed to the panel.[21] But the very continuity of the language for the exotic, with its presumed instruction manuals, leads to the sad conclusion that few artists were directly involved in the creation of fashionable dress: what they did excel in, was the creation of the bizarre, the snake and tinsel-laden, all well within the range of their usual painting practice. For all his 'Moorish' outfits, Hue de Boulogne was chiefly a decorative painter, colouring flags, painting coats-of-arms and doing the mediaeval equivalent of sign-painting. Nowhere is there proof that artists were employed to design everyday dress, despite their obvious and intense interest in it. Without exception, elaborate outfits of this kind were meant to have a limited life-span, being used for court entertainments or public spectacles and impressive by the conspicuous consumption which they involved.

The almost complete removal of the artists' possible part in the creation of fashion forces us to fall back on the evidence concerning those whose livelihood came from the making of clothing. There, the lack of specific directions issued to them is disappointing, but this very lack may reveal that great freedom was accorded to them within the general request for, let us say, a dagged hood or a *houppelande* with closed sleeves. Perhaps it is significant that within the manufacture of clothing there were specialists, unlike the jack-of-all-trades that the decorative painter had to be. One Jehan de Brabant is mentioned as a doublet maker, a '*pourpointier*', employed by Philip the Good in 1433 to make doublets for his pages, while Thierry de Chastel, an embroiderer, Hayne de Necker, a tailor and Perrot Broullart, a furrier, were all *varlets de chambre* (personal servants, a coveted position) to the duke. Apart from making clothes, Hayne de Necker had to carry out alterations: in 1433 he altered one of the duke's doublets and replaced its sleeves, which were too narrow; he took another one to pieces and remade it '*comme tous de neuf*', as well as taking to pieces and remaking six of the duke's *heuques* (see Glossary), because the duke thought they were too old-fashioned, '*de facon trop viezl*'.[22] These employees were usually supplied with their materials from the Wardrobe, although they occasionally had to buy things and then be reimbursed for them, often a long time afterwards.

Colour Plate **5.** The centre panel of the 'Bladelin Triptych' depicts the Nativity. Joseph wears his traditional red gown and cloak, while the Virgin's blue mantle, appropriate to her as Queen of Heaven, slips off to reveal a white smock with openwork seams and neckband, covering a brown dress. Here the donor has not removed his wooden overshoes.

Colour Plate **6.** Petrus Christus' donor is less fashionably dressed than his wife, with his wide sleeves and close necklines. His woodenfold overshoes have been cast aside as he is to be regarded as being on Holy ground.

In general, the specialization of clothes makers seems to have been well defined, if lop-sided, with *cousturiers* making gowns, hoods and clothes in general, with the exception of hose, which were the prerogative of the *chaussetiers*. In 1424, Henry VI extended the privilege of making all garments, as long as they were of good quality, to the *chaussetiers* of Evreux, as they had been in the habit of selling hoods and being *détailleurs* (retailers); on the other hand, the *cousturiers* were still not allowed to be *détailleurs* and *chaussetiers*. In the same year, he confirmed the statutes of the *chaussetiers* of Bernay, under which they were allowed only one apprentice each, for a term of three years.[23] The most interesting injunction to these two guilds is that the hose must be '*de bon biais*', confirming the suspicion that, to fit as well as they seem to, and to need as much material as they did, hose were

generally cut on the bias, a logical development from the bias outer seam on the sleeve of Charles de Blois' doublet.[24] (See page 78.) As well as being allowed to make everything but hose, the *cousturiers* of Bourges were forbidden, in 1443, to make clothes for sale: they were simply to make clothes to order, always from new cloth, while the second-hand dealers were forbidden to sell new cloth. As usual, the inhabitants of the capital came off best: in 1441 Charles VII confirmed a statute of his father's by which the *tailleurs de robes* of Paris were exempt from paying tax on cloth they bought to use for making, decorating or padding clothing, which, by extension, presumably means that *they* could make clothes for sale.[25]

The apparently simple provision of sewing skills to customers who brought along their own cloth appears again in one of the more curious documentary survivals, the accounts of a Parisian tailor named Colin de Lormoye, which cover the years 1423–55.[26] His customers seem to have been mainly middle-class families, clerics, teachers and students at the University of Paris and the occasional aristocrat, like the seigneur de Saint-Simon. Although page after page lists garments, one much like another, with little specific information about any one garment, a few points do emerge which can be useful if one knows what to look for. The available evidence suggests that gowns had stopped being called *houppelandes* in the Burgundian accounts by 1420, although the French court continued to order them until at least 1420;[27] Colin's customers go on wanting garments he calls by this name into the 1450s, showing how slowly changes in fashion percolated down through society, particularly if fashion at the uppermost levels was stagnating, as seems to have happened in France after the English takeover. His clients do not seem to have asked for hoods with padded brims until *c.* 1440,[28] although Philip the Good had ordered them for his *archiers du corps* in 1432, as part of their livery.[29]

The charges also give some indication of the amount of work involved in making each garment: the making of an adult's *houppelande* cost six *sous*, while a *robe* cost six or eight; a child's *houppelande*, a man's *pourpoint* and *jacquet*, and a woman's *cote simple* cost four *sous* each; a workman's smock, or *rochet*, cost two *sous*, as did a pair of men's hose, while a shirt cost one *sou*. One of his more unusual undertakings was the washing and drying, in the early 1440s, of two black *houppelandes*, for which he charged 2s 8d *parisis*.[30] (In towns, clothes were dried by being hung over poles which ran parallel to the fronts of the houses, under an upper window. They seem to have been kept, not in wardrobes, but wrapped, in chests, or on frames: in 1438 the posthumous inventory of the goods of Clement de Fauquembergue, clerk of the Parlement de Paris, includes a '*gibet de boys a mettre robes*'.[31])

The general public's ambivalent attitude of contempt and appreciation was not shared by workers in other, more unhealthy

Colour Plate **7.** The donor's wife is probably to be thought of as wearing dress fashionable a few years after Petrus Christus' 'young couple with St Eligius' of 1449, as the sleeves are neater at the wrists and the neckline is more open. The rich red velvet of her gown is echoed by the red jewels on her cap.

Colour Plate **8.** Jean Fouquet's portrait of the Chancellor of France, Guillaume Jouvenel des Ursins, probably painted well in the late 1450s, is a sumptuous composition made in rose red and gold. The colours of his coat-of-arms at the top of the pillars are repeated in the cushion supporting his pink covered prayer book. Even his cloth-of-gold purse with its flowers and stags has a rose velvet top.

or more arduous crafts: they wanted to better themselves by encroaching on the privileges of the guilds who used their products. Thus, in 1409 there arose a dispute between the dyers and drapers of S. Denis near Paris, because, the drapers claimed, the dyers had slowly begun to make cloths and to dye them as cloths, whereas previously they had done the dyeing in the (unspun) wool and thread stages of manufacture. They were also using dyes like nut shells and pods, without woad, which made the dyes fugitive. Perhaps because the dyers were only six against 140 clothmakers, the dyers were ordered to return to the old rules governing what they could and could not do.[32] It is easy, however, to feel sympathy with the dyers as, apart from being outnumbered, they followed a very unhealthy occupation, working among vats of steaming dyes, some of which were foul-smelling, if not downright poisonous, and ammonia, which was provided by untreated urine. There may have been some consolation for the dyers during the English siege of Paris in 1420, as the cost of dyeing one ell of cloth green rose to fourteen *sous parisis*, much to the horror of the *Bourgeois de Paris* who kept a diary of notable events but failed to tell us what the previous cost was; the price of cloth rose too, '*drapz de* XVI *solz*' costing 'XL *solz parisis*', (a 150 per cent rise in cost), and shoes cost even more than before,[33] the high price of shoes being a very old complaint.

In 1431 the drapers and tailors of Paris prosecuted the second-hand clothes dealers of the town, because the latter were breaking an edict of 1427 by which they were forbidden to make clothes from new cloth. The outcome of the case was that the dealers were forbidden to work with new cloths costing more than twelve *sous parisis* the ell, while the court undertook to make arrangements to prevent any fraudulent dealings to get round this ruling.

Other guilds associated with dress were those of the goldsmiths and the silk ribbon weavers, the former men and the latter women. In 1427, under the need for gold to pay troops to fight the Dauphin, the English Regent issued prohibitions on acquiring it, and Parisian goldsmiths consequently found serious problems in getting hold of enough to allow them to carry out large commissions. Further restrictions were announced in 1429, not this time to prevent the wasting of gold, but to try to maintain standards within the craft. Similarly, Parisian silk ribbon weavers drew up regulations for themselves: in 1422 they founded a confraternity in honour of the Virgin, and in 1425, as a further mark of solidarity, they drew up rules governing the taking on of apprentices and the reception of, in this case, mistresses of the craft. A year and a day of practice of the craft had to elapse before admission as a mistress of the guild; no mistress was to take an apprentice under the age of six, she was not to have more than two apprentices at any one time, and neither she nor her staff was to work at night or on holidays.[34]

The squabbles over the illegal activities of the dyers and old clothes dealers show how jealously guilds guarded their privileges against outsiders, while the regulations drawn up by the goldsmiths and the ribbon makers show how determined the guilds were, in theory at least, to set themselves standards, as well as to stop any one craftsman or woman from acquiring a larger share of the market, by limiting the number of apprentices, and hence the amount of cheap labour, ensuring a maintenance of price levels.[34] The whole guild structure was designed to protect its members from each other and from outsiders, but it could also lack incentives to encourage the production of really good work, as the guilds themselves tended to set any standards to be maintained, at any level *they* chose.

Craftsmen employed personally by the leaders of the French or Burgundian courts were free of the restrictions of the guilds, and their work must have been of a consistently high standard to meet the demands of their fastidious patrons, but the standards maintained by the average tailor, weaver or goldsmith are almost impossible to determine, because of the destruction wrought by time and greed on their products. Virtually no garments survive, as the Northern climate is not conducive to textile preservation over five centuries, and precious metals and stones could always be reused. The gold work which does survive displays a great deal of skill, but it has survived mainly because of that skill, and cannot therefore be considered representative.

While working from reality, artists can flatter and suppress the less attractive, be it in people or objects: eighteenth-century portraits give no impression of the sometimes appallingly slovenly construction of surviving garments, whose patterned textiles were in danger of being outdated almost as soon as they were made up into clothes. There too, every last piece of the precious fabrics was used to make a dress, sometimes without any regard for the vertical or horizontal continuity of the pattern. These flaws were glossed over by the painter, and it is possible that we get another too-tidy or too-frivolous impression of dress from fifteenth-century painters. The feeling which the Limbourgs imparted to dress in their miniatures is different from that of their contemporaries in its light-heartedness, but it is only from artists that we can gain the *impression* of what dress was like at this period: the delicacy or lack of it in the hands of the tailor becomes relatively unimportant, since it is the spirit of a fashion which a good artist of any age can capture. What the Limbourgs *knew* of the structure of dress was one thing, ever present as a framework on which to build 'working' depictions of it; what they *felt* about dress was another thing, and so it is with all their great successors. The skilful tailor may have created the fashion, but the skilful artist gave it its contradictions of the genuine and the ideal, at once real and false, with its basis in hard fact embellished by the unavoidably distorted vision of the moment.

le ciel et

4 International Gothic, *c.* 1380- *c.* 1420

29. The writer Jean de Vaudetar kneels before Charles v of France. The king wears old-fashioned, ceremonial dress, with its cowl-like hood and flipper-like front bands, and a transparent coif on his head.

In chapter 2 it has been indicated that a new form of dress was evolving *c.* 1380 and as this coincides with the spread across most of Europe of the Gothic taste, we may describe this new form, like the accompanying artefacts and architecture, as 'International Gothic'. Across Europe spires rose skywards from churches and turrets clustered round castles. In 1387 building was begun on the Cathedral of Milan in Italy, in the Gothic style, with pointed arches inside and an incredible array of spikes outside; the lack of experience in this type of building among local architects meant that when they encountered inevitable problems in the first few years, northern experts had to be consulted.

Despite troubles like these, the Italians fell completely under the sway of this charming and whimsical style, and the casual glancer at works of art produced during the period of monopoly of the international style can find it very difficult to disentangle national peculiarities in dress, so pervasive was the influence of this 'courtly' style. It can also be termed courtly because its main patrons were the aristocrats and rulers of Europe, linked to each other by a bewildering network of marriages, alliances and debts of gratitude (see diagram, pages 28 and 29). The Emperor Charles IV (died 1378) had lived in Paris, and had taken home with him a love of this spectacular style, which he grafted on to the buildings of his capital, Prague. The centre of all inspiration and activity in this style was the luxurious court of France, with its princes of the blood royal patronizing artists, goldsmiths and tailors of the greatest skill and technical sophistication.

Until *c.* 1380 flamboyance in dress had had to be confined to the use of exotic textiles, ablaze with jewels or embroidery, not very cunningly assembled into garments. As indicated before (p. 43), the most important development seems to have been the idea of setting sleeves with curved tops into curved armholes, instead of attaching nearly straight-topped sleeves to straight body edges, which used to result in T-shaped garments. Once the idea of curved seams had been established, their use could be extended to other seams on the body, particularly on women's dress, to allow clothes to fit as neatly as could be desired to the fashionable outline. Around this date, tailors may have noticed

30. RIGHT: A variety of *houppelandes*, long and short, and uses of dagging *c.* 1402.

that movement of the arms also involves the shoulder blades: the first steps in producing curved armholes clearly involve setting the sleeves into armholes cut deeply into the body of men's doublets and gowns. At the back there is often only a narrow strip, about as wide as the distance between the shoulder blades, to form the back of the garment.

The Musée Historique des Tissus de Lyon displays a doublet said to have belonged to the Blessed Charles de Blois, who died in 1364. Charles, however, is unlikely ever to have seen this garment, because of its later cut, and the museum itself correctly expresses doubts about his ownership. Its shape when worn resembled that in a very early example of the front-buttoned, padded chest, over narrow waist and hips, in the scene (illus. 29) of Jean de Vaudetar presenting his *Bible historiale* to Charles v of France, in 1371.[1] Unfortunately, the garment depicted here lacks any indication of the placing of the armhole, or of any other seams, although the sleeve fits smoothly round the arm and its socket. What is much more usual at this date, and for some years into the 1380s, are the sleeves of the God of Love and his son in the Guillaume de Machaut manuscript referred to above (illus. 15). The body of the doublet wrinkles towards the arm, and the sleeve fits well only round the lower arm, because this part of the garment was sewn closed every day once it had been put on (see illus. 37); the sleeves of the girls in this scene are pulled so tightly round the tops of the arms that the shoulder socket is quite clearly outlined. Neither type of sleeve fits satisfactorily or comfortably. By contrast, the Lyon doublet shows considerable sophistication of cut, which is shown up quite clearly by the changing grain line of the cloth in the doublet's different pieces (see diagram). The lions worked into the textile march horizontally or diagonally over the garment, according to the lay-out of the pieces of the doublet. The armholes are cut well into the body at front and back and the sleeve itself is cut with curved seams at inner and outer arm, giving a bias-cut edge at the elbow, where the stretch imparted to cloth by bias-cutting can be used with greatest advantage. The seam structure matches almost exactly those in a manuscript of Boccaccio's *Des cleres et nobles femmes*, given to Philip the Bold in 1403 (illus. 30);[2] the appearance of the extremely narrow back and front sections is emphasized by the use of different textiles, and the sleeves' inset sections have spread over a larger area of the body.

'Doublet of the Blessed Charles de Blois' (Lyon)

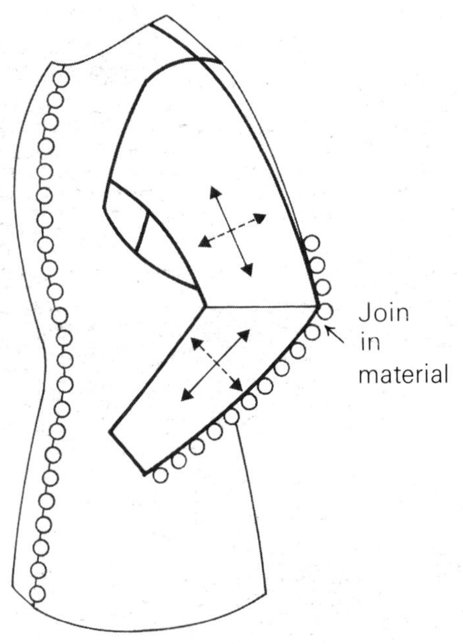

Heavy lines denote seams and grain lines are indicated by broken rule. Number of buttons not necessarily accurate.

Along with the innovations in tailoring around this date, there appear new names for garments in wardrobe accounts. The almost universal term for a gown (the most formal outer garment of men and women) tends to be, not the previous '*robe*' but '*houppelande*': see Glossary. Some other garments survived from earlier periods, together with their original names, and some items of dress had to remain basically unchanged because they had essential functions. In winter, the wearing of fur linings in

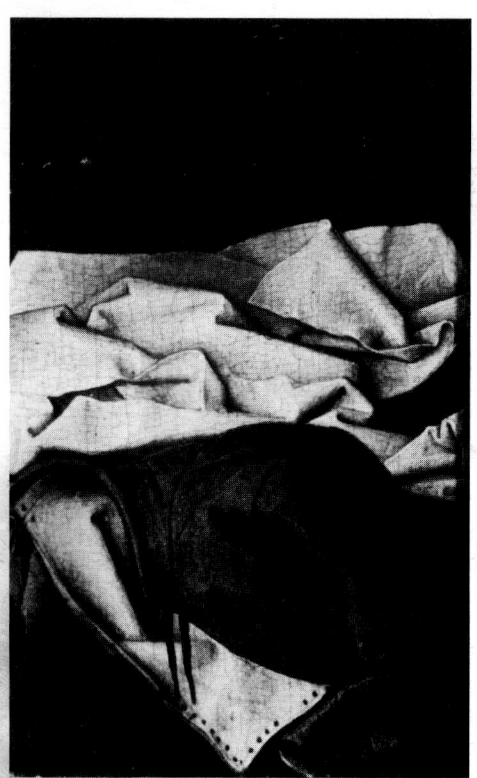

31. St Sebastian's doublet, as painted by Memlinc *c.* 1480. Although points of style within the doublet changed across the century, the basic positioning of lace-holes remained unchanged, down the centre front and around the waist, as can be seen here.

gowns was vital if one was to keep warm in large, draughty castles and palaces, even if all the fur made one look fat.[3] Linen shirts were worn next to the skin by both men and women, probably to protect the outer garments from the body, which was not washed very often. Linen underwear was easily washed, and seems to have been changed frequently, as most inventories list many shirts, and yard upon yard of linen being bought to make shirts and, for men, drawers. Women's shirts were longer than men's therefore it may have been felt that drawers were unnecessary, although the Bible did forbid the wearing of the clothes of one sex by the other. (Anyone who contravened this ruling could be burned to death, as was one unfortunate male transvestite in Lille in 1459.[4]) Although the *Ménagier de Paris* gives various recipes for removing spots of grease (*not* washing) from various textiles, most other garments seem to have been left to their own devices, apart from careful shaking to remove any insect inhabitants.[5]

Between the *houppelande* and the shirt were worn garments which could be displayed publicly, if the situation permitted it. Men of all classes, when engaged in strenuous activities, whether aristocratic archery contests or humbler house building, could appear in their doublets (*pourpoints*) and hose. As doublets grew shorter from *c.* 1370 onwards, it was felt that decency demanded that what had been two separate stockings tied to the doublet waist, over the drawers, ought to be developed into a one-piece garment, like tights, still tied to the doublet waist by vertically laced ties or 'points', whence the French name ('a for-points') (compare illus. 31).[6] These laces, like those closing the front and the lower sleeves of the doublet, are often shown loosened, or every second set of them undone, on men working and bending.

Women's hose were shorter than men's, being gartered below the knee, and were rarely visible. Women could appear in public in their short-sleeved underdresses, but only if they were working women or housewives: upper class women were always subject to more constraints of behaviour, and the inflexibility of these rules increases, in theory at least, in direct proportion to an increase in social standing. These underdresses are usually referred to as 'kirtles' in English, and seem to have been called '*cotes*' in French, although *cotes* are sometimes also respectable outerdresses, as close-fitting as the kirtle but with full-length sleeves (see Glossary). Corseting could be provided by a combination of inserted pieces for the breasts in the shirt and tight lacing of the kirtle (see p. 44).

32. RIGHT: A back view of the kirtle worn by Mary Magdalene in Van der Weyden's 'Seven Sacraments' altarpiece, *c.* 1445, showing the close fit of the garment and its short sleeves, to which the Magdalene in her distress has omitted to attach her false oversleeves.

Above all else, the kirtle was an eminently practical garment: its short sleeves meant that it was a suitable garment to wear when a woman was working, and it is often depicted with a tuck running round it below the knee, or with a presumably detachable frill sewn on to it at this point, the tuck showing that it was too long for sensible wear when working or travelling and the frill showing that the garment could still be worn long after its

33. One of Jean de Berry's castles, that of Mehun-sur-Yèvre, in whose moat swim the duke's beloved swans, who reappear in his jewellery inventories and on his gown in illustration **41**.

hem had been frayed by contact with the ground, the frayed piece simply being replaced. Rich and poor alike employed these expedients on their kirtles.

A head-covering of some kind was essential for almost everybody. Men wore hoods or hats, depending on the prevailing fashion, and if the fashion required it, they carried their headgear instead of wearing it. Only young, unmarried girls could go about bare headed, with their hair loose: every other woman had to cover her head and with increasing age more and more of it. Among married women only queens wore their hair loose, but aristocratic women followed their example by wearing flimsier veils than middle- or working-class women: indecency in attire was always the prerogative of the upper classes.

International Gothic dress was as flamboyant and exuberant as contemporary architecture. Throughout France there are late mediaeval buildings decorated with curling serrated leaves carved on mouldings and pinnacles, looking like pieces of cloth whose flapping in the breeze has been frozen in stone. The edges of *houppelandes* and hoods were slashed in various patterns, such slashing being called 'dagging' in English and in French '*découpeures*' (see Glossary). The almost ragged appearance of this form of dress could be complemented by literally thousands of tiny gold or silver plaques or bells hanging from one *houppelande*. Raising an arm, or taking a step, would have caused the slashed edges to move, each piece hanging slightly differently, while the metalwork ensured that every movement caused a musical clinking. As they are depicted in the *Très Riches Heures*, Jean de Berry's castles are turned into fairy-tale buildings, potentially as mobile as their owner's dress, particularly his favourite castle of Mehun-sur-Yèvre, chosen as the symbol of wordly power with which Satan tempts Christ (illus. 33).[7]

Although Huizinga has denounced the spirit of the late middle ages as degenerate, surely the love of visual and aural splendour in the one object is the expression of nothing more sinister than a possibly rather naive pleasure in two of the senses. Dress began clinking, as well as swishing in its usual way, as early as 1389, when the Duke of Touraine acquired *une chayenne d'or à sonnettes*—a gold chain with bells—and in the following year the king and the duke went hunting in gowns (*robes*) to which twelve small gold and silver bells had been attached by gold ribbon. Indeed the pleasure of riding or hunting seems to have been heightened by the accompaniment of tinkling bells or discs, as cavalcades wound their way through the poets' perenially green woods, in unbroken sunshine, with birds singing cheerfully and fountains sparkling. The poor shepherdess, seduced and abandoned by her noble lover in Christine de Pisan's '*Le dit de la pastoure*' of 1403, was most taken by her knight's attendants and their

> '. . . *escharpes qui bel et gent*
> *Leur estoient avenans, Dont les cliquetes sonnans*
> *Tout le boys retentissoient Pour les sons qui en yssoient.*'

'. . . sashes which were beautiful and became them, with the whole wood echoing to the noise which came from their ringing trinketry.'

These jolly sounds, however could have more sinister applications: the author of a treatise on chivalry advocated that in battle a knight's horse trappings should be hung with bells so that as armour-clad man and beast thundered across the ground, the clanking of all the metal would enable the knight to spread terror before him, while doing wonders for his self-confidence. One can hardly suppose that these bells were the delicate items worn on

34. A wedding ceremony, *c.* 1380, with the female guests in, as would be expected, their most fashionable attire, with ribbon-like sleeves.

festive occasions, which looked like the bells we put on cats' collars today, to try to spread terror before the animals as they charge on unwitting birds.[8]

Now that the main features of International Gothic dress have been established, it is time to consider chronologically their development and application. Despite the improved tailoring techniques which became available *c.* 1380, many men were content to carry on wearing the ill-fitting, hip-length doublets of the past. The short-legged effect created by these garments, seen in the Machaut manuscript, reappears in some of the bas-de-page scenes in Jean de Berry's *Très Belles Heures de Notre Dame* of *c.* 1380 (illus. 34).[9] The cloakless women are half-way between the 'teddy bear' chests and upright stance of the Machaut girls, and the early fifteenth-century stance of round shoulders and swollen stomachs. Their sleeves still bite into the tops of the arms, but the neckline would now reveal quite an expanse of upper chest and shoulders, were the ladies not partially covering this area with a hood. The fronts of the hoods were so deep that they had to be turned back, as here, or were worn forward, shading the face, as on the woman in the cloak. Such hoods, predictably, provoked the anger of Eustache Deschamps, who likened them, very aptly, to louvres or porch roofs.

> *Faire un auvent com ceuls qui font verriere,*
> *Qui leur cuevure leurs visaiges devant*
> *Piet et demi, et semble a leur visiere,*
> *Qu'elles aient le chief d'un cahuant.*[10]

'. . . making a louvre as glass-workers do, which *covers their faces in front for a foot and a half*, [my italics] and, to look at them, they seem to have owls' heads.'

The girls (presumably unmarried) have their hair dressed in the usual plaits; all the women have ribbon oversleeves and fairly

35. Richard II of England seated on a throne somewhat undiplomatically draped with the arms of England *and* France, receives his copy of the proposals for friendship between France and England. Note the doublet of the courtier on the left, which explains the shape of the gown of the long-toed man on the right.

rounded shoulders. The mixture of stances in the manuscript accurately reflects the swift or gradual adoption of any fashion by different people.

By *c.* 1395, the foppishness of men's dress had become extreme: in 1395–6 a Celestine monk called Philippe de Maizieres wrote a treatise to encourage the alliance being discussed by Charles VI of France and Richard II of England in the shape of the marriage of the seven-year-old Isabella of France to the twenty-nine-year-old Richard; the British Library still owns Richard's copy of the manuscript (illus. 35).[11] On the right, watching the presentation of the manuscript to the seated Richard, gestures a courtier of exactly the kind to give Deschamps another attack of outraged decency, with his beard and head wedged against the high collar of his rich, short gown, his wide sleeves, his *mi-parti* (two-toned) hose and his toes, so long that one of them spills out

36. Although metallic leaves had long been out of fashion by the 1470s, when Van der Goes painted the 'Trinity Panels' for export to Scotland, they seem to have remained in use for decorating fancy dress, as here on hanging 'sleeves' worn by St George in the 'Trinity' panels. (H.M. the Queen, on loan to the National Gallery of Scotland, Edinburgh.)

over the edge of the picture! Deschamps' '*Balade contre les modes du temps*' describes very accurately this gentleman and the problems which he must have experienced with his attire:

> *Sont singe, tant sont escourté*
> *Et tant de taiches sur eulx a*
> *Comme panthère loqueté*
> *Sont, et de pluseurs draps brodé;*
> *De leurs manches font chalemiaux*
> *Et se souillent comme pourceaux*
> *Es laides ordures du mont;*
>
> *Adam ne Noé ne chaussa,*
> *Ne noz peres d'antiquité*
> *Telz solers comme on trouvera,*
> *Qui une aulne ont de bec anté,*
> *De denz de balaine enhanté;*
> *S'en reculent com creviciaulx,*
> *Leur cul monstrent et leurs museaulx*
> *Cueuvrent . . .*[12]

'. . . they're monkeys, so short are their clothes, and
there are so many spots on them and embroidered cloths,
that they're like a spotted leopard [literally, panther] they
make spouts of their sleeves and get themselves dirty like
pigs in the ugly filth of the world. . .

Not Adam, Noah or our forefathers of antiquity were
shod by the kind of shoes you will find [today], which
have an ell-long beak in front of them, fitted with a
whale's tooth [actually whalebone?]; walking
backwards like lobsters [the only way possible with
those toes?] they show their backsides and hide their
faces. . .'

They also wore long trains ('*queues*'), or tails, like calves', and, to cap it all, lay in bed till midday, having stayed up at night like owls.

Disparage them as Deschamps might, long trains could prove extremely useful, as Charles VI found out in 1392 at a masquerade at which he appeared with some friends, disguised as wild men. The *Chronique de Jean Brandon* describes these '*sauvages*', after whom the ball was named, as '*pilosis cum caudis vulpium sive cattorum, injecta pice, sulphure et aliis cito inflammativis induti*'—'dressed in the shaggy tails of foxes or cats, with the addition of pitch, sulphur and other things which could burst quickly into flames'. The pitch was the glue holding the furs on to the outfits, but it was generally suspected that Louis of Orléans had seen its other advantage, that it could incinerate the king. He was accused, posthumously, of having deliberately set these *sauvages* on fire, killing some of them, while the king escaped death only because of the presence of mind of his seventeen-year-old aunt, the Duchess of Berry, who smothered the flames with the train of her gown.[13]

As early as 1371 a bishop had preached against men's clothes which were so short that they revealed their breeches and 'their shame', as well as against women who wore horned headdresses, which made them look like snails and unicorns, as well as making horns at (i.e. cuckolding) their short-dressed menfolk. These devices were all likened to spiders spinning webs to trap flies.[14] Despite these remarks, it is difficult to find examples of men as indecently dressed as this until the 1390s, like the de Maizieres courtier, as most men seem to have retained a fairly modest length of outer garment. Similarly, despite the carpings about gibbet-like and snail-like headdresses for women, there is very little visual evidence for this type of headdress much before 1400. One may presume that only a very few, very brave spirits were flaunting themselves in these fashions, which may have lasted too short a time to find their way into general use and hence depiction.

It is difficult to define at what point women in general began to abandon fairly sober hoods and plaited hairstyles in favour of much more elaborate edifices, and the structure of these devices would also remain a mystery if we were forced to rely on wardrobe accounts for information, as they are remarkably silent about what was required. Fortunately, the plaintive Deschamps seems to come to our aid again. Dating his complaints about dress to the latter part of his life may appear to be wishful thinking, but increasing intolerance of the frivolities of fashion is generally a mark of increasing age, and many of Deschamps' descriptions fit too well to belong to any other period of his life: in his '*Balade sur l'estrangeté de l'atour et du chief que pluseurs dames font a present*'[15] he complained of the use of false hair, which housed mice and rats, likening some of the rig-outs to flat, two-handled baskets, while others made women look like cats, wolves or snails. Other fashions required the use of wool or *coton* (cotton wool) to make *bourrelets* (literally 'stuffed things') which were presumably like the padded roll of the woman in illustration 30. Deschamps reveals they could also be made of twisted dried stalks (a '*torche de pesas*'): in 1403 Isabella of Bavaria bought two and a quarter ells of black satin to finish (i.e. cover?) a *bourelet* for her.[16] All these devices were accompanied by *frontiaulx* (ribbons for the fore-head), nets, pins and knots, and their re-assembly every morning required much help, amounting to almost a week's work; along with her ordinary ribbons, the queen bought *frontelles* of black silk.[17] Whalebone may also have been used to maintain the rigidity of the fronts of ordinary hoods when they overhung the face, as the use of 'fish bones' in headdresses also attracted

37. The narrator of the *Roman de la rose* in his bedroom, and in a typically 'poetic' landscape. Note the simple furnishings of the room.

Deschamps' disapproval. At least Isabella's wardrobe accounts do mention the hanging undercuffs of illustration 38 as separate items: in 1403 she had '*une houppelande de veluiau noir et une paire de poingnetz de mesmes*'.[18]

It is a little easier to observe the structure of men's dress at this time. A copy of the *Roman de la rose* presents us with a scene of the narrator dressing himself and setting out across the archetypal sunlit landscape of poetry (illus. 37).[19] As he goes, he sews his sleeves tightly around his lower arm, a detail from the date of the composition of this section (before 1240); the painter has remained faithful to his text in including this, but has updated it by adding the trumpet-shaped cuff of this period. On his head he wears the Balaclava-type hood in the manner then becoming fashionable: the face opening was placed round the head, the shoulder cape was pleated, and wrapped round the whole was the long tail, keeping the pleats in position. Fortunately, the narrator here has not yet completed this operation, allowing us to see quite clearly that the hood is being worn at an angle of 90° from its previous position.

38. A stylishly dressed man tries to distract a studious lady from her books, *c.* 1402.

Deep armholes occur throughout Philip the Bold's copy of Boccaccio's *Des cleres et nobles femmes* (1401–2); illustration 38 shows their use combined with integral dagging on the under sleeves, as well as applied dagging on the contrasting set-in sleeves.[20] (The importance of the armhole is occasionally indicated by its being embroidered round: the green gowns for the royal May Day procession in 1408 were embroidered round the *assiette* of the left sleeve with peacock feathers and branches of may and broom, which spread thence across the body of the gown.[21]) Dagging as a separate item, made from a material other than that of the main body of the garment, occurs in 1397 when Georges de La Trémoille acquired a black satin *houppelande* and doublet with cloth *descoupeures*; the variety of shapes which dagging could take was wide. In 1389 the Duke of Touraine ordered five hoods, one of which had a tail (*cornete*) dagged into a fringe. In 1394 there were inventoried '*houppelandes entaillés menuement ou grossierement, en bandes, à pelz, et en quelconque autre manière*': '*houppelandes* nicked finely or coarsely, in strips, like stakes and in any other manner'. Large slashes were easily cut with scissors, but the more intricate leaf-like edges, where the large slashes were sometimes slashed within themselves, required something more sophisticated, as did large orders of clothing. In 1416, 460 livery robes of vermilion cloth of Ypres for the pages of John the Fearless, his son and his nephew had on each sleeve a black and green band, running from the shoulder to one cuff, the edges of the bands being trimmed with '*larges décopures de fin drap blanc faictes d'une fer dentelé*' (jagged piece of metal): the design of the dagging was set up in a jagged, sharp-edged metal die, which could be hammered through the cloth like a pastry-cutter. In the same year, Philip the Good's vermilion scarlet *robe* and hood were embroidered and then trimmed with black cloth dagging, made in the manner of squares with a *menu fer*, attached by gold thread; after this, small gold discs, with a plane (a Burgundian badge) in relief were placed in each square, and along the gold thread seam line were a large number of *branlant* (loose, therefore clinking) silver planes.[22]

Christine de Pisan commissioned a manuscript of all her poems written before October 1405 and presented it to Louis of Orléans, on whose death it passed into the collection of Jean de Berry.[23] In this manuscript (datable 1405–8) numerous ladies wear their hair coiled over their ears, under veils held almost taut between two 'horns' and falling straight down on to the forehead. As the almost straight upper edge of the veil is a peculiarity of this workshop (the Epître shop), it may reflect the version of the developing headdress which was preferred personally by the master of the shop.

Another workshop, that of the Master of the Cité des Dames, produced, *c.* 1406, three manuscripts of the work of Christine from which his name is derived, the 'Cité des Dames'; the same scenes produce the same headdresses, worn by various women, including Christine. These headdresses consist of a widely-set veil less tightly stretched and less concealing than those in the contemporary Epître master's scenes. The peculiarity of the veils of the Cité des Dames shop lies in their being in two layers, with the smaller veil on top, parallel to the under one at the sides. The other women wear flowers or horned *bourrelets* on uncovered hair, probably as an indication of their age and status (unmarried young women of good families).[24]

The upward and outward growth of the female headdress can be seen in illustration 39, taken from Jean de Berry's *Belles Heures*, which were finished in 1408 or 1409.[25] Although it is of the same type as the Epître Master's, with two corners of the veil brought forward at the temples, it is bigger, and reveals a black loop on the forehead (a *frontelle*?), which may well have been a device attached to the understructure of the headdress to enable its wearer to adjust its position if it slipped. A very detailed examination of the veil also reveals a pin in the right-hand corner at the side, and another one on top, just below the tip of the horn; both pins

39. The Limbourg brothers' version of an exceedingly beautiful woman and a young man determined to resist her advances, *c.* 1408.

anchor the veil to the piled-up hair. What caused the veil to curve over the head as it does cannot be ascertained; perhaps it was a strip of whalebone placed on top of the padded hair, attached to the *frontelle* and held in place by some of the many pins necessary for a lady's wardrobe, perhaps not unlike the silver ones bought for the Princess Isabella of France in 1403.[26] However the edifice was constructed, it must have demanded careful movements of its wearer, as a sudden turn of the head could have dislodged it, particularly if the veil were caught on the surface of a velvet or fluffy woollen cloth. Here there is no danger of the veil's catching on the dress: instead, one wonders how this rose-pink *cote hardie* remains on the shoulders, as there are no shoulder-straps above the tops of the sleeves. Only the very close fit of the sleeves (achieved by bias-cutting?) and of the bodice round the compressed rib cage, as well as a good deal of determination on the part of the wearer, could have kept such a neckline *in situ*. As with most depictions of a *cote hardie* or of a kirtle, the waistline is set almost at its natural level.

40. ABOVE: The respectably dressed, married owner of a Book of Hours kneeling before the Virgin and Child, and presented by an angel.

41. RIGHT: The bustle of life at the French court with aristocrats and liveried servants, as depicted by the Boucicaut Master who has even included the pot plants on the window ledge on the lower right.

The victim's rich blue *houppelande* has *bombarde* sleeves (see Glossary), lined in a sandy-brown fur, which also forms the much diminished collar. Although he is clean-shaven, as was normal by this date, he still has fairly long curly hair, much like that admired in the Poissy poem (p. 41). The egg-shaped torso shows that doublets with padded chests were still being worn, as can be seen in the more upright figures in the book's calendar scenes for April and May (ff. 5 and 6); long toes have disappeared from male fashion.

The use of two veils as seen first in the Cité des Dames shop spread into other painters' shops, as the fashion must have spread among women. By about 1410 it was becoming popular to draw up the two front corners of the under-veil to meet itself on the forehead, making the two horns much more pronounced, in some cases almost like snails' horns. Twice in the same Book of Hours[27] the Boucicaut Master painted the lady who owned the book; on f. 192 she appears with her family, clad in an orange-red *houppelande*, lined with miniver, with wide, open-ended sleeves, and a turned-down straight-edged collar which closes immediately under her chin. Her under veil is drawn together in the fashion outlined above, and over it a second veil is more casually draped, touching her collar. Behind her kneels her young daughter, in a red and gold *bourrelet* and dark blue *cote hardie*. The woman reappears on f. 290 (illus. 40) in a similar *houppelande*, and has some very clearly defined pins in her veils. An extremely long one runs from the tip of the horn towards her face, catching the upper veil on to the lower, while a shorter pin seems to ensure the continued descent of the lower veil towards her ear, after which it passes tightly round the back of her head. A *frontelle* peeps out from under the veils.

The increasing length of the veils meant that the high-standing *houppelande* collars of the first few years of the decade had to give way: with the increasing feeling of control imposed on the *houppelande* by descending veils, the bodice area was stacked into more careful folds, under turning-down or turned-down collars. *Les croniques de Burgues*[28] bought by Jean de Berry in 1407, shows Dido's attendants wearing good examples of both collars, which are no longer part of the gown's v-necked opening: the gowns close to half-way up the neck and square-cornered collars open from the top of the fastening. These ladies also wear *bourrelets*, sitting well clear of their collars. (The turned-down collar and the regular pleating of the gowns are very similar to those of the woman in illustration 40.)

Male dress in the same manuscript also shows the start of careful control of the pleating of the excess material in the body of the *houppelande*, although the folds are more widely spaced. One of the courtiers who attends Charles v in the scene of the manuscript's presentation wears such a *houppelande*, in pink, with *bombarde* sleeves, buttoned on the upper chest by three buttons, above which stands a fur-edged collar, much shorter than those of the women, and therefore not turned down. His outfit is completed by orange hose and a dark blue hood, with a dagged tail and the shoulder cape sitting out at the side of his head; colour combinations are not particularly subtle.

In 1409, Pierre Salmon, at the request of Charles vi, made a compilation of his works.[29] Illustration 41 shows Salmon presenting his *Lamentations* to the king, in the presence of Jean de Berry, while the life of the palace goes on around them. (This scene, attributed to the Boucicaut Master, occurs in what was probably the king's own copy of the compilation, and must therefore be datable to 1409 or shortly thereafter.) The king wears

42. The haughty-looking Duke of Burgundy, John the Fearless, accepts a copy of a manuscript, dressed in clothes resplendent in his personal badges.

his royal attire of baggy tunic under the type of mantle worn by the kings of France, where it has been turned through a quarter circle so that what would normally be the centre front opening has become a side opening, at his right hand; the left hand has to fight its way out by bunching up the cloak on to the upper arm and holding it there. Facially, it is an accurate depiction of the rather long-nosed king, who also had a slightly receding chin. (None of the French royal family in the fifteenth century was over-endowed with beauty, whether by contemporary or modern standards.)

Jean de Berry turns from the scene to address a man in the royal colours of green, red and white, which are worn by the mace bearer in the doorway, the man on horseback in the courtyard and the guard at the gateway. (When the king's *maître d'hôtel* was beheaded in the same year, he was taken to his execution dressed in his livery of red and white *houppelande*, hood, and one red and white stocking. Protocol was observed even to his wearing his gilded spurs.[30]) Berry's *bombarde*-sleeved *houppelande* is made of black satin or velvet into which are worked gold swans, one of his personal badges. His collar, which is higher at the back than those of the other, younger men, touches his fur-brimmed hat; this hat is usually part of the duke's portraits towards the end of his life, as can be seen in the January miniature from his *Très Riches Heures*.[31] This portrait is also a good likeness of the duke.

Outside the palace two men seek admission, both wearing hoods with forward-flipped shoulder capes and dagged edges; the man behind has his *cornete* hanging across his chest, while his companion has wrapped his around his head. At the right walks a man carrying a staff and a flagon, doubtless going on some errand for a thirsty great one. His deeply-cut armholes are among the last to be seen on the outer garments of fashionably dressed figures, although some doublets ordered for John the Fearless's family in 1416 are described as being '*à grans assietes*' (with large armholes).[32] Their later appearances are confined to poorer wearers, who could have bought them from second-hand clothes sellers, of whom there were many.

The question of the accurate depiction of well-known individuals, as well as the inclusion of a typical feature of their dress, as brought up by this scene and others in this manuscript, leads to the obvious conclusion that artists were working from extensive pattern books, in which they would record almost anything of interest which came their way. A patron need not have gone near the painter he was employing, if he was satisfied the painter possessed an adequate likeness from which to work; such must have been the case with John the Fearless, who appears in panel and miniature paintings in approximately the same hat, making the same over-nice gesture with one hand (illus. 42). A scene in the Salmon manuscript shows the Duke of Burgundy in a tall bag-shaped hood, like the one here, with a caped hood worn

in its original manner of the 1370s and 1380s, which it seems to be here, although less clearly.[33] In both scenes one hand emerges from a closed under-sleeve, worn beneath dagged *bombarde* sleeves, to make this strange gesture of apparently holding something small between thumb and forefinger. Although in the Salmon manuscript the duke is standing and facing left, while here he is seated and looking right, there can be no doubt that the same source was used to produce these 'portraits', particularly as both scenes are the work of the Boucicaut shop. Instead of these profile views, a fifteenth-century panel painting of the duke in Antwerp shows him in three-quarters view, wearing the same hat, with the same type of under-sleeve and dagging on his *houppelande* sleeve.[34] Although the hands are neatly at rest in the Antwerp portrait, and there is no hood, all the pictures may derive from one image which could explain his rather bizarre gesture: the Louvre portraits, show him holding a ring, perhaps brought back with him from the crusade mentioned on p. 36.[35]

The scene before us comes from the duke's copy of *Les merveilles du monde* (B.N. fr. 2810) which he gave to Jean de Berry in January 1413 (1412, old style);[36] the duke wears a collar of gold planes which are also worked in gold on his scarlet *houppelande*, as well as being attached to the dagging of his hood, round the shoulders. When Louis of Orléans adopted a knotty stick as his device, symbolizing his intention of clubbing John the Fearless, with the words '*Je l'envie*' (I challenge), John calmly replied by adopting the motto '*Ic houd*' (I accept) and, as his device, the plane with which he would wear away the Orléans club. The whole outfit here is very like that acquired by his son in 1416, even to the use of red and black cloth, as well as the 460 liveries for his pages (p. 90). When faced with this degree of elaboration in male dress, one begins to wonder by what right did men carp about female dress.

An idea of ordinary female dress *c.* 1412 can be gained from a study of the women in a scene from Terence's *Adelphi* in a manuscript now called *Le Térence des ducs* from its having been owned by Louis, Duke of Guyene, who died in 1415, and then by Jean, duc de Berry.[37] The seated, older woman wears an overdress whose sleeves cease at the elbow, at which point they develop a slight tail, possibly a vestige of the ribbon sleeves of the 1380s (illus. 34), and what appears to be a man's hood, with the face opening drawn over the head from the back and the shoulder cape gathered at the back of the neck. The hood has only a short tail, which has been flipped forward, as have the front flaps on the hoods of the younger women. The standing woman lifts the hem of her *cote hardie* to reveal her *cote*. Both she and her companion on the left are wearing typically middle-class hoods, beneath which can be traced the outline of the rolls into which their hair must have been put to allow their hoods to fit closely to their heads;

poor Pamphila, as she twists the sheet in her agony, has been deprived of the dignity of her hood, being left in the scarf in which her hair has been bound, presumably to act as a partial support for the front flaps of her hood.

Not even great ladies were averse to appearing in public in what looks remarkably like hair in rollers, covered by a scarf. The ladies in illustration 43 come from Jean de Berry's most famous manuscript, the *Très Riches Heures*, begun *c.* 1413 by the Limbourg brothers and left incomplete at their death in 1416.[38] They ride out into the woods on May Day, accompanied by their gallant knights, musicians, lap dogs pretending to be hunting dogs and the sound of clinking metal chains and bezants (coin-like sequins) sewn on to clothes and horse trappings. Only one lady has a headdress; all the rest are bare-headed, except for the gold nets and leaves which adorn their horned hairstyles. The leading lady wears a wide, swooping arrangement of veils, in which the tiny under-veil does not conceal her hair, probably because she is much younger than the lady in illustration 40, and Christine de Pisan, who was born in 1363 or 1364 and widowed in 1389. Three of the ladies also wear green gowns, which were considered particularly suitable for the festivity before them. Instead of having slashed edges on their attire, they have gold fringing, on the long blue and gold under-sleeves of the first lady and inset into the back seam of the sleeves on the woman second from the right. Behind her rides a girl in a violet-blue dress decorated with gold crowns: her white under-sleeve trails across her hand, reaching to a point we cannot see. The two *houppelandes* have turned-down grey fur collars, one of which can be seen to be closed no higher than the base of the throat, although the collar itself still sits like the earlier closed ones. The broad gold bands with the hanging gold streamers, worn by men and women, are probably what Christine de Pisan (p. 83) called *escharpes*.

The *houppelande* of the man leading the procession is of rich blue figured velvet with gold leaves scattered across its surface, probably sewn on so that they shake as he moves. It is split up the back, to allow him to sit astride his horse, which no lady ever did, and therefore no lady's *houppelande* ever incorporates this feature; his collar is also much lower than the woman's, even though his head has been shaved half-way up. His white stocking is embroidered with what looks like gold tears or raindrops, a fairly common conceit among lovers: tears decorate the sleeve of a lover in a manuscript of the poems of Christine de Pisan.[39]

Next to him rides a man in black-and-white and red motleyed garment, some of the royal livery colours. Not only are the outer edges of this garment dagged in 'teeth' to which gold tips have been added, but the join of the black-and-white sections has also been treated in this way. His hood's cape has been dagged within its main dagging, and the gold 'teeth' have been added to its *cornete*. Perhaps this sleeveless over-garment, with its elaborate

43. A group of aristocrats riding out into the woods near Paris on May Day. In 1408 the royal tailors had to make and embroider round the left armholes of four green gowns, with matching hoods and dagging, in a week, for the Maying that year.

decoration and livery colours, corresponds to the garment called a *heuque* in accounts, where it is an almost exclusively male garment, often connected with issues of livery. In 1412 John the Fearless ordered '*une paire de manches ouvertes pour mettre soux une heuque*', made of black stain figured with large green leaves and brocaded with baskets in gold:[40] the wearing of open sleeves under another sleeved garment would not have been particularly easy, unless the over-sleeves were also open, and such an elaborate textile, as this was, must have been for obvious display. These factors, combined with the lack of mention of sleeves as part of any *heuque*, suggest that a *heuque* did not have sleeves. In 1413 the city fathers of Paris decked themselves out in violet

44. Brocade- and jewel-bedecked aristocrats in another cloudless landscape, with well-ordered trees and garden, and in the background Jean de Berry's castle of Dourdan.

heuques, covered in silver leaves with, in silver embroidery, the legend '*Le droit chemin*';[41] in the same year Charles of Orléans ordered four, made of Brussels violet cloth, embroidered with the same legend, with gilded leaves attached to them, and a further six embroidered with shrub roots, a reference to his 'knotty stick' device.[42] By decking themselves out in this livery the Parisians were affirming their support of Charles of Orléans in the Burgundian-Armagnac struggle.

Meiss has suggested that the first lady may be Berry's daughter Marie, accompanied by her third husband Jean, duc de Bourbon, who succeeded to the title in 1410, and claims that all the horse trappings contain the badge of the Bourbons, a roundel filled with six small dishes surrounding a seventh at the centre. This is an attractive theory, making the book, which already contains depictions of the duke's castles, more personal, especially since he himself is shown dining on f. 2r, surrounded by his household, his gold plate and his tapestries. Unfortunately, the comparative immodesty of the first lady's dress is incompatible with the age of Marie de Berry at this time, as she would have been middle-aged; perhaps the girl is one of her daughters. It has also been proposed that the protagonists in the April calendar miniature (illus. 44) are the duke's daughter Bonne and her husband Bernard, comte d'Armagnac, leader of the Orléans faction, witnessing the betrothal of their eleven-year-old daughter Bonne to the sixteen-year-old Charles, Duke of Orléans.[43]

The mother, who gently propels her daughter towards her betrothed, wears a black *houppelande* with the opening collar, wide sleeves and gold-brocaded red undersleeves, edged with gold fringing. Dagging is much less common on women's dress than it is on men's: when it occurs in the August miniature on the sleeves of the blue *houppelande* very similar to that worn by the young man here and in the May scene, and seen, in addition, from three quarters back, it is only the presence of a white horned veil on the head which marks the personage as female, men's *houppelandes* being belted almost as high as women's. The mother's hairstyle is the same as the May Day ladies', except for the replacing of the nets with a *bourrelet* covered in gold roses.

The girl at the back of the group is dressed in a blue *bourrelet* with her hair rippling down her back, as does the hair of the other two girls; her sleeves and under-skirt are royal blue, with a black *cote hardie* lined and trimmed in white, including the ribbon sleeves. In fact, the frequency of black garments in this scene is remarkable: few manuscript pictures give the impression that black was as popular a colour as wardrobe accounts reveal it was. Instead, clothes tend to be painted as red, green, blue or pink, probably because black is a difficult colour to introduce into small pictures without its 'killing' other colours. The other bending girl wears pale pink lined with blue-grey, with tight black under-sleeves peeping from under her wide gown sleeves, which spread beside her on the ground.

The dress of the fiancée is particularly interesting because of the fairly unusual features which it incorporates, including the use of yellow for the underdress. Yellow is not at all common in accounts or in illustrations: the objection to its use cannot have been purely aesthetic, as many women, including those present in this scene, have hair of almost the same shade as the *cote*. The objection was probably mainly social, as Jews were expected to wear yellow, to proclaim who and what they were, although it is difficult to see why this colour should have been singled out for them. The gown with its décolletage presents another miracle of engineering, especially since the sleeves hang straight from the shoulders to the ground, like two broad bands, complete with white fur lining to add to their weight and downward drag.

The gown itself is too long to allow normal unimpeded walking, and is bunched up under the stomach, thereby continuing the diagonal slant of shoulders and pelvis into the folds of the skirt. The hem of the skirt, which passes behind the untrimmed sleeve, appears to be dagged at the point where the violet-blue damask meets the white fur hem and lining, but it is far more likely that the uneven edge is caused by the use of a row of small animal skins, like ermines, without their black-tipped tails but with the fur of the heads; the snout and sides of the heads would then give the trefoil-like upper edge to the white band. (Rogier van der Weyden used such skins, complete with legs and ears but minus the tails, to trim the dress of the youngest Magus in his 'Columba Altarpiece' of *c.* 1460–2).[44]

Hats were fairly common items in the female wardrobe: in 1412 the Duchess of Burgundy had her feather hat, which probably looked like the one here, altered to make it lower.[45] The free-hanging false sleeve is not particularly common in French dress at this date, although it appears for many years afterwards in Dutch dress and German dress, where it can take on the shape of a cloak which is attached to the gown at the shoulder seams (see illus. 52).

Returning to the April scene from the *Très Riches Heures*, we find little to note in the men's dress, except for the fantastic forms into which the hood could be twisted, and the introduction of regular gathers on the top of the sleeve of the father's gown. The fiancé's sleeves may have their patterns woven in ('brocaded') or the design may be embroidered: a repeated design, such as this, is less likely to be embroidered, since its repetition could be achieved by mechanical means on a loom. Even 'one-off' pieces of cloth could be ordered, woven with the badges or motifs of the commissioner (see p. 102). If the fiancé is indeed meant to be Charles of Orléans, his attire here is almost sober beside a gown he ordered in 1414,[46] which was almost an advertisement for his interest in poetry: all along the sleeves were embroidered the words of the song '*Madame je suis plus joyeulx*', with decoration provided by 960 pearls. A further 568 pearls were required to make the 142 notes of the song, each note being four pearls set in a square. For the pearls alone he paid 276l 7s.6d. *tournois* (the pound of Tours, which was worth four-fifths of the pound of Paris, the *livre parisis*. Neither was a coin, being simply money of account, much as the guinea and crown were for many years. The *franc* was a coin worth one *livre tournois*). It is impossible to translate costs accurately: suffice it to say that for just part of the decoration on one garment, this was a costly acquisition, especially since almost the same sum (276 *francs* 5s. *tournois*) was paid for the gold and silk threads and the work involved in decorating a black satin *houppelande* with wolves and ants on the background, the application of his six livery colours in a screw-shape, on front and back, all in embroidery, and, in gold and pearl embroidery, a large crossbow on the left sleeve.[47] Still, propaganda of any kind is rarely cheap, and no doubt Charles considered the money well spent, whether he was trying to impress a lady or intimidate John the Fearless.

Despite the deadly seriousness of the thoughts which prompted such bizarre displays, there was a superficial frivolity in its structure, which probably guided most people in the assembling of their wardrobes. Soon, however, the fairy-tale feeling behind International Gothic dress was to disappear, leaving behind only its outward appearance used in a more heavy-handed way. The French defeat at Agincourt in 1415 cannot be held to be directly responsible for altering fashion, but the mood of panic and despair which it engendered most certainly could have put paid to the attitudes which guided the light-hearted fantasies of this style. Men's and women's clothes became much more solid, if not more sensible, in their construction.

Before the podgy-faced Queen of France kneels Christine de Pisan, presenting her with a complete set of her works, commissioned again from her favourite workshop, that of the Master of the Cité des Dames. Meiss dated this manuscript *c.* 1410, then *c.* 1415–20, without its final date ever being established except that it must be after 1409, because the Master has collaborated on and was influenced by the 1409 Pierre Salmon manuscript (illus. 41).[48] Clearly, a manuscript which requires to be bound in two volumes as this does, must have taken some time to execute, and the presentation miniature may have been executed towards the end of the campaign, as few people, on receiving their portrait in a new book or picture, would care to see themselves as already out-dated. Comparisons with the *Très Riches Heures* ladies lead to the conclusion that this scene, at least, must have been produced after 1415. There are subtle variations in the dress of the women in the manuscript, suggesting a fairly lengthy programme of work on it: on f. 150 a queen wears a wider *bourrelet* than those of her ladies, whose turned-down collars still sit a little high off the shoulders, whereas on f. 376 the young lady standing in a garden with her lover has a *bourrelet* to match the queen's, as well as a slightly lower-set collar. The ladies in the queen's chamber in the presentation scene all wear the wider *bourrelet*, Isabella's naturally being bigger and better than anyone else's. Throughout the manuscript, the use of the *bourrelet* coincides with two puffs of hair sitting out on the temples and, in the case of, presumably, married women, a small filmy veil is wrapped round the back of the head and tucked under the puffs of hair. All the *bourrelets* also require a *frontelle*; perhaps the whole structure is now like a hat, from which the wearer's own hair appears only at the temples, the rest at the sides being false and covering the under-structure of the edifice.

The gown collars sit more neatly on the shoulders than in the *Très Riches Heures*, and to protect the fur collars from the neck and vice versa, the shirt collar begins to make itself seen, lying neatly on top of the fur. Before this date, one is hardly aware of the existence of the under-shirt, probably because tailors were careful to make them according to the type of dress with which they were worn: presumably it was to wear with a *cote hardie* that the queen ordered '*iiij chemises a bas colet*' (four low-collared shirts) in 1404.[49]

The degree of elaboration of the materials worn by the queen's ladies is an indication of each lady's rank: the queen herself wears a gold patterned brownish-red *houppelande*, lined with ermine, while two of her ladies wear matching outfits of black patterned in gold and white, and the decoration of their *bourrelets* is as elaborate as the queen's. Their outfits must reflect the issue of a livery, since even the great could not be expected to wear out their own clothes in the service of the royal family. In humbler attire and on lower seats, are four more ladies-in-waiting, three of whom wear plain, probably woollen, *houppelandes*, with smaller and less elaborately decorated *bourrelets*, or 'stacked' veils held high above their heads in two horns. The difference between the veils painted by the Cité des Dames shop and the Limbourg brothers need not imply a vast difference in the dates of their works, simply in the taste of the artists, as seems to have been the case with the Epître shop. The use by the Boucicaut and Cité des Dames Masters of the same type of veil headdresses *c.* 1410, in the Book of Hours (illus. 40) and the Christine de Pisan manuscripts, is a further proof of their connexion mentioned above. Although he too seems to have been involved in the British Library's Christine manuscript, the Epître Master did not introduce his own preferred dress patterns: instead his bizarre colour schemes of, for instance, orangey-red set against pink, make his presence felt, as on f. 376, where the lover wears a pink hood and a vermilion *houppelande*.

Throughout her life, Isabella delighted, as did her contemporaries, in lavish brocades and velvets: for instance, in 1403 she bought some green satin and velvet patterned with little white and vermilion flowers and figured velvet woven with the royal badge in gold, i.e. broom and chestnut branches interlaced, with great lozenges full of besants (light hanging metal discs). Valentina, Duchess of Orléans, had owned, among other fancy textiles, a length of azure blue *baudequin* (the most expensive cloth of gold) worked with lions, crowns brocaded in gold and vermilion silk roses.[50] Given this love of exotic textiles, the painter has done justice in this scene to the queen's tastes.

Christine's own attire alters little throughout the years in which she was commissioning manuscripts: she usually wears a closely-fitting mid-to-royal blue dress, with short, square-ended hanging sleeves, as here. That this dress is meant to point her out instantly to the viewer cannot be doubted, as a complex visual language was part of the relationship between painter and spectator, but its continued use must have met with her approval, and may even be a reflection of her own way of dressing. Although her headdress alters little, it does alter more than her gown; sometimes it is possible to discern a white scarf filling in the space between the veils and the gown neckline, as would befit the widow she was. The relative stability of the form of her dress, while useful to the painter, may actually have been caused by the tendency of widow's dress to 'freeze' women in outmoded fashions. (Thirty years later, the widowed Michelle de Vitry (illus. 71) was painted in attire not markedly different from that of her daughter Marie, who was a nun at Poissy.) However Christine's outfits are to be interpreted, they are not full mourning, of which we get a glimpse in the Duchess of Orléans' inventory in 1408: we know from Monstrelet that she was given to making great display of her mourning (see p. 16). She owned seven '*mantelez crespés*' and '*deux trusses crespés, avecques les barbettes*' (crêpe or crinkled cloaks), and two crêpe-covered head rolls (*trusses*: *tourses*: twists), with the chin cloths.[51] Although the duchess was conforming to the demands of the need to cover her neck with cloths, and wear crêpe, she was not prepared to give up the fashionable *bourrelet*, except that calling it a *trusse* disguises slightly its relation to contemporary fashion. Deschamps had talked of *bourrelets* and *torches*, as he spelled it, side by side (p. 87).

Although the approach of the Master of the Cité des Dames was not as ethereal as that of the Limbourgs, they did depict contemporary fashions, as the similarities between the *bourrelets* show, rather than the differences between the veils. The Master outlived the Limbourgs, and his less joyful depiction of dress reflects what happened in dress itself, as solidity became more important. The *bourrelets* became top-heavy, as did the veils; the dagging of gown textiles and linings, instead of meeting neatly in a seam where each struck to its own side of the garment, increasingly became outlined by a roll of fur turning over from the lining, thereby stiffening the edges of once mobile sections of garments. The increasingly grim situation in France deprives us of visual information on the scale in which it has so far been available to us, although wardrobe accounts give the impression that dress was as frivolous as it had been; only the scrappy pieces of visual information tell us of this hardening in the dress, which the wardrobe accounts cannot convey.

5 'Sober Frivolity', *c*.1420–*c*.1440

In this chapter we shall look at the gradual disappearance of the International Gothic style from dress, from its more sober post-Agincourt form, until all that is left of it is a small strip of dagging on hoods. A new aesthetic value takes over, that of control of dress, which shows itself in men's dress by an increase in the amount of material, allowing the gown to be set into ever-neater and more pronounced vertical folds, and in the imparting of a permanent shape to the hood's rolled edge. In women's dress there is a more gradual process, almost the reverse of what happens to men's dress: the tiny folds on the gown bodice are removed by the reduction of the amount of material required, and after a few years of uncontrolled bagginess, the bodice becomes so skimpy that it has to be left open to the belt.

The increase in surviving visual material from the Netherlands, as well as a few very loosely datable manuscripts from France, makes it possible to speculate on the extent of differences in dress from region to region, even from city to city: thus, Ghent and Bruges were both in the county of Flanders, but is it a difference in age or a difference in cities which causes the differences in the veils of the donatrix of the Ghent altarpiece (illus. 58), finished in 1432, and of Giovanna Arnolfini (illus. 59), painted in 1434? In which aspect of women's dress was regionalism most marked, and how far did this affect aristocratic dress? We shall not find complete answers to these questions, but indications that although gowns may have differed from region to region, and been worn with these differences by aristocrats, it was the type of headdress which really marked off various groups. Thus aristocratic women may have been more advanced and uniform in their taste in head decoration than their lower-class contemporaries, who lagged behind and were more parochial in their tastes. Men's dress too, outside court circle, seems to have been subject to regional variations, albeit much more subtly.

One of the most impressive depictions of International Gothic dress in its post-Agincourt (or post-Limbourg) form is the Eyckian drawing (illus. 45)[1] of John IV, Duke of Brabant, grandson of Philip the Bold, who was born in 1403 and died in 1426. With the lack of enough comparative material to suggest a date,

45. The young John, Duke of Brabant, second husband of Jacqueline of Bavaria and grandson of Philip the Bold of Burgundy, in the heavier type of *houppelande* which appears by *c.* 1420.

46. The commemorative or epitaph painting of Yolande Belle, who died in 1420. Epitaph paintings were very common in northern Europe, but comparatively few have survived, and their use tends to be unknown to the general public.

we must content ourselves with an examination of the main features of the dress.

The young duke makes his dignified way across the page, with his great *houppelande* sleeves trailing heavily towards the ground, their edges quite different in weight and feeling from those of the men in the *Très Riches Heures* (illus. 43 and 44): they almost seem to have been padded, as does the front of his hood, although it is doubtful whether it would retain a circular shape off the head. The *cornete* has been attached to the hood, having first been folded in four, and the entire hood very closely resembles that of the donor of the 'Seilern Triptych', one of the earliest works attributed to Robert Campin (illus. 27), although there the gown is not as heavily trimmed with fur. (The 'Seilern Triptych' is usually thought of as being *c.* 1415.) The duke's belt is slipping towards the natural waist level, where it retains folds of vertically increasing size, such as would result from the gown's being cut in flared panels, or gores, to form a segment of a circle: the first available reference to the use of gores ('*girons*') in a *houppelande* occurs in 1416, when John the Fearless acquired one '*faicte à XXIIII girons*', almost as though each fold of the gown was cut as a separate piece, which is still not its most extravagant feature, since the sleeves of this particular gown were covered in embroidery and goldsmith's work, making it a very lavish garment. A few items later, the accounts mention a similar *houppelande*.[2] The 'padded' feeling of hood and sleeve edgings, the greater control of the folds and their splaying out, and the lowering waistline, help to give this outfit the air of being *c.* 1420.

Even children's dress was not exempt from this increasing rigidity, as illustration 46 shows.[3] In 1420, in Ypres in Flanders, died Yolande Belle, wife of Joos Brid, and to commemorate her, her family set up this painting over her grave. Before the Virgin and Child kneels the family, with the patron saints of the parents. To complement her husband's knightly attire of armour and coat-of-arms, Yolande wears a grey cloak (a *mantel a parer?*) over her red *houppelande*, while the four sons wear what appear to be *heuques*, all with the fur lining turned out at the edges and trimming the scale-like dagging on the eldest son's red *heuque*. (In March 1420 the Dauphin ordered an embroidered *heuque* of vermilion scarlet, brocaded with gold; its lower part was covered in black woollen cloth, dagged in the manner of scales, which were *pourfilées* [edged] and *nervées*—veined, with thin narrow trimming?[4] Perhaps this garment should be regarded as providing evidence of the hardening of dress, but if it does, it is almost alone in its usefulness: the rest of Charles's *heuques* for that year are as frivolous-sounding as earlier examples.) The second son wears his blue *heuque* belted round the hips, in keeping with the dropping male 'waistline'. All the men still have their hair cropped very short, although the disappearance of the high collar would have allowed them to grow their hair longer. Closed sleeves, like purses with drawstrings, become normal everyday wear for men, being shrunken versions of the great closed *bombarde* sleeves of earlier years.

Yolande's cloak hides most of her *houppelande*, but enough is visible to show that it is similar to those of her two elder daughters, with their *bombarde* sleeves, high-set belts and flat fur collars, over which lie the collars of their under-shirts. (In Paris, in 1420, a landlord seized a servant's possessions to pay her mistress's rent: not unnaturally, the servant retaliated by appropriating some of her mistress's belongings, including a *houppelande* '*a colet renversé*', probably very like those here, as the defaulting mistress was of a similar social level, being the dowager lady of Miramont.[5]) The third daughter, being only a child, wears only a *cote hardie*. All the daughters wear *bourrelets* with *frontelles*; the two older girls have curls of hair sitting out beyond the nets under their *bourrelet* like those in the Christine de Pisan manuscript, as well as very fine veils sweeping on to their temples. Yolande's headdress is much more modest than those of her daughters, but is no less acceptable, incorporating as it does items we shall see more of, linen veils with crinkly edges set over small, netted horns of hair. To minimize any wrinkles, she has a finer veil on her forehead with three tiny pendants hanging from the hairnet. The Virgin also wears a crinkly-edged veil draped over her head and shoulders.

As if to compensate for the move away from light-heartedness in most aspects of dress, women's headdresses became more and more bizarre in the 1420s. *Bourrelets* remained in use, as did veils supported by unseen devices: the former grew taller and wider, while the latter managed to outdo them, by taking up even more space at the sides of the neck and resembling white doves in flight. Once again, the variety of veil arrangements is considerable, and the lack of firmly datable evidence increases the difficulty of deciding whether we are looking at two contemporary versions or two consecutive versions, with the additional problems of workshop preferences and regional variations.

Both a flat fur collar and a belt were items forbidden to prostitutes: in 1422 they were ordered not to wear '*habit fourré de gris a colet rabatu*' and in 1426 one was deprived of her '*houppelande de drap pers, fourrée par le collet de penne de gris*' and '*une ceinture sur tissu de soie noire avec garniture d'argent*'; in 1425 the provost of Paris defended himself, when accused of officiousness, of having simply diligently searched out '*des ceintures et habis dissolus, defenduz aux femmes amoureuses*'.[6] If the wages of sin were not to be a respectable wardrobe, then why was even an '*habit dissolu*' forbidden, one wonders.

Many of the women in the *Bedford Hours* still wear wide sleeved *houppelandes*, as do the attendants in illustration 47, depicting the 'Legend of the Fleur-de-lys'.[7] The attendant holding the queen's cloak in both scenes is dressed in red, with a very tall, deep *bourrelet*, and, most importantly, an increase in vertical emphasis on the upper body, with a deliberate showing of the gown's centre-front closing. To the left in both scenes stands a lady in green, with a red belt, and M-shaped veils, while in the upper scene there is a lady in an open-necked black gown with *bombarde* sleeves, carrying the queen's prayer-book and rosary: on top of all this, she wears the kind of headdress which drove two itinerant preachers, Brothers Richard and Thomas, into frenzied denunciations, extended with the aid of small children, who were enlisted to run after offenders in the street, mocking them.

In 1428 Brother Thomas Couette created a sensation by preaching for five or six months in Flanders, Artois, around Tournai, Cambrai, Amiens and Ponthieu, against women of any rank who wore high headdresses, which had been the custom of noble women in that area. By promising days of pardon to the children, he encouraged them to yell at the women '*Au hennin!*' until the unfortunate women were chased to a place of safety. (*Hennin* seems to derive from the Netherlandish *henninck*, a cock.) Any grand lady who went to the friar's sermons had to appear in the attire of working women, '*de petit et povre estat*'. Many of them underwent a genuine change of heart after these sermons, burning their tall headdresses before his pulpit, and taking to wearing simple headdresses, like those of the *béguines* (a lay sisterhood); this change, however, says Monstrelet, lasted but a short time, as once the danger was past, like snails they put forth their horns again, at least as tall as they had been.[8]

47. Out for a stroll with her ladies in their 'snail' headdresses and voluminous gowns, the Queen of France encounters a hermit who gives her a miraculous lily-strewn cloth, with which she drapes her husband's shield. Because of his victories thereafter, the king, Clovis, becomes a Christian.

Encouraged perhaps by this, albeit transitory, success, a Brother Richard condemned the women of Paris in 1429, forcing them to burn, in public, their headdresses, such as *bourreaux* (*bourrelets*), *truffeaux* (= truffles, false hair at temples?) and pieces of leather or whalebone which were put into their hoods to make them stiffer or turned over in front: the ladies gave up their horns, their trains and all attendant display.[9] Brother Richard was himself burned for heresy in Rome after criticizing the pope.

The *Bedford Hours* headdresses must approximate very closely to what Brother Richard was attacking, particularly the great

48. While somewhat unrealistic in its scale, this little scene gives a lively picture of the speed of hunting parties, although the ladies' headdresses must have made speed rather difficult in woodlands.

dove-like one of the third lady, with its enormous starched outer veil pinned on to the understructure on the front of the centre dip. The understructure may well be a *bourrelet*, like her companion's, with a small veil wrapped round from the back and left open at the front, before the great top veil was attached: all the veils used seem to have been simple squares or rectangles, any deficiency in shape being remedied by pins, as cutting the veils would have restricted the variety of forms into which they could have been made from day to day.

Pins play a very pronounced role in the headdresses in the *Hours of Marguerite d'Orléans*, datable between 1426 and 1438:[10] the dress is probably of *c.* 1435. As the hunting party (illus. 48) hurtles across the bottom of the page, one is left wondering how the great edifices remained on the head; they must, in these cases, have had *bourrelet*-type under-bonnets with two veils wrapped round the back, one long and narrow, brought forward and folded backwards to leave its short edges above the level of the other veil. Pins have been inserted in the front to keep the lower veil attached to the understructure. Fortunately, hermit saints were prone to attack from demons disguised as fashionable young women: if corroboration of the depravity of these headdresses were needed, it could be provided by the deviless tempting St Antony on f. 173 in the same manuscript.

The gowns no longer display many features of the *houppelande* proper, as their volume has been greatly reduced in the body and, more markedly, in the sleeves. The collars are developing a V-shaped spread, but more slowly than in Netherlandish dress (see p. 114).

Yet another version of the monstrous female headdress occurs in the Book of Hours which belonged to someone in the family of Ralph Nevill, Earl of Westmorland, among whom were members of the English forces of occupation (illus. 49 and 50). At the back of the group of mother and daughters appears one example of the

usual wide *bourrelet*, with the usual decoration of spots and central rosette, but the other headdresses are quite unlike anything seen in French art until now. For all their size, there had been a certain elegance and lightness in French headdress, imparted by their division into two definite 'horns'; on the other hand, these headdresses worn by Englishwomen are as unfortunate by the aesthetics of their own time as they are by ours: they are almost certainly English importations, as national and regional peculiarities are most marked in headdresses.[11]

The mother, as befits her rank of daughter of John of Gaunt, son of Edward III, wears an ermine-lined cloak over her V-necked, narrow-sleeved gown and, as befits her widowhood, a plain linen-covered version of her daughters' headdresses, with a widow's neck and chin covering. Behind her, her daughters seem to be ranged according to their seniority. Immediately behind the countess kneels the daughter who should be identified, from the arrangement of the coats-of-arms below, as Cicely, Duchess of York, mother of Edward IV and Richard III: she wears a *bombarde*-sleeved *houppelande*, with a wide, square-edged collar, while the other gowns, with their straight sleeves, appear to be more advanced versions of this *houppelande*. The two daughters at the back, despite the appearance of their coats-of-arms as married women, wear *bourrelets* without veils, and one wears only a *cote hardie*: they may be the youngest daughters, perhaps not long

49. LEFT: The widowed Countess of Westmorland and her daughters. The arms of the countess are those on the extreme left (the royal arms of England with Nevill) and next to them, the Duchess of York's (Nevill with England).

50. ABOVE: The Earl of Westmorland and his sons. The only deviation from the fashionable norm of *c.* 1430 is in the dead earl's gown, but his 'portrait' may depend on one taken earlier, in his lifetime.

married. Not content with a jewelled fretwork cover for their headdresses, the ladies have outlined them round the face, across the top and at the side-front of the 'horns' with jewelled ribbons, while in sharp contrast to this glittering splendour are opaque rectangular linen veils, secured to the upper edge of the headdresses.

Let us now turn our attention further north, where the availability of visual evidence becomes widespread enough to allow us to distinguish regional differences in women's dress, as well as the concessions to the demands of pictorial composition which had to be made by wearers of large headdresses.

In March 1430 in the northern Netherlands Lysbeth van Duvenvoorde was married to Symon van Adrichem, and it was apparently to commemorate this event, that her portrait (illus. 51)[12] was painted. Her dress is staggeringly old-fashioned for such a date, but there are other examples from the north to confirm its authenticity. She still wears a *houppelande*, with dagged *bombarde* sleeves, too-long damask undercuffs with applied lettering, collar still not flat to the shoulders, and bells hanging from her belt, all features which could be expected to date the painting to *c.* 1415. However, the emphasis on the length of the front closing is quite in keeping with taste further south *c.* 1430, except for its continuing as far down as we can see. The *houppelande* is tied closed below the bells and again at the point at which the hanging undercuff crosses the gown opening. Her hood, with its dagged *cornete* and shoulder-length *pate*, is much more like a man's than the versions seen in French manuscripts until now, but it again is in keeping with the more Germanic and hence more masculine taste which prevailed in women's dress in the northern Netherlands (compare the 'Tiefenbronn Altarpiece' of 1432).

51. One of the standard excuses for having one's portrait painted was one's betrothal, and here Lysbeth van Duvenvoorde holds the ring which marks this as a betrothal portrait.

In 1430 the thirteen-year-old Catherine of Cleves was married to Arnold, Duke of Guelders, with whom she went to live in 1431 and whom she left in 1445. She owned a Book of Hours, produced in Utrecht, in Holland, which has been dated, because of the lack of her husband's coat-of-arms, as widely as *c.* 1428–31 to *c.* 1440–45:[13] despite the various arguments, the dress in it, particularly that of the men, points to a date *c.* 1430, mainly because of the very slight emphasis given to the *bourrelets* of their hoods.

There are examples of deeply-set armholes, which we have not seen since the 1409 Salmon *Lamentations* (illus. 41), on a carpenter (M945, f. 64) and in illustration 52 on a beggar child. Although neither figure is at all likely to be fashionably dressed, we may have before us examples of regionalism in men's dress, as well as of second-hand clothing: when Philip the Good visited his newly acquired Dutch subjects in 1432, he ordered doublets '*à grandes*

Colour Plate **9.** The devil's underdress is made from cloth-of-gold as is the Bishop's cope and such extravagance is a mark of extreme vanity on the devil's part.

52. Daintily holding her trailing gown away from the grimy beggars, Catherine of Cleves dispenses charity, with a suitably beatific expression on her face.

assiettes'[14] along with other garments which were specified as being in the Dutch fashion (see p. 132).

The lady distributing alms is probably Catherine herself, in her aristocratic scarlet cape-sleeved gown, with its ermine lining and cloth-of-gold undersleeves. Her collar still stands high, from a slightly V-shaped neckline: this feature almost matches Lysbeth van Duvenvoorde's collar, while the cape sleeves recur in this manuscript on the dress of St Apollonia (M917, p. 304), much like those throughout Guido da Columna's *Historia destructionis Troiae*, illustrated *c.* 1445–50, probably in Vienna. Catherine's hair is drawn into horns on her temples, kept under control by a black net, with a veil on top; the white bird which strives to keep its balance on her head should not be interpreted as being part of her headdress, it being representative of the Holy Spirit which has urged her to perform this act of charity.

The beggar child's patched doublet, worn more like a coat, has eyelet holes for laces down the front and along the hem, even though he has no hose to attach to it. It also has a curved outer arm edge, which twists to the left on the sleeve as it hangs, while the curious zigzagged lower sleeve suggests that such a garment must have had an interesting existence, having been passed down from a wealthy original owner, through servants to whom it would have been given as a cast-off, then perhaps second-hand clothes dealers and no-one knows how many owners, until it reached this beggar.

Colour Plate **10.** Rogier van der Weyden's portrait of an unknown lady. The unassuming colour of her attire belies the probability that she was well-to-do if not an aristocrat, with her fine gauze veils and elaborate gold buckles and tag on her silk belt.

53. Ysabeau de Roye, one of the grand ladies of the court of Philip the Good, with St Catherine, in a heraldic mantle over a gown, datable *c.* 1430.

Nearer the centre of fashionable activity was Ysabeau de Roye (illus. 53), wife of Philippe, seigneur de Ternant, one of Philip the Good's household. It has been proposed that this portrait, coming from an 'Altarpiece of the Life of the Virgin', must be connected with the Ternants' establishment of a chapel to the Virgin in 1444 in Ternant,[15] but Ysabeau's dress suggests a date shortly after their marriage in 1431. The horns of her heavy heart-shaped *bourrelet* would have been drawn together in the 1440s, and her sway-back posture, apparently balanced on one forward-placed knee, as though she were standing, is one of the archaic features of this panel with its pre-Eyckian perspective, but it need not imply that the whole thing was painted a decade later, archaic in every feature: very soon after 1430 such a stance would not have been fashionable as women increasingly stood straighter. Although her heraldic mantle hides most of her gown, we can see that it has small 'purse' sleeves, a series of regular folds falling from the high-set belt, and something not yet seen in France, a truly V-shaped neckline, with the collar being only an extension of the shape of that neckline. It is this V-neck, where it can be distinguished, which seems to mark off more fashionable dress in the Netherlands from that in France.

Having said this, I wish now to consider three examples of Netherlandish dress, all from *c.* 1430, which do not fit in with this rule, for two different reasons. Around 1430 Robert Campin painted the portraits of an unknown couple (illus. 55 and 56).[16] Although the woman is clearly still very young, she has swathed her head almost as completely as we would expect of the average middle-class woman, twice her age: that this may well be a regional feature is indicated by the similar headdress of another young woman, the donatrix of the 'Mérode Altarpiece' (illus. 54), painted by a follower or pupil of Campin.[17] Both women have small, almost horizontal, horns at the temples, supporting an under-veil, to which is pinned at the sides a second small linen cloth, folded so that its selvedges, with their vestigial frill, lie across the base of the neck; over the top lies a much longer and wider veil, this time folded at the side. All three veils in the Campin portrait have a very slightly crinkled edge, almost more like added blanket stitching than an excess of fullness in the cloth at that point, and two of the gold pins which hold together the four layers on top of her head can be seen quite clearly. The Mérode donatrix has only two layers of veils on top of her head, but she too requires, as far as we can see and conjecture, a pin in the centre and one above each horn to hold the layers together, and on to something underneath, perhaps just her hair. The fluting on the selvedges of her veil is more pronounced.

Both women wear gowns whose bodices are set in regular folds: the cloak of the Mérode woman and the veils of both of them make it impossible to determine whether, in the first case, the gown collar extends to the shoulders, and in both cases,

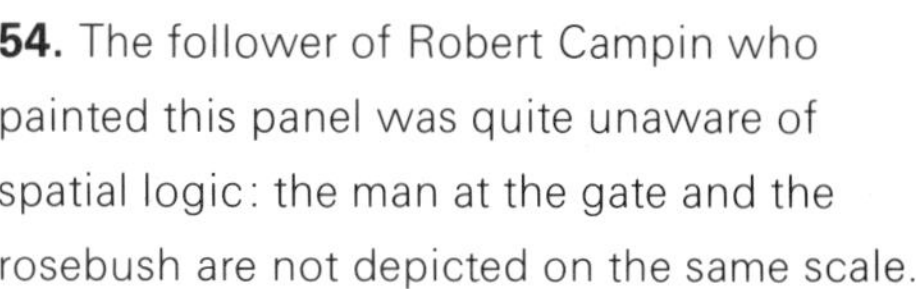

54. The follower of Robert Campin who painted this panel was quite unaware of spatial logic: the man at the gate and the rosebush are not depicted on the same scale.

55,56. OVERLEAF: These portraits are two of the most striking works on display in the National Gallery in London, with the detailed play of highlights and shadows on the faces. Although of paramount importance in the composition, the dress is at first almost unnoticed by the viewer.

57,58. Set like coloured statues in cool stone niches in front of the 'Ghent Altarpiece' are its commissioners, Joos Vijd and Isabella Borluut, in their red and pink gowns.

whether the necklines are V-shaped. At least with the Campin woman we can see no trace of the wide collars of contemporary French dress.

The Campin man is interesting because of the degree of elaboration now being incorporated into the winding round of the hood by the *cornete*: indeed, it will shortly cease to be a proper hood, although retaining the name *chaperon*, but become a hat, because of the permanence of its shape, whether worn on the head or not. The *pate*, with a clearly visible seam, is bunched on to the man's left shoulder (viewer's right), while the *bourrelet* is almost completely hidden, except on the forehead, under the turban-like wrappings of the *cornete*, before it finally descends on to his right shoulder. (The resemblance of the hood to a turban, once the *cornete* has been wound round it several times, is so great in a Van Eyck portrait, dated 1433, that it is always erroneously referred to as 'The Man in the Turban'.[18])

Because of the shortness of this man's neck, the square-edged doublet collar curls forward behind his gown's furry collar; the fur reappears down the centre front opening, which is held closed only below the collar, by a knotted 'point'. Where fifteen or twenty years previously the gown had fitted smoothly across the shoulders, bunching into folds only from mid chest, here slight folds are beginning to appear on the shoulders, making an increase in bulk in the upper half of men's clothing: in 1432–3, one of Philip the Good's gowns was assembled from eight gores, set in twelve folds (*'de* VIII *gerons à* XII *plois*').[19]

The Mérode donor's shoulders are effectively hidden under his hood, worn in its original form, but his gown shows quite clearly the other new feature in men's dress, the stacking of the bulk of the gown towards the front and back, leaving the sides flat; with the addition of a belt to hold the folds in place, the flat sides can make the waist seem narrower as the folds fan out from above and below the belt, which in turn can make the shoulders seem wider.

In the Campin portraits we have a fine example of the problems of scale which contemporary fashion must have posed for painters: to paint something concentrated on as small an area of the body as the head and shoulders meant that little space could be sacrificed to a woman's elaborate headdress, particularly if balance were to be maintained between two pictures painted on panels of a similar size, as these are. Perhaps it was fortunate for Campin that Brother Thomas had been storming around the neighbourhood, denouncing elaborate headdresses, and making these modest nun- or *béguine*-like veils acceptable. The Mérode Master may only have been following his master's lead in this matter, as scale worries him little: the donor and donatrix would have to shuffle on their knees through the door to the right to enter the room in which the Annunciation, the subject of the altarpiece, is taking place.

The dress of these fairly young people can be compared with that of the elderly donors of Van Eyck's 'Ghent Altarpiece' (completed in 1432) which also provides the third variation in female headdress (illus. 57 and 58).[20] The donor Joos Vijd and his wife Isabella Borluut were members of old Ghent patrician families, and Isabella's headdress, and its freedom, beside those of the two we have just looked at, may be a reflection of modes current in Ghent, although her *houppelande* is more probably a reflection of her age and conservatism. The rose-pink wool gown has wide, straight sleeves, turned back to reveal their green lining, which reappears at the neck on the flat square-edged collar. Above this stands her shirt collar, again square-edged, both collars being quite *passé* beside Ysabeau de Roye's attire, and the *Ménagier de Paris* would certainly not have approved of the way in which her collar is rumpled on the left.[21] The straight-edged upper veil sits on top of a curious flesh-coloured veil which

59. Giovanni and Giovanna Arnolfini, the archetypal fifteenth-century married couple, without whom writers in this century on subjects ranging from symbolism to population explosion would have had less to say and less to illustrate their books.

is forced into a tiny horn on the viewer's right; here the puckering seems to betray the existence of an understructure to which the black band, on the temple, must be connected. A fine gold pin has been inserted from front to back on the centre of the forehead, while a much coarser pin seems to run downwards at ear level, passing twice through the lower veil. The headdress is remarkably immodest for a woman of about fifty.

Joos Vijd is, like his wife, a little behind the times (if one assumes that donors' dress was not allowed to look outdated in their own eyes, as soon as their portraits were finished). His belt is worn low enough to cause the same fanning of the folds of his red gown as in illustration 54, but the gown lacks the continuation of the folds on to the shoulders of illustration 55. The sleeves, while conforming to the prevailing mode for the 'purse' shape, are too deep and long and would have been more acceptable in these dimensions when he was twenty or thirty years younger.

Let us now consider probably the most famous and misinterpreted Netherlandish painting of the fifteenth century, Jan van Eyck's 'Arnolfini Marriage Portrait' (illus. 59) from 1434.[22] Although Giovanni Arnolfini was one of the Italians resident in Bruges who supplied the ducal court with luxurious cloths of silk and gold, he and his bashful bride wear very ordinary textiles: his wife's gown is of a bright green wool (*'vert gay'*?), while her underdress is mid-blue. The marks on the under-sleeve today may give the effect of a damask patterning (see Glossary), but the shapes which they make are not consistent enough to match the formalized patterns in damasks, popular throughout the century: they are perhaps indications that the sleeves were made of something like crushed velvet, although there is nothing recognizable today as this fabric in wardrobe accounts. Giovanni's over-garment is of a purple brown material, which today has a curious 'bloom' on it, because of the aging of the pigments; this has given the cloth a velvety appearance which it was probably not meant to have. This garment is a type of *heuque*, whose cut is shown quite clearly by the uninterrupted fall of ever-deepening folds from smooth shoulders to a 'ric-rac' hem. His hat, doublet (with square collar), hose and shoes are all black.

Any ordinariness of textile is more than compensated for by the splendour of Giovanna's dress, with its great train and sleeves, which have marvellous examples of the late use of applied dagging as the continuing form, but not the spirit, of International Gothic features. The sleeve itself is enormous, set into a neat raglan sleeve on the shoulder, from which it swells rapidly, curving at knee level and then being gathered into the lower end of the fur-edged slit through which her arm passes. The curve of the sleeve is decorated with vertical strips of dagging, cut into almost complete Maltese crosses, set on top of one another, with their edges 'pinked' to prevent fraying, and to be decorative. Just under the gathering of the sleeve into its slit, the strips have

60. RIGHT: One of Rogier van der Weyden's earliest paintings distinguishable from those of his master, Robert Campin. The dress is more probably middle-class than aristocratic, and may therefore show how Rogier's own wife dressed.

been placed in three overlapping layers, each three crosses wide, as an echo of the 'bunching' of the sleeve. The straight lower edge of each strip marks the point at which the cloth has been doubled: if opened out, each strip of dagging would form a loop.

The round neck of the dress is most unusual, but this is a most unusual dress, cut probably as nearly a complete circle: the folds gather between the breasts, and are shortest where there is most flesh; the side of the gown, under the arm, is smooth, as in men's gowns. All these features would occur on a gown of circular origin, if worn by a woman. The round neck is aesthetically the most obvious way of creating a neck opening which would continue the shape of the gown, and the fine gold chains worn as a necklace are as much as this gown and its furs would have permitted her to wear round her neck.

Giovanna's hair has been drawn into two horns on her temples, kept tidy by reddish nets trimmed on the face by tiny plaits. Her five layers of veils are in fact just the one cloth, folded backwards and forwards on itself five times (see diagram: this is the only possible explanation of the lack of two free ends in an uneven number of layers, as the edge on her forward shoulder is a tidy fold). Because of the way in which the straight edges of the veil are curved across the front of the head, there is an excess of material further back which has to be distributed: the usual solution adopted throughout the 1430s and 1440s was to draw the excess into the two folds which can be seen, like additional horns, on the centre of Giovanna's head.

Superficially, the colours of Giovanna's outfit—green and blue—as well as their being set against a red-covered bed, are in accordance with the colour schemes found in dress in other paintings and wardrobe accounts, but they may have a symbolic use as well. The pursuit of colour symbolism was, in the hands of the intellectually weaker, a pseudo-science of the worst kind, but its use, when properly controlled, cannot be ignored. According to Sicily Herald in his *Le Blason des couleurs*, written at Mons sometime between 1435 and 1458, green symbolized (as well as Thursday!) youth, the planet Venus and marriage, and was a colour particularly suitable for the clothing of newly-weds; azure, the sky-blue of Giovanna's underdress, symbolized loyalty, and was a becoming colour for girls to wear, that age-group stopping at fifteen by his reckoning.[23] These points, although sometimes stretched to the ridiculous, would be at the back of the mind of a contemporary observer.

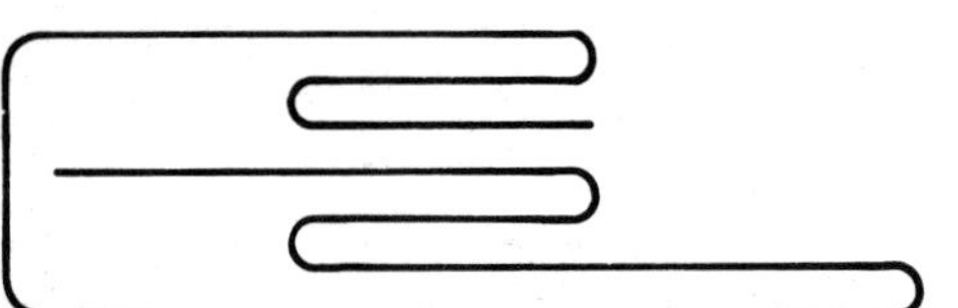

Possible structure of the veil of Giovanna Arnolfinin in 1434.

Next let us consider two works attributed to Rogier van der Weyden, lacking, as all the works said to be by him, both his signature and a definite date. Nonetheless, they both fit in well to the general pattern of dress in the 1430s, without being precisely datable, again like most of the artefacts of this decade. Rogier's wife, Elisabeth Goffaerts, was a native of Brussels, and she is generally supposed to be the woman in illustration 60.[24] Art

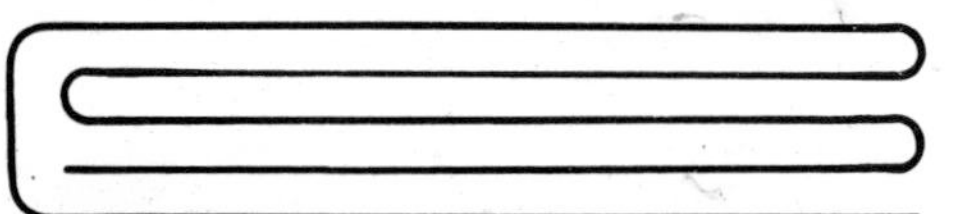

Possible structure of the veil of Margaret van Eyck in 1439.

61. A certain stiffness in the drawing may indicate that an anxious copyist rather than an artist working from life produced this likeness of Jacqueline of Bavaria, but the depiction of the headdress is careful enough to suggest that the artist was familiar with such constructions and was working fairly close to the date of the original.

historians make this assumption because of the direct gaze of the sitter at the spectator (compare Van Eyck's portrait of *his* wife, illus. 64), and because of the lack of starchiness which passes for dignity among his more aristocratic sitters. To this argument the dress historian can add the points that a grey woollen dress, with its high fastening and plain linen headdress, concealing the neck of this young woman, would not have satisfied an aristocratic patron after the danger of the travelling preachers had passed. This young woman is undoubtedly middle-class; an aristocratic sitter would have worn at least *scarlet* wool. The awkwardly-placed ring on the second knuckle of one finger is part of fifteenth- and sixteenth-century fashion, and need not mean that her hands were normally idle because of their jewellery.

Immediately on top of the head sits a linen veil, starched and folded into two horns which extend to cover the ears; the ridges in the centre of the head are at least partly caused by the folding of the excess of upper veil, as in illustration 59, but there may well be yet another peak in the under-veil. Once again, a straight-edged top veil is curved round the forehead and kept in place by pins: note the one visible on the left horn. This veil is slightly transparent, allowing the outline of the under-cap to appear through it. On to the under-cap is pinned a gathered chin cloth, with the pinhead showing on the corner, at ear level.

Art historians tend to call this an early work by Rogier and date it *c.* 1435, which is borne out, as far as can be determined by the dress, but where was this type of dress worn? If we could determine a date, we could suggest a location, and vice versa, but we cannot. If the Campin and Mérode women were painted in the district of Tournai, this is perhaps the form which their headdresses would have assumed, but they already looked as though they were going to evolve in the more 'open templed' direction of Giovanna Arnolfini's, with a chin cloth. However, the use here of three separate cloths to form this headdress does reflect the Campin and Mérode structure. If this is a reflection of middle-class dress in Brussels, was it worn by Rogier's wife after their marriage, during their stay in Tournai, or is it Brussels dress after their removal to Brussels? Ysabeau de Roye (illus. 53) was painted in Brussels, but presumably wearing what was worn, not in the painter's own circle, but at the ducal court. Wherever this headdress was worn, it reappears minus the neck cloth, on the donatrix of Rogier's 'Crucifixion' in Vienna[25] and with the only example I know of vertical slits on the sleeves of a woman's gown, which otherwise resembles that worn in illustration 60.

Further questions of regionalism and class distinction in women's dress at this time are raised by the drawing of the ill-starred Jacqueline of Bavaria (illus. 61), and the manuscript painting of the sin of lust (illus. 62), from the *Hours of Jean Dunois*, the Bastard of Orléans and companion-in-arms of Joan of Arc. Jacqueline of Bavaria, cousin of Philip the Good, and rightful heiress of the county of Holland was born in 1401 and died in 1436; this drawing of her is the most accurate, as far as the detailing of dress is concerned, of several drawn and painted versions.[26] Jacqueline is clearly no longer a girl, although she looks rather older and more tense than the thirty-five years of her life should have made her, but her exceedingly troubled life may well have aged her prematurely (see p. 24). (The problem of 'youth' and 'age' in women is difficult to settle in the fifteenth century: Jacques du Clerq talked of a young woman of about thirty-four who married a twenty-year-old man the day after her husband's death, to avoid being married off to one of Philip the Good's household in 1457, and yet Olivier de la Marche described Marie of Anjou [then forty] and Isabella of Portugal [then forty-eight] as '*desjà princesses eaigées*' when they met in 1445.[27]).

It is, however, in the headdress that Jacqueline has outdone her middle-class contemporaries. Being a member of the ducal family she can show much more of her hair than Giovanna or 'Elisabeth van der Weyden', although she is probably much older. Her hairnet has the same diamond-shaped knots as Giovanna's in 1434 and Margaret van Eyck's in 1439, and is similarly trimmed with a plait, which runs from the top of the head, round the base of the 'horns'. Outlining the other edges of the horns she wears a pearl-trimmed band, which would help, by its weight, to keep the net forward. Not until near the plait does her hair seem to grow; her hair must have been plucked out to this point to ensure a completely smooth forehead. (It is therefore hardly surprising that false hair should have been needed to supplement thinned locks which had somehow to form 'horns'.) At the point at which the hair begins to grow, a pinhead is visible, and from it hangs her veil.

The dimensions of the horns are certainly greater than those worn by a very young Bruges woman in 1434 (illus. 59), and as large as those worn by a thirty-three-year-old Bruges woman in 1439 (illus. 64); because of the sitter's family position, she is far more likely to be fashionably dressed in some respect than either of them, and certainly this factor would tend to make this headdress a few years earlier than 1439. However, the yoke on the gown is a most unusual feature, and the collar is downright old-fashioned. If the sitter is Jacqueline of Bavaria (and she has been identified thus for at least three centuries), she may be wearing Dutch aristocratic dress: she married Frank van Borselen in 1432 and spent most of the rest of her life in the northern Netherlands. Once again, we have more questions than we can answer, but the apparent age of Jacqueline makes it probable that the drawing should be dated *c.* 1435: perhaps, instead of worrying about the apparently advanced headdress, worn with an old-fashioned gown (compare the pronounced horns and standing collar of Catherine of Cleves in illustration 52), we should regard this as an example of how what really mattered in class distinction, as in

62. Another, invaluable depiction of the Sin of Lust, complete with King David and Bathsheba, and an elaborately dressed lady in the high fashions of *c.* 1435.

regional distinction, was the headdress. Thus, the Eyckian women in the 1430s may have imitated the gowns of the ducal court far more quickly than the headdresses, while the aristocrats of all regions may have adopted headdresses far more quickly than they did gowns, because of the degree of facial exposure which the former allowed.

The second example of female dress comes from the *Dunois Hours*, produced by the Bedford Shop in Paris, *c.* 1436.[28] In the background is King David spying on Bathsheba, while in the foreground, seated on a goat, symbol of lust, is a woman epitomizing the sin of lust. She wears a cloth-of-gold *houppelande* whose gold front lacing shows against her black undergarment; the undersleeves are red and are probably therefore pinned on to the underdress (compare the Magdalene in illus. 67). The gown is lined in a light brown fur, which now forms a plain V-shaped collar, over which her white under-shirt still lies. However, it is the headdress which is most remarkable, with its immense bulbous horns, topped by nets, *bourrelet* and a tiny veil. Although the horns' lower edges are as wide as examples from the late 1420s, such as in the 'Fleur-de-lis' scene (illus. 47), they are both thicker as the *bourrelet* draws itself together. This type of attire must have been the most fashionable, and therefore most sinful, which the painter, or his director, could evolve: the visible front lacing certainly was new, and rather unsubtle as a means of attracting attention.

Far more practical female headdresses appear in the background of Van Eyck's 'St Barbara' (illus. 63);[29] to the right of the seated saint is a group of ladies, out for a walk to inspect the Gothic tower which is being built to incarcerate the saint. These ladies wear hoods almost like men's, with *bourrelets* and *pates* draped round the backs of their heads, although women never wound the *pates* and *cornetes* round their heads, and thus never really copied men. In 1439 the trousseau of Agnes of Cleves, who was to marry Charles, Prince de Viana, included a number of hoods, at least two of which had *bourrelets*; perhaps they all had *bourrelets*, but these two were mentioned because of their elaboration, one being of black velvet, decorated with thirty-one rubies and thirty-one large pearls, the other, also of velvet, worked in peacocks' feathers and gold sequins with large seed pearls.[30]

Barbara herself sits unconcernedly reading her prayer book, almost lost within her too-long skirt and sleeves: in contrast the bodice is losing its bulk as the folds do not run right up to the armhole. Sleeves on women's gowns seem to have been in a transitional stage at this time: Agnes of Cleves' trousseau included a large number of gowns, some with '*grans manches*' and some with '*petites manches*'.[31] Confusingly, this less-controlled stage leads to very tight bodices in the 1450s and 1460s; the seeming lack of control is caused by there being less material to

63. A drawing which Van Eyck meant as a finished work, and to which another, thinking he knew better, added the blue sky at a later date. The figures below the tower show people in everyday attire.

64. Van Eyck's wife Margaret in her best attire in 1439.

control consistently, and too much to produce a neat fit.

The red gown of Margaret van Eyck (illus. 64)[32] has more controlled gathers above the green damask-woven belt, but also a smoother fit on the upper half of the bodice; the sleeves are as bulky as St Barbara's, but two years is not really a sufficient time lapse, given the paucity of other dated material, in which to distinguish significant changes. Where the most noticeable and unmistakeable change has taken place is in the headdress; the small horns of Giovanna Arnolfini's hairstyle have grown outwards, although still encased in a black net. The veil itself has been folded seven layers deep between the horns, and three deep on the right where it hangs over the shoulder. Both free ends are initially baffling in that they are both folded edges: the whole edifice can, however, be created from one long veil, divided into twelve imaginary sections (see diagram).

In our pursuit of regional dress, let us consider a painting of undoubted origin, from Brussels. In 1437 there was founded a chapel to St Hubert in the church of Sainte Gudule in Brussels; connected with this event seems to be the panel of 'The Exhumation of St Hubert', attributed to a follower of Rogier van der Weyden (illus. 65). Friedländer's date of *c.* 1450 would mean that the affected young man on the right was a decade out of touch in his dress, and it is much more reasonable to assume the connexion between the chapel's foundation and the painting. At last, we may well have a definite picture of the headdress of the women of Brussels, tucked into the groups flanking the altar, and meant to be of only secondary interest beside the ecclesiastics in their vestments, and the King of France, Louis le Débonnaire, in his royal mantle.

Martin Davies, in identifying the scene as being the second exhumation of St Hubert in 825 from his grave in the church of Saint Pierre, Liège, also denies the possibility of the interior depicted here being an accurate representation of the Liège church, as the architecture is Brabançon; since no-one seriously believes this panel to be by Rogier himself, the lack of regionally accurate architecture may well be reflected in a lack of regionally accurate dress.[33] If Brabançon architecture satisfied the painter, so may have Brabançon dress. Furthermore, later versions of this headdress seem to occur in a painting by an anonymous Brussels master showing a Brussels (?) family (illus. 132) painted towards the end of the century, where both elderly mother and considerably younger daughter wear radiating chin cloths.

Colour Plate **11.** Petrus Christus' portrait of an unknown girl shows admirably the delicate work of which fifteenth-century jewellers were capable. So sheer is her gauze undercollar that the lustre of the pearls is scarcely dimmed.

The headdresses here are not identical to the ones worn by the Berlin and Vienna ladies mentioned above, but they are certainly quite different from the Bruges examples in illustrations 59 and 64; this latter pair is much closer to the Ghent example of Isabella Borluut. The 'St Hubert' women have linen undercaps, to which slightly radiating neck veils are pinned at ear level, with an upper veil drawn over the top of the head in two ridges, rather than

proper 'horns'. The disparity between these veils and their truly Rogerian counterparts is perhaps inevitable, as artists quite clearly (see p. 90) extracted one particular element of fashionable dress which appealed to them and used that in preference to the available alternatives. All we can deduce is that there are better grounds for supposing the 'St Hubert' headdresses to be from Brussels and/or Brabant, than we can assemble for the other pair, which art historians think of as lying chronologically one on either side of the date of this painting.

However, lest we think that only women's dress was subject to regional eccentricities, let us note here that men's dress too had its peculiarities, distinct to contemporaries but perhaps less

65. In a church crowded with spectators, St Hubert's remarkably well-preserved body is exhumed. The spectators are of all classes, as their clothes indicate.

Colour Plate **12**. The temple is draped with striped cloth bearing Kufic Script of the type which Rene d' Anjou collected.

Colour Plate **13.** This lady is almost the only person within the René Master's work who manages to present a passable imitation of the fashion of the 1460s for ladies to resemble Gothic spires.

66. One of the middle-class women watching the exhumation, probably in the dress of Brussels. Beyond the screen are other women in similar headdresses.

noticeable today. In 1433, the tailor Hayne de Necker made '*une robe . . . à* VIII *gerons trois doubles pour les plois de la façon de Brabant*' for Philip the Good: that is, a gown assembled from eight gores, three of which seem to have been twice as wide as the others (one for the back and two for the front?), to give enough material to create vertical folds. This seems to have constituted the 'fashion of Brabant', the duchy in which Brussels was situated.[34]

Shortly afterwards, when Philip was planning to visit his newly and illegally acquired Dutch subjects, he flattered them by having two gowns made '*à la façon de Hollande*'; both of them had five folds ('V *plois*'), presumably five on the front and five on the back. One of these gowns was made of '*brunette*', as were the twenty-one gowns, each '*à* V *plois*', ordered for his attendants on this expedition.[35] (*Brunette* could, despite its name, be black, as it was ordered for the mourning liveries to be worn in 1432 for Philip's sister Anne, Duchess of Bedford.[36]) Perhaps careful counting of gown folds in many examples of known origin and similar date would prove that regional differences lay in the number of folds in a man's gown: certainly, by dressing his cavalcade in what appears to be Dutch dress, Philip seems to have been trying to reconcile his new subjects to him, declaring more subtly than by words alone, that he was as interested in Holland as in any of his other possessions.

The elegant young aristocrat on the right demands, and warrants, considerable attention. That his head has been partially shaven to produce this beret-like hairstyle is betrayed by a 'shadow' round the edges; the dropping of the gown's back neck to a V betrays that the aim of the haircut and dress is to appear to elongate the neck, much in the way that his shoes elongate his feet. The arrangement of the folds on his red velvet cloth-of-gold gown are clearly not being left to chance and the low-slung belt: the folds run neatly and stiffly from his shoulder blades to the hem and are drawn in by something behind them, at natural waist level. It was only a matter of time before the 'purse' sleeve became an unacceptable nuisance, or boring, or both; the solution, of which this must be one of the earliest examples, was to slit it to allow the arm, in its neater doublet sleeve, greater freedom of movement, at least forwards and sideways.

The hood too is an improvement, in that its *bourrelet* is capable of retaining a circular shape when not in use; this seems to have resulted in an ability to treat it much more casually, and the fashion grew for slinging it over one's shoulder, while holding on to the *cornete* at the front. In 1433, iron hooks (*crochés de fer*) had been bought to put in the front and back of Philip the Good's hoods, to 'block' (*enformer*) them, but exactly how they were of use is not explained.[37] Dagging is now almost exclusively a decoration of the hood's *pate*; here the grey hood has an extremely elaborately cut *pate* composed of ringlet-like strips of dagging which have been attached, dagging being regarded now

as decoration, not an integral part of the garment. Except for the dress of the clergymen, and the 'historical' beards of the king and one of his courtiers, the rest of the dress in the painting is purely contemporary.

67. Rogier van der Weyden's 'Descent from the Cross'. The woman standing behind the Virgin wears an everyday gown and kirtle with a tailed hood wrapped round her head. It is possible to trace the side seam of the weeping man's cloth-of-gold gown from under his arm to the front of his body as the gown crosses it.

From this unimaginative use of ordinary dress, let us turn to the use made of it by Rogier van der Weyden in one of his early works, the 'Deposition' (illus. 67), presumably done after 1432, when he became a master, and certainly before 1443, when a dated copy was produced.[38] In this work, the secular and contemporary, by their unobtrusive ordinariness, are used to heighten the intensity of the pathos: the contemporary plays no part in the emotional interplay in the 'St Hubert' scene, a solemn but not tragic event, which is only to be expected if it was painted by someone following Rogier from the outside, without having the faintest notion of why he sometimes stuck as closely as he did to contemporary dress.

Although Rogier had studied under Campin, the latter's flamboyantly striped and bejewelled orientals are quite alien to Rogier's taste, particularly when he is faced with depicting acute suffering. Martin Davies remarked on the inclusion of details like seams to add veracity to the scene;[39] what he did not remark on was the everyday-ness of the dress, with the careful screening of the few 'oriental' touches. The omission of standard details like seams (and hence of standard dress?) would possibly have been more distracting than their inclusion, on the principle of things being rendered more conspicuous by their absence; the exotic elements in Campin's 'Entombment' (illus. 27) are still too interesting today to focus as much attention on the body of Christ as could be given to it. The attire in the 'Deposition', on the other hand, is in fairly straightforward blocks of colour, undisturbed by stripes, and is as mundane as the figures' status will allow. The scene gains in immediacy from the dress within it, even if the dress was not Rogier's first concern. Cramped within a gold box, like a section of a carved altarpiece, slump various figures, like polychromed statues. At the back left is a weeping woman whose headdress consists of the standard arrangement of three veils, with one free end of the upper one flipped back to give a turban-like knotting of the cloths, while she wipes her eyes with the other free end: the effect of the 'oriental' is achieved without theatrical tricks, by a natural twist in normal dress, such as could have been seen happening to any woman's headdress in a high wind. Leaning in front of this woman, to support the swooning Virgin, is St John the Evangelist in his traditional attire of red tunic and cloak, buttoned at the neck by a few buttons, some of which are nearly always left undone; the Virgin's shapeless blue overgown is also traditional, as was the swathing of her head in this manner. To have dressed either of these figures in more contemporary dress would, strangely enough, have destroyed the illusion of reality Rogier was trying to create: this was how people were used to seeing these figures dressed in depictions, and any departure from these norms would have alienated him, rather than drawn the spectator into the scene.

Almost hidden behind the cross and the least involved in the scene is the attendant who has removed the nails from Christ's hands; he is the nearest to a Campinesque prototype with his heavy features, mop of hair, head band with its striped ends and fringed armholes on his white damask doublet. Immediate inspection, however, does not reveal this figure, just a zigzag of white well enough hidden not to intrude, and yet just 'Saracen' enough to satisfy anyone who observed him. Similarly, the elderly man supporting Christ's shoulders is in toned-down 'Saracen' dress, in dark blue and red, sombre enough to provide a background against which Christ's pale body can stand out, and 'Saracen' enough for the really observant: it must be significant that the two most unusually dressed, and potentially most histrionic figures, although centrally placed, are very well hidden, and their emotional involvement less overt than that of the others. (Compare the dress of the men supporting Christ's body in the Uffizi 'Entombment'.[40])

Propping herself against the right-hand wall of the box is the most stunningly dressed figure of the group, Mary Magdalene. As she raises her arms, her lilac cloak slips off, revealing an incredibly complex dress, which has to be a kirtle, or *cote*. Her red sleeves are of damask, pinned into the kirtle's sleeves; for someone who could have afforded damask sleeves, to be so overwrought as to appear in public without a suitably impressive overdress, is in itself a mark of the distraction of the Magdalene. The intricacy of the tailoring of the kirtle is presumably yet another mark of her rank, while the use of a normally short-sleeved garment is an infinitely more subtle way of producing the short sleeve often incorporated in exotic dress, as worn by the man in red and blue.

Under the square neck is a very fine gauze scarf or 'collar', the neckline itself being outlined by a series of narrow bands of cloth, in which the stitches strain visibly at the back as the Magdalene draws her shoulders forward. The exceedingly tight fit of the whole bodice ensures that it can act as a corset, helped by the lacing which continues down the front of the skirt. What is difficult to reconcile with the high-waisted outer dresses is the fairly natural waist level of this garment, but within the next twenty years women's belts became wider, thereby making it easier for an observer to accept that the waistline could lie anywhere between bust and pelvis. (One of the forces at work throughout the history of dress is the struggling outwards of garments: thus, a man's shirt was never seen to any great extent in the fifteenth century, more of it was seen at neck and wrist in the sixteenth and seventeenth centuries, until today, when far from being an undergarment, it is socially acceptable on many occasions as an outer garment. So too the change in the female 'waistline' seems to have worked its way outwards.) Just above the waist seam is what appears to be a second row of stitching, an essential reinforcement if this seam is to carry the weight of the skirt with its increasing width and fur hem. The centre front bands, on to which are sewn the rings for the lacing, continue down into the skirt, while the skirt itself is composed of many small gores, increasing in depth and width towards the hem. The most obvious material for this patchwork treatment would be a fur or leather from small animals, and the buff colour of the kirtle does suggest this. Whatever the prototype of this dress was made of, and whether or not it is a true kirtle and not a vamped-up fur-lining for a gown skirt, it is something that Rogier uses again, in his Antwerp 'Altarpiece of the Seven Sacraments' (again worn by Mary Magdalene), *c.* 1445,[41] and the Magdalene in his 'Braque Triptych' (*c.* 1452: illus. 78). It is used also by his and Campin's imitators, the underdress with fewer gores and this low-slung belt with the two clasps, appearing in a 'Lamentation' in Berlin, but with the addition of very Campinesque diagonal stripes in the overdress.[42]

Thus everything worn within this painting falls into one of three categories, that of traditional attire, like that of St John and the Virgin, of modified 'traditional Saracen', or recognizably contemporary dress, complete in most cases with painstakingly observed and realized details, while the urge to involve figures in purely contemporary dress, and hence to involve the spectator even more closely, finds its most legitimate expression in the approximately contemporary and as emotionally enclosed Vienna 'Crucifixion' referred to above (*c.* 1440). The donors kneel, not in the wings, which are occupied by solitary saints, but immediately beneath the cross, and the donor has been deprived of the standard donor's expression, the vacant stare through everything which passes for pious contemplation: instead he looks up at the body on the cross, as though he were actually present within the scene, instead of seeing it in a vision. In Rogier's so-called 'Bladelin Altarpiece' (illus. 79 and 81), there is no need to suppress the theatrical elements, as the foretelling of Christ's birth to Augustus and the journey of the three kings are joyful events, as is the Adoration of the Kings in his 'Columba Altarpiece', where fringes, jewels and red velvet cloth-of-gold can be used without restraint,[43] in direct opposition to his complete removal of clothes from the terrifyingly vulnerable souls in the Beaune 'Last Judgment' (p. 47).

Rogier could be as obsessed with accuracy of detail as Van Eyck, but the complex thinking which drove him to produce a work such as the Prado 'Deposition' separates them. Van Eyck, if he painted the New York 'Crucifixion',[44] used more theatrical forms of dress and could probably never have used what he observed with such restraint for such an effect, and will probably therefore always be more approachable and popular than Van der Weyden, who requires today so much more thought to be understood as completely as he intended to be. Van Eyck could enjoy dress and its frivolities for their own sakes, Rogier perhaps never. It is fitting therefore that the signs of International Gothic dress should have been fading when Van Eyck died, leaving Rogier to face a form of dress which catered less readily for fantasies of painter and painted, in his greater search for psychological realism.

6 The Body Imprisoned, *c*.1440–*c*.1460

In the previous chapter, we saw how International Gothic dress gradually lost ground before a more heavy-handed style, which introduced greater weight to the outlines of garments, male and female, as well as forcing greater depth and immobility into the garments themselves; in this chapter we shall consider how this new feeling works itself out in different ways in the dress of both sexes, women's dress being always the less comfortable, first because of its uncontrolled bulk and latterly because of the loss of too much of that bulk, making gowns too tight.

Erwin Panofsky attempted to use a mass of documentary evidence to support his theory that Van der Weyden's 'Altarpiece of the Seven Sacraments', commissioned by Jean Chevrot, Bishop of Tournai, must date from *c.* 1453–5, but the place in the evolution of dress which this work occupies, militates for its being *c.* 1445, the more traditional dating.[1] The whole altarpiece is set, without regard for spatial and temporal unity, inside a Gothic church; behind a pillar lurk a couple (illus. 68), the woman in a deep-opening purple gown, with visible front lacing, a black cloak and a gauzy veil set on top of a mildly horned undercap. The man wears a mid-blue gown, with slightly puffed shoulders, fairly straight sleeves, and something essential if as much material as possible was to go into the folds on the gown skirt, a slit up the side of the skirt. His doublet collar has been rounded off at the front, and his hood is slung over his shoulders, his right hand holding its *cornete*.

At the wedding (illus. 69), the bride wears a scarlet gown, with miniver lining in her great sleeves, her gown opening below her green damask-woven belt, her hair worn loose, a token of her virginity, and on top, a coronet, a token that she is a bride. Her husband wears a gown of the same colour, flat at the side and split further up than that of the man among the pillars: this young dandy is also more advanced in wearing his gown open at the front neck to reveal what is probably meant to be his shirt, except that his doublet collar continues forward, *behind* the 'shirt'. Along with the puffing of the shoulder has come an apparently sway-back stance, caused mainly by the sleeve's being fuller at the back

68. Almost lost within the church are this couple, devout but uninvolved spectators of Rogier's 'Seven Sacraments'. The woman's cloak and linen-covered headdress probably mark her as a well-to-do bourgeoise.

69. FACING PAGE: Unusually, this wedding is taking place *within* the church; the young couple are dressed in gowns of scarlet.

70. LEFT: A rather well-to-do family watch the baptism of their newest member.

than at the front. Two bars of lacing at the neck are supposed to keep the gown closed: instead, they must have allowed a further slipping of the gown towards the back. Behind the bridge stands probably her mother, in a curiously stacked set of veils with fluted edges, almost as though Margaret van Eyck's headdress had sprouted of its own accord. Another example of Eyckian stacked veils is worn by the mother in the baptism scene (illus. 70), where a lot of re-painting has done much to destroy the original effect of this headdress, leaving it looking more like a honeycomb than a series of veils. Clearly, the control of so many layers must have presented considerable problems, and it must have been a welcome relief to abandon them in favour of a cap which provided the same outline, although it may have had its own problems, like hurting the ears as it clamped itself round them: such a cap is worn by the godmother, although the bands at the side front seem merely decorative, continuing as they do up on to the horns. Something invisible must have performed their

71. Strung out against a cloth screen is the Jouvenel des Ursins family, staunch supporters of the French royal family and the Church, painted in the later 1440s in all the variety of dress to which their occupations and rank entitled them.

original task. The horns themselves are no longer making any pretence of being formed from their wearer's hair, being a jewel-fretted hat instead: this extra weight, coupled with the extra size of the horns, has made it necessary to re-introduce the loop in the centre front, which was used to re-position the horns of the 1410s whenever they slipped. (In 1447 René of Anjou's illegitimate daughter Blanche was given '*ung rigotier*' of hair: this apparently refers to some kind of wig, probably to be worn in conjunction with a headdress of this type.[2]) Both women wear the kind of gown we have come to expect, with shrinking sleeves, and the bare neck made slightly less bare by the wearing of fine chain necklaces lying more or less in a T-shape.

The godfather stands with his back towards us, allowing us to see that his scarlet gown still has a V-shaped back neckline, that its folds are as neatly stacked at the back as other men's gowns are at the front and that his olive green hood, by its retention of its shape, is really more like a hat. To the *pate* are attached narrow strips of intricately-cut dagging, the *pate* itself being arranged in layers.

A comparison of the types of dress in the 'Seven Sacraments' with those in the 'Exhumation of St Hubert', *c.* 1437 (illus. 65), and those in the 'St Eligius' panel of 1449 (illus. 77), shows that there is a progression from the 'St Hubert' low-slung belt to a rounded hourglass figure with a natural waistline for men, just discernible in the 'St Eligius': the dress of the men in the 'Seven

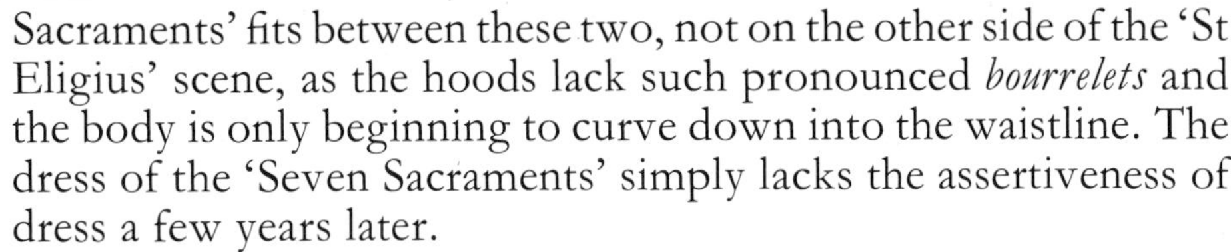

72. One of the daughters of the Jouvenel des Ursins family, in her robes of rank.

Sacraments' fits between these two, not on the other side of the 'St Eligius' scene, as the hoods lack such pronounced *bourrelets* and the body is only beginning to curve down into the waistline. The dress of the 'Seven Sacraments' simply lacks the assertiveness of dress a few years later.

All the plunging necklines of women, no matter how carefully filled in depictions, greatly worried Jean Juvenal (his own spelling) des Ursins, a noted French ecclesiastic and brother of Guillaume Jouvenel des Ursins. When Guillaume became chancellor of France in 1445, Jean took the opportunity to write to him of his responsibilities, as he, Jean, saw them, and, not unexpectedly, one of them included the suppression of wickedness in women's dress: he urged that the king (already under the sway of the décolletage-mad Agnès Sorel, let us remember) should not allow women in his household to wear front openings which revealed their breasts and nipples, or great fur trains or fancy belts. Later, he equates these women in (or out of?) their revealing necklines with old horses tricked out to increase their market value.[3] Perhaps some, if only partial, notice was taken to these strictures; in 1446, once again a sumptuary law forbade the prostitutes of Paris to wear silver belts, turned-over collars, or furs of '*gris*' (grey squirrel) or miniver (grey squirrel belly) in their miniver (grey squirrel belly) in their gowns.[4]

Sometime between 1445 and 1449 the Jouvenel des Ursins family commissioned a family portrait (illus. 71),[5] including their

73. A Flemish illustration to one of the most popular romances of the day, that of Girart de Roussillon, showing how even royalty lived in fairly sparsely furnished surroundings.

father Jean, who had died in 1431, their mother and the nine living offspring. The attire of the men is singularly useless for those seeking civilian dress, as they are all in military or ecclesiastical attire; the mother and one of her daughters are widows, while another is a nun.

The two married daughters are in *cotes hardies* and *surcotes ouverts*, the latter having trains so long that they can be looped over their arms: so much for their brother Jean's pronouncement. Their apparently royal robes need not distress us too much, as this rather parvenu family seems to have gone in for dressing beyond its station on official or ceremonial occasions: in 1449 Guillaume, according to the chronicler Jacques du Clerq, appeared with the king '*vestu en estat royal de robbe et chapperon fourré, et ung mantel d'escarlate*', which is more elaborately described by Jean Chartier, brother of the poet Alain Chartier, as consisting of '*le manteau, la robe et le chapeau d'escarlate vermeil, fourré de menu vair, et portant sur chacune de ses espaules trois rubans d'or, et trois pourfils* (bands?) *de laitices*' (a fur).[6]

The headdresses of these women seem to have little to do with ceremonial dress, although the paucity of dated material in France at this time makes it difficult to be sure. They are elaborately jewelled horned headdresses, with a small *bourrelet* on top and the bizarre addition of a very fine veil wrapped round the back and pulled up beyond the points of the *bourrelet*, the veils seeming to be wired at the back and the other three edges of the veil having tiny beads sewn on to them. The curious wrap-around effect of these veils echoes veils of twenty, even thirty, years earlier and calls to mind nothing so much as the headdress of the Countess of Westmorland in the *Nevill Hours* (illus. 49): perhaps English taste had not been entirely eradicated in the decade since the re-capture of Paris.

The daughter who was the nun at Poissy, where Christine de

74. The starchy, male-dominated court of Philip the Good who deigns to accept a copy of the *Chroniques de Hainaut*, probably in the late 1440s. The richness of the textiles in this scene is remarkable.

Pisan's daughter had been a nun (p. 40), kneels behind her splendidly dressed sisters; the only significant differences between her attire and that of her mother and other sister lie in the lack of white edging to her black veil, the way in which the other two have draped their veils back on the points of the shoulders, and the widows' attempts to introduce some kind of horned effect into their widows' weeds, much like Valentina Visconti's refusal to give up fashionable headdresses in 1408 (see p. 104). (In the twilight of a chapel in the south-east of Notre Dame in Paris kneel statues of Jean Jouvenel, *père* and his widow, both dressed as they are here, and the horned effect of her headdress is unmistakable.)

Behind his mother kneels Jean Juvenal, denouncer of the décolletage, while immediately to the right of the nun kneels what passes as a representation of Guillaume Jouvenel, the chancellor; a far more realistic and less idealized, likeness is to be found in the portrait by Jean Fouquet (illus. 88), which will be discussed shortly.

In a Flemish *Romance of Girart de Roussillon* (scribe paid in 1448: illus. 73[7]) we find the delightful scene of the disgraced and worried-looking Girart and his wife waiting outside the royal bedchamber while the queen persuades the bearded (therefore 'historical') king to re-instate Girart: people normally wore nothing but night caps in bed, but to ensure that the spectator recognizes their majesties, the painter has put their crowns on top of their night caps. Meanwhile Girart is fully dressed in the manner of the late 1440s, with sheared-off doublet collar, puffed and too-long sleeves, and pleated gown with flat, slit sides. His only eccentricity lies in his not having a pronounced *bourrelet* to the hood.

His wife's attire seems more fashionable, with the closed blue *bourrelet*, and its split *pate* and *cornete* lying over her shoulder, to the left. Tucked under her pink gown is a very fine gauze collar,

75. OVERLEAF: Etienne Chevalier, who became Treasurer to Charles VII of France in 1452, with his patron saint, St Stephen. This hollow-cheeked young man appears again as St Stephen with Chevalier in Chevalier's Book of Hours.

76. OVERLEAF RIGHT: The least Virginal of fifteenth-century Virgins; is this actually a portrait of Charles VII's mistress, who died in 1450? The dress suggests it may well be.

77. The interior of a fifteenth-century jeweller's shop, with rings kept on spindles in a tray. The young couple are wealthy: the girl's cloth-of-gold gown had its very expensive counterparts in court circles.

while her gown, with its green collar and cuffs, fits comparatively neatly on the bodice and sleeves.

In 1446 was begun a translation from Latin by Jean Wauquelin of a work to become known as *Les chroniques de Hainaut*: one copy was to be given the famous frontispiece attributed to Rogier van der Weyden or his shop (illus. 74).[8] Under a pink and gold canopy edged in green, stands Philip the Good, dressed in a black figured velvet gown lined with brown fur, a black doublet, and black hose and hood. To the right stands his heir Charles, later to be called 'the Bold', and in front of the group of courtiers kneels probably the translator, presenting the duke with a copy of his work. Among the courtiers have been recognized, to the left of the duke, his chancellor Nicolas Rolin, the donor of the 'Beaune Altarpiece' (compare illus. 82), and beside Rolin his friend and colleague Jean Chevrot, the commissioner of the 'Seven Sacraments Altarpiece'.

Because of Rolin's age and consequent conservatism, his gown is belted at the level of the 1430s, although it is as carefully pleated as anyone else's (except that of Chevrot standing beside him). His hood also lacks the extremely rigid *bourrelet* of the duke's. Philip and the younger courtiers wear their gowns tightly belted at the natural waist level to give an hourglass figure, and opened from neck to waist to reveal the shirt; it is impossible to tell whether it is the gown or the doublet which is fastened at the neck by the two bars of lacing. All the men in knee-length gowns have stork-like legs, which, as was suggested in chapter two, was probably meant to make them look long, with the help of the pointed toes on their boots and pattens (wooden over-shoes). With their open-fronted gowns, nipped-in waists and up-standing sleeves, these men of the ducal court resemble very closely the young man in the Bruges painter Petrus Christus's 'St Eligius' (illus. 77),[9] and cannot therefore be far removed from its date of 1449. It would have been ideal to be able to include a contemporary portrait of the duchess, Isabella of Portugal, but the wall painting in the Butchers' Chapel in Ghent, which includes her, and which is dated 1448, has suffered so much from restorers that its value as an accurate record of dress must be regarded as minimal, while a Rogerian altarpiece (before 1450), which included the ducal family, is known only from a nineteenth-century drawing:[10] there the duchess's outfit is not radically different from that of the woman in illustration 77.

Within the shop of the goldsmith–Saint Eligius stands an aristocratic young couple, the man wearing a red patterned velvet doublet under a blue gown: it is quite clearly the doublet whose edges are held taut by the double lace. Partially filling in the gap under his gown is a black undergarment, apparently called quite simply and sensibly a 'piece': in 1458/9 Charles VII of France was to acquire several, often matching his doublet and described as '*une piece a mettre devant son estommac*' or '*devant sa poitrine*',[11] even

though they were no longer visible in fashionable dress. The saint is much less fashionably dressed, his red gown lacking support for his pleated sleeve tops and the folds in his gown body not curving into the waist, although his acorn-like hat will become increasingly important in fashionable dress as the hood becomes too bulky.

The dress of the young woman has caused a lot of problems, not least because of the appearance and disappearance of the pins in her headdress across the years:[12] in our reproduction there is only one pin, on the top of the right-hand horn. Such are the problems caused by misguided restoration; it cannot be decided so readily who is responsible for a common flaw, the lop-sided way in which the forehead band is deeper at the base of the right-hand horn, as well as being beaded in the same way as the left horn. Also the veil, transparent over the forehead and jewelled horns, suddenly becomes solid towards the back.[13] Perhaps there *is* a heavier veil at the back, set into the under-cap, with a finer veil over the lot. There is, however, little basically wrong with the way in which these 'ear phones' and horns are structured.

The green cloth-of-gold gown has, at last, a neatly fitting bodice which is, however, extremely small, the raglan sleeves, with their gathered tops, covering most of the shoulder. The sleeves are lined in red, as is the collar, and because of the sleeves' length, the cuff on the right has been turned up to allow its wearer to take a ring from the jeweller. The areas in which the lining appeared to spill over on to the surface of the gown was becoming increasingly important: in providing the Dauphine's sister, Eleanor of Scotland, with her trousseau in 1448, Charles VII gave her a number of gowns, of various textiles including cloth of gold, lined with ordinary sable (a black fur), and with the collars and '*gectz*' (border at hem? from old French, *gésir*, to lie?) of sable which is specified as being completely black ('*bien noires*');[14] this implies that flaws in colour were tolerable where they would have no chance of being seen. Instead of the usual fine T- or Y-shaped necklace the woman wears a gauze under-collar which has been cut to lie in a Y-shape before it passes under the zigzag lacing of her gown. (Compare the gowns in illus. 70.)

In 1449–50 Jean Miélot translated *Le débat sur l'honneur* and a copy was produced for presentation to Philip the Good (illus. 12);[15] from the appearance of the dress, this may well have been one of the earliest copies. The duke and his courtiers posture in broad-shouldered gowns of various lengths, with the duke himself in the shortest gown and with the most sway-backed pose. Hoods are being abandoned in favour of 'acorn-cup' bonnets, while toes, with the aid of wooden clogs, are growing to ridiculous lengths. In all, this scene appears to be a caricature, possibly a couple of years later, of the scene in illustration 74. Inside the manuscript, a much less stylish illustrator depicted the events of the story, in which an impoverished but noble Roman

78. Mary Magdalene in the type of dress and loose belt she usually wears in depictions by Van der Weyden, and which Memlinc continued to use for her.

youth competed with a wealthier rival for the hand of a beautiful Roman maiden (illus. 13); on the left stand the two heroes, in almost identical outfits to those of Philip the Good's courtiers, but with none of their exaggeration. Perhaps it is significant that these two young men, embodying all the ideals of chivalry to which Philip and his court fondly imagined they themselves were attached, are the only figures dressed in the attire of Philip and his court, without 'oriental' touches.

Let us now look at two paintings which inform us of the techniques of cutting women's clothes; one Netherlandish, the Magdalene from Van der Weyden's 'Braque Triptych' (illus. 78)[16] and the other French, the 'Madonna' from Jean Fouquet's 'Melun Diptych' (illus. 75 and 76).[17] The Van der Weyden paintings seem to commemorate Jean Braque who died in June 1452, while the Fouquet panels contain a portrait of Etienne Chevalier, treasurer of France from 1452, and a Madonna who is supposed to be a likeness of Agnès Sorel, Charles VII's mistress, who died in

February 1450; the probability of this identification will be considered shortly, in relation to another Virgin of *c.* 1450, in Van der Weyden's 'Bladelin Triptych' (illus. 80).

The sorrowing Magdalene is dressed more fancifully than in the Prado 'Deposition' (illus. 67), but her sorrow is more generalized, i.e. the Magdalene was usually sorrowful, and there is no central depiction of the Crucifixion by which her sorrow can be intensified and her dress played down. Her curious fringed ribbon hat recurs on a female attendant in the same painter's 'Columba Altarpiece', where the woman also wears a kirtle, complete with deep fur hem, and on the Youngest Magus in the Boutsian 'Pearl of Brabant' altarpiece in Berlin;[18] fringes, however employed are, as we know, signposts for exotic and, quite often, glamorous personages, and her hat can therefore be dismissed from this discussion. Her main garment is tightly laced and its grey fabric seems to have stretched to mould itself to her body; there are narrow sections of cloth round the neckline, a dart *above* each breast, and in the centre front every second lacing hole is left unused. (Criss-cross lacing does not occur in the fifteenth century, and rings had to be sewn on to garments, or holes punched into them and bound by stitching; not until the invention in the nineteenth century of the metal eyelet hole, punched into the cloth, was really tight and deforming lacing possible. Perhaps it was necessary to alternate from day-to-day the rings or holes through which the lacing passed, to avoid continuous stress on the cloth and stitches: there seems to be no other good reason for having half the lacing holes lying idle). The low-slung belt with its two great clasps is a typical motif with this type of dress, although its use is not confined to Rogier. An enormous gold pin catches the red velvet cloth-of-gold false sleeve on to the short sleeve while between them, at the back, her shirt sleeve portrudes. Clearly, by its use as a corset and a support for normally less visible items, like a false sleeve to be shown only at the cuff under a gown, this garment is an under-garment, and must be, like the Prado Magdalene's garment, a kirtle.

It is less clear exactly what kind of garment we have before us in the Melun Diptych (illus. 76): is it a very elaborate kirtle, or is it an extremely sophisticated gown, far in advance of the rest worn at this time? Examination suggests that it is a *cote hardie*, that close-fitting garment, neither gown nor kirtle, rarely found in art or literature at this date: the fur-lined white damask or velvet cloak would have been too bizarre an addition to a simple kirtle. The Virgin is, in addition, depicted here as queen of heaven: a *cote hardie* was part of a *robe royale* and the omission of the *surcote ouvert* is quite logical in terms of the Virgin's pose. The dress has curved seams running across from the armholes on to the breasts and down into the kilted-up skirt; the centre front opening can be laced shut through a series of rings placed just inside the edges, so that, if the dress ever managed to shut across this incredible bosom (let us remember, Agnès Sorel flaunted hers), all that would be visible would be what appears to bet yet another seamline; the sleeves fit as neatly as the bodice, and fall over the hands. The under-shirt is of such a fine gauze as to be practically invisible, and only adds to the blatant exhibitionism of the figure. On her head she wears another transparent veil, over a black loop to which would normally be attached an elaborate headdress.

If we summarize the main features of this Madonna and compare them to the far more typical Madonna of the ' "Bladelin" Triptych' (illus. 80,[19] we see that there is every reason to accept the traditional, and downright blasphemous, identification of the 'Melun' Virgin with the outrageous Agnès Sorel. The 'Melun' Virgin's knowing and supercilious expression, the immodesty of her flaunting pose, the sophistication of the tailoring of her grey dress, her damask cloak and the vestiges of a fashionable headdress are all too worldly for this figure to be considered as belonging among the normal Virgins of the fifteenth century. The 'Bladelin' Virgin is demure, a guileless child, whose clothing owes little to the skill of tailors, except for the insertion of a triangular side panel, sewn in with open-work seams in her white over-shirt: such seams on shirt-like over-garments are common in religious or 'historical' scenes, and must be a reflection of current tailoring practice in shirt-making. The clergy in the 'Seven Sacraments' wear surplices with seams of this kind, and scenes of the Crucifixion or the Lamentation often include at least one female figure dressed thus (e.g. the Rogieresque 'Crucifixion' in the Abegg Collection and Petrus Christus's 'Lamentation' in Brussels.[20]) With 'historical' scenes it appears that the participants have reversed their normal order of putting on their clothes, but there are other explanations for this mode of dressing. In the case of the Virgin, particularly at the Nativity, it would be desirable to introduce as large an area of white as possible into her attire, as a token of her continuing virginity: that indefatigable seeker of symbols, Sicily Herald (or his continuer), proclaimed that the wearing of white was ideal for children until the age of six or seven, as befitting their innocence, while white was also worn extensively by village girls and shepherds '*en beaulx roquetz*'.[21] *Roquetz*, however spelt, were presumably what we should today consider peasants' smocks or overalls: in 1432 Chartres was captured by a band of soldiers disguised as carters wearing '*roques*', and '*guietres*' (leggings, rather than properly tailored hose), and in 1441 the same trick was used to capture Courville, by English soldiers, each dressed in a '*rocquet*', as though on his way to market.[22] Here the Virgin's over-garment resembles nothing so much as a smock, and is probably to be regarded as a '*rochet*', its colour and style being in keeping with her purity and humility.

This very mundane garment also had its place in the theatrical wardrobe: in 1454, at the famous Feast of the Pheasant, held at

79. LEFT: The turbaned and short-sleeved Sibyl gives the Emperor Augustus a sight of the child who will save the world; in reality the poet Virgil wrote of such a child, but he was referring to the hypothetical product of the marriage of Mark Antony with Augustus's sister Octavia.

Ghent by Philip the Good, among the figures in fancy dress were twelve ladies (men in disguise?) representing the virtues, each dressed (somewhat ungrammatically) in '*cottes simples de satin cramoisy, bordées de letices, et par dessus avoient* en manière d'une chemise [my emphasis] *de si fine toille, qu'on voit la cotte parmy*' (crimson satin kirtles, edged with lettice [a white fur]; and on top they had like a shirt of such fine cloth, that one saw the kirtle through it). This is the description given by Olivier de la Marche,

one of the actors at the Feast; another account, in almost the same words, was written by Mathieu d'Escouchy, probably at second hand, in which the ladies' *cottes* were covered in the manner of a '*rochet à la fachon de Brabant*' (a Brabançon *rochet*), trimmed with long gold thread fringes.[23] Despite the link between the attire of the Bladelin Virgin and the theatre we cannot dismiss this Virgin's attire as flashy, like that of the 'Agnès Sorel' Madonna, as, after all, the theatrical ladies were *virtues*, even if they were

80. CENTRE: With everyday life in a Flemish town behind them, Mary, Joseph and Pierre Bladelin(?) worship the infant Christ.

81. RIGHT: The Three Wise Men, resplendent in cloth-of-gold and jewels, kneel before the Star-Child who will lead them to Bethlehem.

more flamboyantly attired than the Virgin. In the *roquet's* resemblance to a clerical garment, there may also be a veiled reference to one of the more obscure themes of religious painting, that of the Ministry of the Virgin: in 1437 a citizen of Amiens commissioned a panel[24] which depicts her in the bell-trimmed vestment which passed for the attire of the priests of the Old Testament, as in illustration 26.

Dressed in deacon's robes, St Stephen presents Etienne Chevalier, executor of the will and organizer of the funeral of Agnès Sorel, to this 'Agnès Sorel' Madonna: Chevalier is not particularly fashionably dressed, but his scarlet gown is remarkably dignified beside those of his younger contemporaries. The cloth of the gown, with its brown fur lining, is unyielding as the out-moded 'purse' sleeves bunch across his body, but it also creates sculptured folds on the chest and rises in an unbroken line as the gown's collar, dispensing with the usual break in the neckline caused by the rising of the doublet above the gown. Across his left shoulder he has slung the *cornete* of his black hood, which reappears behind him.

In 1443 Nicolas Rolin, Philip the Good's chancellor and one of the least lovable characters of his day, in an outburst of piety, founded a hospital (Hôtel-Dieu) for the sick poor of Beaune in his native Burgundy: perhaps increasing age (he was then about sixty-three years old, and was to die aged about eighty-two) was causing him to worry about getting his particular camel through the eye of the needle into heaven. In 1451 the Hôtel-Dieu's chapel was dedicated to St Antony, who appears on one of the wings of the altarpiece commissioned for the Hôtel-Dieu from Van der Weyden; in 1452 the dedication was changed to St John the Baptist, who does not occupy an unusually prominent position in the altarpiece: the altarpiece is therefore generally assumed to be datable between 1443 and 1451.[25]

Although neither Rolin nor his wife, Guigone de Salins (illus. 82 and 83) was of an age to be highly fashionable (and in illus. 74 we saw how outdated was Rolin's taste in dress), they may still have regarded their dress as fashionable enough by their own standards when the paintings were first brought to Beaune from Brussels, where Rogier worked and the Rolins lived, and their attire may therefore have been subject to last-minute alterations: for some reason, the left horn of Guigone's headdress has been lowered. Perhaps it was originally too high and too modish for her taste. Rolin's black gown with its low-slung belt and unpadded shoulders, is as old-fashioned as that in illustration 74 (possibly from the same original drawing?), both depictions confirming his remoteness from the latest fashions, as does his eccentric insistence on propping his hat behind his head, keeping it in place by wrapping the *cornete* round the collar of his gown: he seems not to have caught up with the fashion for slinging the hood over the shoulder. His wife's gown is pulled closely shut

across the bodice, with the gap at the neck being filled in by an opaque linen scarf which stands well up her neck; the sleeves are shorter than those of the young woman in illustration 77 (dated 1449), and the whole gown seems more old-fashioned, but not as outdated as Margaret van Eyck's (illus. 64, 1439) would have seemed in 1449.

82. LEFT: Nicolas Rolin, the grasping founder of the charitable Hôtel-Dieu at Beaune, in a sober black gown, perhaps an affectation in the face of this attempt at piety.

83. ABOVE: Guigone de Salins, Rolin's second wife, also clad in black, who looks capable of cynical amusement at her husband's motto *Vous la seule estoile* (You are my only star).

The earliest dated example of a headdress which has the same outline as Guigone de Salins' is, once again, that of the young lady of 1449, although Guigone's much greater age demands that the under-structure be less glittery and the veil less transparent: it is not, however, as opaque as those of the younger, but middle-class women painted by Rogier in the 1430s (illus. 60). The veil shows quite clearly that the folds which would have been pressed into it

84. Seated among their elegant courtiers, Count Thomas and Countess Joanna of Flanders graciously grant privileges to the citizens of Ghent, as doubtless their descendants hoped Philip the Good would do after perusing this manuscript of Flemish privileges.

in storage are an important part of the appearance of the headdress, as they are at the same height at the sides, and extra folds have been ironed in on the temples, to ensure the projection of the veil at the correct angle. Despite the eight-year gap (1443 to 1451) into which the altarpiece can be placed, its size (central panel, three wings on either side with two smaller wings on top, and on the outside four wing-sized panels with the reverses of the two smaller top panels) must mean that it took several years to complete, and the donors' portraits may well have been executed towards the end of that period, *c.* 1450, as is implied by the latest feature in their dress, Guigone's headdress. That Guigone was not so far out-of-touch with fashion can be seen by comparing her attire with that of the much younger donatrix of a northern French altarpiece, dated 1451.[26]

After Philip the Good crushed the 1453 revolt of his troublesome subjects in Ghent, the citizens, who had had to ask his pardon, half-dressed, decided to vindicate their claims to certain privileges by presenting the duke with a book (*c.* 1454–5?) listing the concessions granted to the town by his predecessors, including Count Thomas II of Savoy and Countess Joanna of Flanders (illus. 84) and Philip himself, up until 1454.[27] Although this scene took place in 1241, everyone is in modern dress: the count and his male courtiers wear gowns of various lengths, ranging from his formal floor-length one to the hip-length gowns of the court dandies on the left. All the torsoes of the men retain a slight convex curve down to the waists, inherited from the longer 'figure-of-eight' gowns of illustration 74, but the waist has risen slightly and the centre-front has closed, giving the bodice folds less opportunity to sag into curves to match the outline of the gown: these folds will very rapidly run into the waist in straight lines. The hood with its padded *bourrelet* is being replaced increasingly by shaggy hats, like upturned saucers or bowls, their roughly parallelogram shape echoing, on a smaller scale, that of the upper body of the new shape of the gown. (The aging Charles VII was still acquiring hats with *bourrelets* in 1458.[28])

The countess and her ladies are more flamboyantly dressed than the men, with their tall *bourrelet* headdresses, either with the *cornete* strapped under the chin or hanging loose with the pleated *pate*, as worn by the two women on the right: both methods of wearing this headdress parallel contemporary treatment of the male hood. The woman with her back to us is particularly useful in providing us with one of the rare glimpses of the back of a woman's gown: conditioned by the aesthetics of our own century, we would expect the back of the gown collar to be only as deep as the front, whereas it dips into a deep V of fur, which hangs free over the high-set belt; perhaps it was weighted inside to help draw the very wide neckline back over the shoulders. Both this gown and that of Countess Joanna have trains with pointed ends, a further echo of the pointed collar at the front and the back, and the summits of the headdresses when seen from the side. The Countess's bare shoulders are partially covered by a necklace of red beads and the bosoms of all the ladies seem in danger of popping forth above their necklines. On her head Joanna wears a gold horned cap studded with white and red beads gleaming through her white veil, on top of which sits a tiny veil at the tips of the horns, as on the white *bourrelet* of the lady behind her. Although her cuffs fit neatly to her wrists, her sleeves are still baggy above the elbow.

85. Lust, this time without King David and Bathsheba, but with the addition of an ill-favoured crone.

Approximately contemporary must be the dress in a French manuscript of poems by Alain Chartier (illus. 85)[29] where the poet kneels before a figure representing Lust, and the dress of the men lounging against a river wall overlooking the Seine, from the '*Retable du Parlement de Paris*'.[30] Lust and her companion wear gowns with open necklines, filled in by a patterned cloth; between the patterning and the gown lie transparent gauze scarves. The sleeves are narrowing, as are the horns on their heads. These headdresses are bizarre, seeming to be tall bonnets, as though the previous horns were drawn together, but slit along the centres to allow the veils to be inserted between the two sections, before being drawn up beyond the 'horns' to stand like flags or butterflies' wings in outline. Again, as in illustration 77, there is inconsistency in the transparency of the veils, which suddenly become very fine where they are in danger of hiding the pattern of the bonnets; where they form a double layer at the tops of the horns, like those of Countess Joanna (illus. 84), they necessarily obscure the bonnet. Despite their strangeness, they

86. RIGHT: The man leaning over the wall shows what happened when a narrow strip of cloth was set into the tops of sleeves, and the two layers pleated together.

87. FACING PAGE: Louis of Savoy, as he appeared in statuette form on the tomb of Louis de Mâle, with the padded shoulders of the late 1440s–late 1460s.

88. FACING PAGE BELOW: Guillaume Jouvenel des Ursins, Chancellor of Charles VII of France, by Jean Fouquet. His family liked to believe they were related to the Italian aristocrats, the Orsini, whose badge was a bear, and they obtained permission to use the Orsini bear, which appears above.

may well be fairly accurate depictions of one of the forms taken on, briefly, by the veils-and-horns headdresses before the horns were finally drawn together to form a steeple-shaped bonnet, covered with a veil set in 'butterfly wings' or simply draped with a veil: Lust was unlikely to be depicted as anything other than modishly dressed, particularly if we recall that men liked to think women dressed up fashionably simply to attract them.

The men in illustration 86 display fashionable and outmoded official dress: in the centre stands a figure in a full-length, structureless gown and in his hand he clutches a document, while over his shoulder is slung a hood, and on his head is an 'acorn-cup' hat. Perhaps he should be regarded as a lawyer or a member of the Parlement de Paris, for whom this altarpiece was commissioned; some of the judges in Fouquet's depiction of the trial of the duc d'Alençon (illus. 91), which took place in the autumn of 1458, wear full-length gowns without padded shoulders, hoods in their original 'Balaclava helmet' form, and acorn-cup hats. The man on the right wears a similar cap and clutches a shaggy hat in one hand. His doublet collar stands well clear of his neck, perhaps being forced back by his casual pose, and his short gown, laced twice across his shirt, is more casually drawn together at the front, one side being held over the other by his sword belt. The third

man, as he leans over the parapet, shows us how short the gown had become and how the back was as carefully drawn into diagonal folds as the front, the outline of the folds being emphasized by the triangular dip in the back above which the doublet collar rises. The tops of the sleeves are pleated into the armholes: illustration 87, a drawing of Louis, Duke of Savoy,[31] shows why this pleating was necessary, as the duke's doublet sleeves are composed of two parts, the upper parts being puffed and causing his cloak to sit, on the right, much in the manner of gown sleeves. As this drawing seems to record a figure on the tomb of Louis de Mâle at Lille, erected in 1455, we have a *terminus ante quem* for the original depiction of the duke, which accords well with the examples we have been considering, *bourrelets* on male hoods vanishing soon after the Ghent *Privileges* manuscript. Split doublet sleeves are first discernible in Petrus Christus's portrait of the Englishman Edward Grimston, dated 1446,[32] although the puffing there is no more than the effect of pleating the lower edge into the main part of the sleeve: Louis of Savoy was thus probably drawn sometime around 1450 and the 'Parlement Retable' a couple of years later.

The angle of the gown sleeves to the shoulder seems to have depended mainly on the material and lining used, and it may be a mistake to try to date men's dress in the 1450s by the size of the shoulders: safer aspects, when considered together, seem to be the types of folds (i.e. diagonal or curved) in the gown and the length of the hair. The earliest reference which I have found to padding the sleeves of a gown (as opposed to simply letting them rest on the puffed upper sleeves of the doublet) occurs in 1454–5, when Philip the Good's tailor made him a gown, with the aid of $\frac{3}{4}$ ell black woollen cloth '*pour estoffer les manches*': thereafter many gowns have sleeves which are '*froncées*' at the top (pleated), including, in 1458, Charles VII's dressing gown.[33]

A dated source (1455) which depicts a young man's gown is a manuscript of the *Miroir de l'humaine salvation* in the Hunterian Library, Glasgow University (ms. 60): there the youngest Magus wears a short white gown with flat sides and folds drawn towards the centre front at the belt, the front is closed, the black doublet collar rises above it and the sleeves are too long. Despite this, the gown does not seem unnecessarily bulky, in marked contrast to that of Guillaume Jouvenel des Ursins (illus. 88),[34] Chancellor of France.

The chancellor's gown is made of a deep rose-pink velvet and lined with a brown fur which must be partly responsible for the great bulk of the sleeves; on the other hand it cannot follow every fold of the gown as the shallow folds on the shoulder must be of the velvet alone. If the lining of the body of the gown fitted the figure fairly closely, the outer layer could have been sewn to it at the waist and at dips in the folds, to keep them in position. The sleeve top has barely discernible pleats running towards the

89. In this portrait of Charles VII, Fouquet perhaps captures more of the weariness than the wiliness of his rapidly aging monarch. Charles often wore plush-covered bowler hats like this one.

91. RIGHT: A crammed courtroom for one of the most celebrated trials of its day, that of the powerful duc d'Alençon. The dress is observed from a useful variety of angles, on a variety of age-groups.

90. The painter of this stunning portrait is sunk in undeserved obscurity, being known only as The Master of 1456, from the date on this painting.

armhole, and the back of the sleeve at this point must have been cut extra fully, to give men the appearance of being almost more sway-backed than their women folk: the shoulders of men's gowns slip off their real shoulders towards the back and the side. Guillaume's hair, did it not insist in curling outwards at the end, would cover the tip of his ear, as would that of the man painted in 1456 (illus. 90), had he not brushed it behind his ear. We have here a portrait of this member of the Jouvenal des Ursins family painted within a decade of the family portrait (illus. 71: between 1445 and 1449), being produced probably *c.* 1455.

Much more tidily dressed is his King Charles VII (illus. 89),[35] probably painted about the same time, although in a completely different setting, almost as though we are being accorded the privilege of a glimpse of the sullen, weary-looking king in his carriage or at a window. On his head he wears a plush bowler hat on to which has been stitched, in zigzags, a gold braid with tiny loops on one edge. This is an unusual variation on the fashionable, flatter shaggy hat, but it may have been warmer as Charles seems to have felt the cold badly towards the end of his life: in 1458 and 1459 he ordered '*hocquetons*' (short jackets?) to wear under his gowns '*quant il fait frais*', made of $1\frac{1}{4}$ ell grey damask, one being lined with '*carize*' (kersey, a woollen cloth),[36] and there were also several '*pieces*' for him to wear on his chest when it was cold (see p. 146), although it was nearly a decade since the fashion for open-fronted doublets and gowns seems to have created the need for '*pieces*' in the first place. If the king was as determined to keep warm as the accounts suggest, there may be so much fur in the gown sleeves and body that there is no chance for the shoulders to drop between the collar and the sleeves.

One of the most startling portraits of the fifteenth century is that by the anonymous French 'Master of 1456' (illus. 90).[37] Set against a gold background, with one hand on the wall before him, is a serious, bony-faced young man dressed in a black wool gown over a reddish brown doublet. The gown has its own standing collar, above which rises the doublet collar; between the collar and the raised sleeve tops are four folds, overlapping each other towards the sleeves. His ginger hair is long enough to lie on his forehead and to touch his doublet collar at the back, showing that it is indeed the length of hair we should pay most attention to in depictions of men from this time onwards.

Before we return to considering women's dress, let us look at the Fouquet miniature which depicts many men from many angles (illus. 91).[38] The trial of the powerful duc d'Alençon excited a great deal of interest, and Fouquet has implied how widespread that interest was by including among the spectators two Germans, the figures on the bottom right in long curly blond hair and green 'Robin Hood' hats, with green gowns which are pleated in an inverted fan-shape on the lower back only, and a non-European near the bottom left in a pointed red hat and long

92. The Church was a useful ally in keeping the lower classes in their places, particularly if one had to beg for its help to get rid of a devil called up through aping one's betters out of pride.

black hair and beard. One or two of the natives wear or carry hoods with *bourrelets*, but most of the men wear or carry shaggy hats or felt acorn caps; on the left, next to the usher, one man wears a shaggy hat and an acorn cap on top. Resting an arm on his shoulder is a man whose gown has a small collar set into the V-shaped back neck, while above it stands his black doublet collar, much like that of the 1456 'Man'. Other gowns hang clear of the doublet at this dip, like that of the man on the left of our subject. Despite their short gowns and long-toed shoes and boots, most of these men look quite stocky and not as emaciatedly elegant as their Netherlandish counterparts.

Seated at the centre back is Charles VII, in another of his bowler hats and a pleated azure gown which seems to be threatening to slip backwards and choke him. (In fact, when Charles entered Vendôme for the trial, he was described as wearing a '*robbe sanguine à plois*' [pleated red gown] under his breastplate.[39]) On the left sit several of his lords, in similar straight-necked and straight-shouldered gowns. Careful scanning of the sleeves of the gowns at the front of the scene suggests that the sleeves were pleated at the back, to take in the excess material which gave the sway-back appearance, and then left almost smooth at the front. This may explain the apparent divergences between the gowns of Etienne Chevalier and Guillaume Jouvenel des Ursins, and Charles VII, as they are depicted from angles different enough to make the gowns appear less uniform than they perhaps were. The predominant colours are still blue, green, red (which tends to be pinkish in manuscripts) and, increasingly, black or grey. It may therefore have been around this time that Sicily Herald commented on the overwhelming popularity of black '*pour la simplicité qui est en elle*', and made a remark that would have endeared him to René of Anjou, saying that black and white made a beautiful combination of colours, but black, grey and white together were *very* beautiful (see p. 71 for René's colour preferences); blue with green and green with red were very common, but were not beautiful,[40] implying that at the time of his writing tastes in colour were changing from the cheerful unsubtle schemes of the first half of the century to the more sober schemes of the second half.

About 1456 Jean le Tavernier illuminated Jean Miélot's *Miracles de Nostre Dame* for Philip the Good, and the miracles were many and strange. Apparently, one day in Bethlehem St Jerome and a friend saw a devil sitting on the train of the dress of a middle-class townswoman, proof of her sinfulness in aspiring to the attire of her betters (illus. 92).[41] The woman here apes upper-class fashions only in the long train, which resembles those of Countess Joanna of Flanders and her ladies in illustration 84; her headdress is far more in keeping with her relatively humble status, in being low linen-covered horns, like a sugarloaf in outline.

That the main function of a long train was to proclaim one's elevated rank, by requiring another human being to spend her time carrying it for one, is illustrated by Aliénor de Poitier's accounts of the meeting of the Duchess of Burgundy and Marie of Anjou, Queen of France, in 1445 and of the baptism, in 1456, of Philip the Good's granddaughter, Mary of Burgundy. (Although Aliénor was writing between 1484 and 1491, her mother had been present at the events as one of the duchess's Portuguese ladies-in-waiting, and had told her daughter a lot of the daily history of the ducal court.) When the duchess reached the queen's door, she took her train from the hands of the woman who had been carrying it, and when she walked through the doorway she let her train trail behind her. By 1456 she had given up wearing trains and silks, so that no train-carrier was needed for her '*robbe toute ronde*'. Her niece Beatrice of Portugal, the Lady of Ravenstein, was dressed in blue cloth-of-gold, furred with ermines, and her train was hitched up, carried by no-one.[42] (Beatrice was in the habit of wearing a hair shirt beneath her gowns of cloth-of-gold.[43]) Aliénor does not say so, but Beatrice was probably not entitled to have her train carried in the presence of her aunt since her aunt had no-one attending her as train-bearer, even though such a person was unnecessary. Thus we gain some idea of the presumption of the '*bourgeoise de Bethlehem*' in assuming any aspect of the dress of her betters.

Probably of similar date is the Rogierian portrait of a young woman (illus. 93).[44] The gown's closing is so low that it has necessitated the use of an insert to retain a semblance of decency:

Sicily Herald, in listing the attire of a lady in a common fifteenth-century conceit which linked a women's clothing to her virtues, lists first the shirt, then the *cote* and then '*la piece de devant soy*' of ardent thought for God, which she should have always in her heart, a lace, a half-belt, and over all this, her gown.[45] This list presumably reflects more or less the order in which garments were put on: the '*piece*' must correspond to the inserted area, as well as to the similar, just fading, fashion in men's dress. (The lace and half-belt were used to keep the *piece* in position, according to Olivier de la Marche, in his treatise on the attire of ladies and its significance.[46]) The black line under the gauze scarf, which stops at the *piece*, must be the lace, holding it up, while the invisible half-belt must have been attached to the lower edge of the *piece*. Her hair is enclosed in a simple net with a loop at the centre front, almost lost between the veil's folds and her hair which grows out beyond the net. By continuing her veil in a smooth sweep down to her eyes, the girl makes her forehead appear even longer than it is.

Belts of zigzag damask patterns with heavy, elaborately worked buckles and ends become increasingly common, particularly as the belt becomes wider: such a stiffening would be necessary to prevent the belt from curling between the bust and the pelvis, particularly if the wearer bent forward (and the discomfort of being jabbed by the buckle would have discouraged that). Among the goods inventoried in 1453 after the disgrace of Jacques Coeur was the '*ferreure*' (what we see here at the free end?) of a woman's belt, worked all over with hearts (*coeurs*, punning on his name) and enamelled.[47]

As thin veils became more popular, the understructures which clamped their supporting caps on to the head or which held them out in various shapes, became more visible. Petrus Christus's 'Portrait of a Donatrix' (illus. 96)[48] shows a woman in a rich red velvet gown, wearing a gold cap, studded with jewels and clipped on below the ears by a band which runs down from the top of the cap. The noble ladies in the *Fleur des histoires* attending the wedding of Charles v of France and Jeanne de Bourbon (illus. 97)[49] wear taller bonnets, above which soar fine veils, held out in wings by curving wires at front and back.

The tightening and upward movement of women's dress is very pronounced in an altarpiece of the life of St Bertin, usually attributed to the Valenciennes (Flemish) painter Simon Marmion, and thought to have been dedicated in 1459.[50] Fortunately, St Bertin was yet another holy man who attracted the attentions of Satan, yet again in the guise of a fashionably dressed young woman (illus. 98): from the very close resemblance of this deviless's attire to that of the Duchess of Orléans in a miniature on a document of 1460 in the Archives Nationales, Paris, we may conclude that the painter equipped the temptress with the last word in sinful modishness, *c.* 1460. The 'lady's' tight red gown

93. LEFT: A portrait of a lady by Rogier van der Weyden, in rich but sombre clothing, marking an increasing movement away from gay colours after *c.* 1460.

94, 95. ABOVE: Staring down from above the main entrance from the street on Jacques Coeur's house are this lower class man and woman, probably servants, carved in false windows.

96. ABOVE: The arms on the wall behind this lady by Petrus Christus suggest that she may have been an Italian, but her dress is Northern.

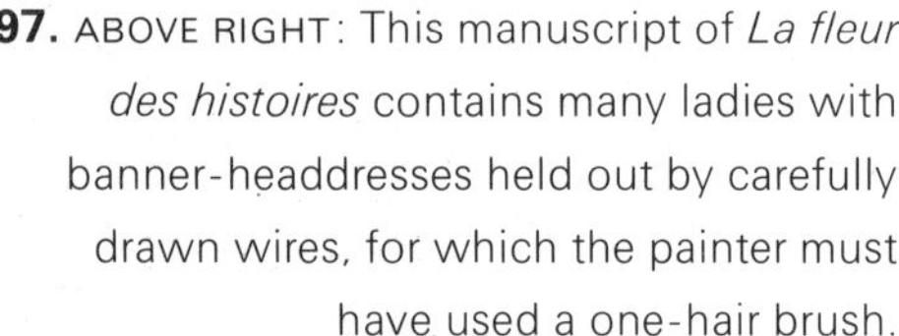

97. ABOVE RIGHT: This manuscript of *La fleur des histoires* contains many ladies with banner-headdresses held out by carefully drawn wires, for which the painter must have used a one-hair brush.

98. RIGHT: This time the devil has taken greater risks, and appeared in public as a fashionable young woman to tempt a saint.

almost slips off her shoulders, and her breasts are only just covered by a shallow *piece*, with a transparent scarf above it, and another on the points of her shoulders. To fill in this great expanse of bare flesh, she wears a wide collar-like necklace, delicately wrought. Pressed against her side, an elbow holds up her pointed train to reveal its grey fur lining, the cloth-of-gold underdress and, most significantly, the deviless's clawed feet. On her head rises a tall bonnet, its veil running straight up from eye level to two peaks on wires above the cap, as though the folds in the veil of the Rogierian 'Young Woman' (illus. 93) had risen with the headdress. (Compare the shorter headdresses of the Duchess of Burgundy and her ladies in the probably roughly contemporary *Breviary of Philip the Good* [illus. 99].[51])

99. Somewhat prettied-up portraits of Philip the Good and Isabella of Portugal at prayer in dress fashionable *c*. 1460.

Once we enter the 1460s we find ourselves in another wilderness, as far as firmly dated or datable works are concerned: Rogier van der Weyden died in 1464 and Hans Memlinc had not yet established himself; Dirk Bouts' dated works in this period are scarce, and although in France the Master of René of Anjou was hard at work, nothing he produced is dated. This dearth is particularly unfortunate, as there is little readily available documentary evidence on dress either, and important changes occur in men's dress during this decade. At least the decade got off to a good start, with another religious maniac denouncing female fashion in 1460: this time the denouncer was a girl from Le Mans in north-western France, allegedly possessed of the devil and the subject of what we would call poltergeist activity. She created enough interest for the queen to ask for an episcopal investigation which, having discovered that, far from being the innocent she had pretended to be, she had been a priest's concubine, sentenced her to prison for seven years. This poor girl was clearly suffering genuine and neurotic remorse for her sinful life, as she tried to persuade others to give up aspects of her wicked past, including horns on their heads, and bared bosoms.[52] In 1461 François Villon forcefully reminded all of their mortality, including:

> *Dames a rebrassez colletz*
> *De quelconque condicion,*
> *Portans atours et bourreletz*[53]

(ladies of whatever rank, with turned-over collars, wearing *atours*—a specific type of headdress?—and *bourrelets*): all in all, two fairly good years for moralizers.

It was probably around 1460 that Van der Weyden painted the portrait of Antoine, the 'Grand Bâtard' of Burgundy, son of Philip the Good, at the age of about thirty (illus. 100).[54] Antoine's

100. The great champion of chivalry and organizer of splendid tournaments, Antoine, le Grand Bâtard de Bourgogne, half-brother of Charles the Bold.

101. A torch-lit dance of knights and their ladies, whose eyes disappear beneath their veils.

gown is of a black voided velvet, set in narrow folds across the body and held shut less securely than the gowns painted by Fouquet. His 'artistically' shaggily cut hair is creeping over his forehead and over his ears, its lower edge parallel to the edge of his lengthening plum-coloured acorn hat. Around his neck he wears the collar of his father's Order of the Golden Fleece, bestowed on him in 1456: his entitlement to the collar places the portrait after this date, and, as Rogier died in 1464, before this latter date. Because his cap is taller than those of the men in Fouquet's trial of the Duke of Alençon in 1458, it is likely that this portrait was painted around 1460, or slightly later.

François Villon's reference to *bourrelets* in 1461 shows that they were still being worn by women, but they were rapidly ceasing to be depicted: perhaps their last appearances occur in the Wavrin Master's illustrations to *L'histoire de Girart de Nevers* (before 1466).[55] In far more common use among the ladies in this book are 'steeple' headdresses on which are draped veils, which, by one of the stylistic quirks of the painter who reduces everything to an impression, appear to blindfold the ladies, as indeed they do at first glance in other paintings. Thus the queen (illus. 101) and the dancing ladies appear to be totally withdrawn from the scene, an impression increased by the way in which the fur cuffs are used as great muffs at the end of very thin arms. The men's legs are as thin as their ladies' arms, curiously at variance with their great bulky shoulders, wing-like collars, pushed-up sleeves and, at last, gowns released from their folds at the waist. It

is as though long sleeves and nipped-in waists have become boring, and as a sharp contrast to its previously rigid control, men's dress has assumed a casually negligent air, to match their lengthening 'untidy' hair. Fashionable women's dress, as usual, retains longer the nuisance value of the train, apparently until 1467 (see p. 176): the Wavrin miniatures are probably to be thought of as being from the early 1460s.

102. Our hero, Girart de Nevers, unsuspectingly drinks the poison which the villainess has prepared for him. The servant's dress, although worn by an older woman, is correct in being almost two decades out of date.

We have, in this chapter, traced the tightening of women's dress, from its first unconvincing attempts *c.* 1440, when the bodice is reduced in size, followed by the sleeves, until *c.* 1460 the chest and arms seem crushed. The veiled headdress became taller, and also more closed in outline: the *bourrelet* headdress simply closed, to achieve a similar outline, until only the tall undercap was left *c.* 1460. The narrowing of all aspects of the female wardrobe gave women a smoother, more elegant appearance, but the new clothes must have been exceedingly uncomfortable, as they themselves controlled the body: in men's dress, only the dress itself was controlled, leaving the body fairly free as the gown acquired ever more carefully set folds. As women's dress reaches a new point of immobilization and svelte elegance, men's dress appears to take the opposite course, by becoming relatively untidy: such a device had been used to release women's dress from *its* folds *c.* 1440, although men's attire will lengthen and become narrower much faster thereafter, and for a much shorter time.

7 The Decline of the Gothic World, *c.*1460–*c.*1500

In the last forty years of the century there is available a vast amount of visual material, but not a comparable amount of readily available documentary evidence to expand on and explain fully what we see: part of the blame for this shortage must lie with historians who tend to find less to interest them in the Netherlands after the death of Charles the Bold in 1477, or even after the death of his father ten years earlier. As a result, we have in most cases to grope our way by the 'feel' of the dress, balancing the appearance and the disappearance of various factors in male and female attire, where possible in the same, dated illustration.

103. Petrus Christus's portrait of a girl shows clearly how the collar of the gown was really just a turning over of the gown to show its lining.

The most unfortunate aspect of the one-sidedness of the availability of the information lies in our being deprived of positive evidence of what happened to alter fashion's governing Gothic aesthetic value of slender height, to the diametrically opposed Italianate appreciation of bulky square or oblong outlines, which must surely be one of the most revolutionary changes ever undergone by fashion. Oddly enough, men's dress moved from an occasionally untidy bulk of excessively wide shoulders, but counterbalanced by a Gothic taste for excessively long toes, in the 1460s, through a fined-down silhouette in the 1470s, almost matching the aspirations of contemporary Flamboyant Gothic (or in England, Perpendicular) architecture, and in the 1480s and 1490s leaving behind the last vestiges of the Gothic past of their dress, into a contrived untidiness which yielded a new bulky outline. Women, because of their more restricted contact with the outside world, moved much more slowly towards the Italianate look, although they may have reached in the 1460s the Gothick extreme which men adopted in the 1470s.

Apart from these extremely obvious changes, a more subtle one took place in the colour ranges depicted. Wardrobe accounts throughout the century showed that black was always a popular colour, but artists did not reflect accurately the occurrence of black in everyday life; at the end of the century, black had taken over as the main colour used in depictions of garments, showing a complete shift in the thinking not only of the public, but of artists,

104. The preparations in a great armoury before a tournament, showing how the women's headdresses must have deserved their name of 'banners'.

of incorporating large areas of this possibly 'deadening' colour. In one respect Huizinga was right to emphasize the late mediaeval obsession with death and damnation, as out of this there arose in the north of Europe a pre-Reformation interest in what the individual could do to ensure his own salvation, without the intervention of the increasingly suspect and corrupt Catholic Church. In the northern Netherlands this expressed itself in the *devotio moderna* of Thomas à Kempis, foreshadowing Reformation ideas that each human being was directly answerable to God in his or her own conscience, and the Church had no right to come between heaven and earth in the way it had been doing.

Although in the North this idea of man as an individual responsible for his own actions, throughout his life, found a religious expression, it was basically no different in impulse, though quite different in outcome, from Italian Renaissance humanism, with its interest in the development of the individual through education and learning, though relying mainly on the writers of pagan antiquity. Intellectual life in the South became a serious but delightful scholastic exercize in classical obscurities, while in the North it became much more intense and eschatological, and life was theologically a much more worrying business than it had been earlier in the century. Against this almost Protestant background it is easy to place Van der Goes's portraits of strained-looking donors, clad in black, and his own nervous breakdown into religious melancholy. All this, however, is not yet obvious at the start of the period 1460–1500, when dress was still a subject for imaginative twists to its structure or its surface.

The breaking up of the controlled structure of men's dress seems to have begun in the late 1450s: in 1458 and 1459 Charles VII added to his wardrobe many gowns which had a slit in one sleeve, the most informative wardrobe account entry being for a gown of crimson velvet lined in the body, and one sleeve with ordinary '*gris de Bruges*', while the other sleeve, which was '*fandue*' (slit), the *getz* (hem?) and *paremens* (edges?) were all trimmed with a more expensive *gris*.[1] (Compare the black marten fur used for Eleanor of Scotland's gown in 1448, p. 148.)

René of Anjou's *Livre des tournois* was probably illustrated *c.* 1460 (illus. 104 and 105), the men's dress being slightly looser than that in his *Livre du cueur d'amour espris* which was written in 1457, and probably illustrated soon thereafter, displaying some gowns with one slit sleeve.[2] In the armoury stand a number of the competitors in the tournament, most of them wearing acorn caps or shaggy hats, short gowns whose folds are being allowed to move out from their earlier central gathering point and at the same time imparting an egg-shape to the torso. Their sleeves are much too long, and are rolled up or slit to allow one arm through: even one doublet sleeve has been slit, showing the shirt sleeve. The toes of the shoes are reaching new lengths of inconvenience, just as the problems of the sleeves are solved. The men in the centre are probably to be regarded as officials of the tournament, as they wear somewhat outmoded *bourrelets* and full-length gowns, whose folds are again less insistently controlled.

105. In such a torch-filled room it must have been easy for Louis of Orléans to have set fire to the clothes of Charles VI and his companions in 1392.

On the right enter the ladies to inspect the paraphernalia of the tournament: leading the procession is the most important lady, as she has the only train bearer, ermine-trimming on her gown and the deepest hem. Generally, the women are squeezed into trailing tight-sleeved gowns which have minimal bodices, their necklines being filled in by *pieces* and collar-like necklaces, while on their heads they wear either tall caps with a single veil, or the same type of veil held up in 'wings' or 'flags': Olivier de la Marche, writing in his old age, remembered the various horrors with which women decked their heads throughout his life, including '*les haulx bonnetz coeuvre chifz a banieres*',[3] which describes very accurately the effect of the headdresses here, particularly when seen beside the banners in the armoury. Further varieties of headdress are displayed at the tournament and in the torchlit scene of the presentation of the prize (illus. 105) where two of the ladies have gowns whose centre-front opening remains visible below their belts.

The girl who acts as train-bearer in illustration 104 wears the under-cap of the banner headdress without the potentially troublesome veils and wires, a concession to her youth and comparatively active existence as an attendant. Another example of slightly more sensible headwear, although worn with an adult's gown, is worn by the 'Girl' by Petrus Christus in

illustration 103, where we see a 'flowerpot' hat strapped on under the chin, much in the way that men had sometimes worn their padded hoods in the 1440s and 1450s, when their size began to render them troublesome.[4]

Banner headdresses seem to have had a fairly short vogue, probably *c.* 1455–*c.* 1465, as they must have been almost impossible to control, particularly now that tight sleeves and bodices must have made it impossible to move the arms high enough to re-position the bonnet when it slipped. Into increasing favour came the bonnet with the single veil draped over it, the veil increasing in length, until it too, by catching on the fur or velvet of a gown, could have dislodged the whole headdress of a woman who turned her head too carelessly. The 'steeple' and veil also elongated the human being more successfully than the 'banners' did. The little figures wandering through the borders of a Book of Hours (illus. 106 and 107),[5] probably reflect the early stages of the adoption of the 'steeple' and veil: the ghostly lady by herself is a splendidly exaggerated example of the narrow-armed and wasp-waisted ideal at which the elongatory aesthetic was aiming, while the less ethereal, but equally constricted lady in illustration 108 shows the wrinkling inevitable on such tight sleeves and armholes whenever the body within it tried to move, as well as the lengthening veil (probably *c.* 1467—certainly before 1473).[6]

Probably shortly after working on the original manuscript of the *Livre des tournois*, the René Master illustrated a copy of *Théséide*, a translation of Boccaccio (colour illustration 13;[7] according to a note in the manuscript, it was dedicated to Jeanne de France, daughter of Charles VII, in 1468, although the lady receiving the book in illustration 109 should probably be regarded as his patronness and the man as Boccaccio himself. Over her gold bonnet the lady wears a waist-length veil, and her black gown has the usual scooped-front neckline of the 1460s, filled in with a red *piece* which has a white edge, matching the white fur of her gown. Instead of holding up her train she has lifted the front of her skirt, to allow her to walk and, by the way, allowing us to see her black underdress and shoes which, for obvious reasons, cannot be as pointed as the author's boots. The author's attire is also fairly sober in its colouring, his egg-fronted gown being blue, his hat, boots and doublet black, and his hose brown. Little has altered in his appearance from that of the men in the *Livre des tournois*; it is in the women's dress in this manuscript that changes have taken place.

In colour illustration 12 the heroine, in her blue *robe royale*, and her two suitors pray before pagan gods, in the company of a crowd of various ranks. Although most of the colours are the usual pinks and blues, there are also brown and black gowns, reflecting current changes in colour preference. Two noble women wear 'steeples' with waist-length veils, and one of them

106, 107. FAR LEFT: Fashionably dressed people engaged in ordinary occupations, like walking, are rarer than more 'grotesque' scenes, such as the man and the bird in **108**.

108. LEFT: A fashionably dressed man shoots at an outsize bird, in the tradition of border grotesques.

109. ABOVE: A noble lady accepts a book from the booted author, in her chamber. Boot-clad figures are particularly common in the works by the Master of René of Anjou.

clearly has a V-shaped fur collar at the back of her gown. Behind them kneel more humble ladies, the farther one in a 'sugar loaf' veil and brown gown, with a presumably younger companion in a blue gown, kilted up at the waist and a much more sway-backed posture than we have seen in aristocratic women for a couple of decades. On her head she wears a version of the tailed hood which we first encountered *c.* 1380 in illustrations 16 and 34, and which was worn, remarkably unchanged, throughout the fifteenth century by those middle-class and peasant women who in France and the Netherlands kept to the dress which befitted their station in life.

According to Jacques du Clerq, and another anonymous chronicler, probably reliant on du Clerq, radical changes in dress took place in 1467, although comparison of the changes specified as belonging to that particular year, with the changes that had been taking place over the previous seven or eight years, suggests that perhaps du Clerq failed to realize what had been happening until 1467.[8] Basically, both chroniclers agree that in France and the Netherlands women abandoned their long trains in favour of deep hems of furs or velvet, as wide as velvet (i.e. about eighteen inches wide, as it was woven on the loom); they took up wearing wider belts, four or five inches wide, with wider and richer metalwork on them and changed their headdresses to round bonnets, which narrowed towards the top, at least half or three-quarters of an ell long, from which their veils trailed behind them to the ground: only du Clerq says that they also began wearing wide gold collars of several fashions. All these features, except for the deep hem instead of the train, were present in Marmion's she-devil of 1459 (illus. 98) and worn increasingly from that date onwards: a breakdown of the component parts of these changes in fashion gives an overwhelming impression of bands encircling the body, all except the hem, at the narrowest points on the body, and all tending to elongate these areas.

Men's dress, according to our sources, altered in some respects towards the same ideal: their shoes had toes a quarter or three-eighths of an ell long, everyone had a gown which trailed to his heels, as well as the alternative (which would also appear to elongate the legs), gowns and doublets so short that their wearers looked like monkeys in short coats, displaying their buttocks. Nearly everyone wore silk or velvet doublets which, along with gowns, had slashed sleeves through which showed the wide, loose sleeves of the shirt, and the shoulders of the gowns and doublets were padded to make them seem bigger. Their bonnets were as tall as their shoes were long, and their hair got into their eyes and hit the base of their necks at the back, an element comparable to the headdresses of women. Once again, only du Clerq remarks on the jewellery: noble and rich men wore great chains of gold round their necks. We, however, have seen that one sleeve on a gown was slashed as early as 1458, and that padding had been introduced into sleeves a few years before that, suggesting that, as with his observations on women's dress, it took nearly a decade for du Clerq's mind to absorb and finally be aware of the changes which had been taking place around him, but that he was at least intensely aware of the upward striving of dress at that date.

In keeping then with this spiky aesthetic would seem to be the lady reading her prayer book at the window of a soaring Gothic

Colour Plate **14.** In this scene of a lady often identified as Mary of Burgundy, the painter, known from this work as the Master of Mary of Burgundy, has shown the fashionable desire to compress women's arms and rib cages into as small a compass as possible. He has made their heads appear overgrown and their tall bonnets precariously perched adjuncts to them.

110. Mannerism is carried to its extreme in the figures of the men with their impossibly long legs, and knee-caps so lumpy that they look like armour knee-coverings.

church (colour illus. 14).[9] She is usually identified as Mary of Burgundy and attributed to the great illuminator the Master of Mary of Burgundy; why this dress should be considered as belonging to the late 1460s, and not the late 1470s as some have argued, will become clear. Her gold patterned bonnet is covered by the filmiest of veils which spreads on to the window ledge; the bonnet itself sits far back on her head and the veil has been drawn up from her eyes and folded into a 'roof' over the forehead: a heavier front band of black velvet is part of steeple headdresses in the 1470s (see illus. 11). The finely-stranded necklace is more in keeping with those worn by ladies from Marmion's devil onwards, rather than the lumpier ones of the 1470s (see illus. 11). As the next decade advances, necklines seem to draw back together into a V-shape from the very wide U-shapes of the 1460s: (see illus. 109). At the back of the church are two tiny figures of young men, one with a floor-length gown whose folds, now only on the shoulders, have been released from control by the removal of the belt, while his sleeves are too long, as throughout the 1460s.

The ultimate expression of this elongated ideal must be afforded by the Flemish illustrations to Quintus Curtius's *Historia Alexandri Magni*, translated into French in 1468;[10] the copy from which comes illustration 110 was made for Engelbert of Nassau, one of the great bibliophiles of the end of the century, and it must

Colour Plate **15.** Detail from the centre panel of Hans Memlinc's 'Donne Triptych' probably of the late 1470s shows Lady Donne and her daughter with St Barbara before the Virgin. The way in which St Barbara's green attire retains most of its colour behind Lady Donne's veil shows how transparent silk veiling could be.

111. ABOVE: An elegant couple, probably members of the aristocracy or upper middle classes, perhaps in Brussels.

112. ABOVE RIGHT: Walking seems to be a difficult undertaking for these men with their pointed toes.

have been one of the first copies illuminated after the translation. Almost lost within a lofty hall move Alexander's courtiers, their bodies stretched upwards as though they were in a hall of mirrors, and the carefully set folds on the men's gowns, with or without belts, turn their bodies into fluted columns, beside which the steeple-hatted women seem insignificant. Their insect-like figures acquire the final touch of the insubstantial from the strange bird's-eye viewpoint from which we see them, as the gods might have looked down on these self-important mortals.

Somewhat similar attire, apart from a shorter bonnet, is worn by the woman in illustration 111, attributed to the Brussels Master of the Legend of St Barbara,[11] while the man's dress, as far as we can see, almost exactly typifies that described by Jacques du Clerq, with his tall bonnet, wide shoulders and split gown *and* doublet sleeves which just manage to retain his shirt sleeves behind four sets of laces; only his shortish hair departs from du Clerq's outline.

Almost everything which du Clerq outlined occurs in the miniatures by the Bruges painter Loyset Liédet for the *Histoire de Charles Martel*, written in four volumes between 1463 and 1465, the third volume being illustrated in 1468;[12] illustration 112, being from the second volume, was presumably painted in 1467 or 1468. There we can see Duke Guerin de Mes and his nephews taking leave of the duchess: the men's hair reaches their collars, their shoulders are clearly padded, while the gowns' folds are confined to the sides, curving round the egg-shaped torso, and the gowns themselves are as short as du Clerq implied. Other men in the manuscripts wear gowns with similar folds, belted or hanging free, in the latter case resembling that in the background

113. A surprised lady smitten by Cupid in a heart-shaped book.

of colour illustration 14. Although the ladies' headdresses are not set as far back on their heads as is 'Mary of Burgundy's', their veils are tucked back to clear the face and the bonnets are at least as tall as du Clerq implied, almost to the point of caricature.

One of the most curious forms taken on by books was heart-shaped (illus. 113 and 126); the first example is a song book which belonged to Jean de Montchenu, a member of the household of Jean-Louis of Savoy, Bishop of Geneva, and probably illustrated in that area, not quite France, Italy or Switzerland.[13] The Queen of France was Charlotte of Savoy and links between the two regions were strong, dress probably therefore being fairly Gallicized. Here we see, on the left, Fortune on her wheel, in her fair and forbidding aspects, while on the right we have a lady smitten by Cupid's arrow. The lady's gown is of black damask with a belt and a very deep hem of red velvet cloth-of-gold, and no train. The bizarre, possibly non-French, elements in her dress are the lacing on her lower sleeves (a trace of Germanic influence in the dress of Savoy?) and the complete filling-in of her neckline, perhaps another Savoyard feature: her tall gold-brocaded bonnet with its long veil and black front cloth would have passed as French or Netherlandish, *c.* 1470.

By 1473 the Parisian painter Maître François had finished illustrating a copy of St Augustine's *City of God* for Charles de Gaucourt, the governor of Paris, and included a scene of the Heavenly City above an earthly city, in which people perform acts of vice or virtue: once again, it is with the vices which we have to concern ourselves (illus. 114).[14] The fashionably dressed men, in the midst of the vices, wear short gowns, pleated-down over the body from the shoulders, and some have long-toed shoes. The

114. An assembly of saints sits above a city full of virtuous and sinful mortals.

industrious woodworker in the centre has loosened the ties which bind his hose to his doublet, while to the left front, one of the men who have stabbed each other under the influence of Anger, has doublet sleeves split and then laced closed again at wrist and upper arm. The women tend to wear *cotes hardies* or wide-necked gowns, although only the figure of Pride, in the top-left division, wears a train. Their headdresses, if not veil-covered 'steeples', are bourgeoises' hoods, with the front flap turned back, as are the bands on the bonnets of Pride's attendants: this front band, usually of black velvet, becomes a mark of the headdresses of the 1470s.

About this time Tommaso Portinari, the Medici bank manager in Bruges, and his wife, Maria Baroncelli, commissioned bust-length portraits of themselves from Hans Memlinc: Tommaso's black gown and plum-coloured doublet, set against a dark background, serve admirably as a foil for his paler face and hands, but make it futile to look at his dress for information. Maria's portrait (illus. 11)[15] fares rather better, as her plum velvet dress is lined with a short-haired white fur and girded by a white belt. Her scooped gown neck closes just above the belt, and is filled in with the usual *piece* attached to a lace which disappears rather disconcertingly behind her elaborate necklace of intertwined gold cords, pearl and enamelled flowers, pendants and beads. Her more realistically sized 'steeple' cap, with its veil, protrudes from what looks like a flapped bourgeoise's hood, opened at the top to allow the steeple through.

Between 1471 and 1473 Dirk Bouts produced a panel depicting 'The Justice of the Emperor Otto' (illus. 115)[16] for the town hall of Louvain. Kneeling before the Emperor, is the widow of a count unjustly executed as a result of the malice of the Empress; cradling her husband's head in her right arm, the impassive countess grasps the red hot bar of metal which does not, by God's intervention, blister her hand, thereby proving that her husband was innocent of the charges brought against him. Simultaneously, in the background, the perjured Empress, clad only in shirt, kirtle and kerchief, is burned to death.

The courtiers wear tall felt bonnets or small shaggy bowler hats, and the sleeves of their gowns no longer stand higher than their natural height: instead, the old bulk of the top of the sleeve has slipped down, continuing the slope of the shoulders. The cloth-of-gold gown of the middle-aged dandy on the left does not owe the shape of its folds to his sword belt, and the tight fit of his gown over his hips is something we have not encountered before: its form is echoed in the full-length gown of the courtier at the other side of the doorway, making his figure as elongated as that of the slender young man in the foreground. Even the men's faces do not escape entirely from this rather mannered elegance and length.

The countess wears a reddish-pink woollen gown (is this the

115. The variety of faces assembled by Dirk Bouts in 'The Ordeal by Fire' is remarkable, from that of the middle-aged dandy (**116.**) who tries not to register an unbecoming degree of surprise, to that of the young countess (**117.**) who seems to have gone beyond suffering any emotion, even triumph at the vindication of her husband.

116. ABOVE LEFT: The outline of the cloth-of-gold sleeve on the left has been lowered and narrowed, probably to match the latest fashion when the painting was delivered in 1473—this can be seen in the darker paint around it on the door frame.

117. ABOVE: From beneath the velvet band of the countess's headdress peeps a tiny loop, probably to allow her to reposition the edifice if it slipped.

less-red red called '*incarnal*' by Sicily Herald?[17]) lined with *gris*, over a black kirtle, and her cuffs have been turned back to allow her to use her hands. The extremely wide open collars seem to have been losing popularity, as the countess, not content with a gauze scarf and black *piece*, seems to have put a wider black collar over her gown's collar, and her headdress is of the more sensible dimensions of Maria Baroncelli Portinari's.

In July 1473 the Bruges couple Jan de Witte and Maria Hoose were painted in a charming triptych with the Virgin and Child in the central panel (illus. 118 and 121).[18] The self-satisfied Jan wears a black damask gown which is allowed to hang freely from his wide but sloping shoulders; the sleeves are still too long and are turned back at the cuffs to reveal the brown fur lining. Over his shoulder peeps his shaggy black bowler hat, still attached to a *cornete*.

Although Maria's black velvet gown seems more sombre than her husband's, which has some play of light over the satin of the damask, it is in sharp contrast with its white fur lining which appears down the skirt as the centre front opening, and with the red velvet *piece* crushing her bosom, its action continued by the unrealistically constricting red satin belt. Around her neck she wears a necklace of the heavier type we encountered in illustration 11, here composed of drop-shaped rubies set in gold. Her headdress is a truncated version of that of 'Mary of Burgundy', set at the same angle on the back of the head with the almost transparent veil drawn up to a ridge above the forehead: the cap's decoration consists of thistles worked in coloured embroidery threads and pearls. Altogether, her outfit seems excessively uncomfortable, with the rib cage compressed from arm socket to its lower edge, the hat precariously balanced at the back of the head, and the extremely tight sleeves, which could

118. ABOVE: The smug Bruges citizen Jan de Witte painted with his wife (**121**) in 1473.

119. ABOVE RIGHT: Salome, by Hans Memlinc in 1479, from the 'Altarpiece of the Two Saints John' in the Sintjanshospitaal, Bruges. Her necklace is breaking away from the solid collar form of the early 1470s to the single main strand of the 1480s.

120. RIGHT: René of Anjou, late in life, and his wife Jeanne de Laval, in sombre dress which completely belies their rank.

have been achieved only by cutting the cloth on the bias, to give the sleeves enough stretch to pass over the hands and then return to a glove-like fit over the narrower arms. The only concession made to common sense by this seventeen-year-old girl is in hitching her cuffs back slightly from her knuckles, an idea which becomes widespread in the early 1490s. It is debatable whether the truncating of the 'steeple' headdress here is purely a result of the demands of the aesthetics of the picture space, although the balance of probabilities is in favour of an accurate depiction of the wardrobe of this demurely self-conscious young lady in her best finery.

In the case of Jeanne de Laval (illus. 120),[19] painted with her husband René of Anjou, perhaps by Nicolas Froment, we can be sure that it must have been the demands of the picture space which prompted the assumption by the titular Queen of Sicily of a headdress half-way between that worn by lower-class women and that worn as the front part of a 'steeple'. Indeed, so small are these two panels (about 17·5cm by 13·5cm each) that the painter had to regulate very carefully the proportion of exposed flesh to dress in each: René's black cap stops further up his head than Jeanne's, but his fur collar rises higher than hers. It is fortunate that in having to make Jeanne's gown close nearly as high up the neck as her husband's, the painter was able to resort to the contemporary mode for filling in the bare neckline with something more substantial than a scarf and a necklace.

Sometime between 1473 and 1478 the Portinaris commissioned an altarpiece of the 'Adoration of the Shepherds' from Hugo van der Goes, in which they appeared with their three eldest children (illus. 122).[20] Once again, Tommaso's attire is disappointing in its black obscurity, but with his little sons' outfits we can see that some concession has been made to their tender years, in that their gowns are sleeveless, and hence less bulky. Maria wears a headdress similar to that in illustration 11, this time decorated with triangles and the letters T (Tommaso) and M (Maria) worked in pearls. Around her neck she wears exactly the same necklace as in her earlier portrait, this time over black-covered shoulders. Her rib cage is as compressed as Maria Hoose's (illus. 121) but her gown's collar crosses her shoulders and such bosom as the dress allows her to have, in a proper V-shape, without any of the earlier curves into a U-shape. Her daughter Margherita has also had some allowance made for her being a child, in that her hair is, not very successfully, held back from her face only by a modified version of the front section of her mother's headdress, complete with the loop at the centre front, and her green gown has a wider front opening whose lacing could have been undone as the child required more mobility or as she grew, which must also be the reason her sleeves are less tightly fitting than her mother's.

The hair style of Mary Magdalene, the figure standing behind

121. Maria Hoose, wife of Jan de Witte, perhaps in her wedding dress, as the painting bears a precise date, 27 July 1473, and may commemorate such an event.

122. Tommaso and Maria Portinari and the three children who were born to them during their years in Flanders. The family all wear Flemish dress.

the child, is interesting, perhaps a reflection of how women were currently wearing their hair under the headdresses. Such a head of hair might well have provided some kind of anchorage for the bonnet, and the stiff black strip at the front, as well as holding back stray locks which threatened to peep out on to the forehead, could well have taken a couple of pins inserted from under the bonnet's velvet flap. In addition, her hair looks rather greasy, as it would quickly have become under a hat day after day: usually women's hair is only painted as soft and loose, as in depictions of the Virgin, which it would have been just after drying, washing it perhaps being the only reason for having it down for any length of time. (It is not known how often women washed their hair at this date: in Boccaccio's *Decameron* in 1348 the young Florentine noblewomen washed their hair every Saturday, and in 1542 the French Duchess of Guise urged her daughter, the Queen of Scots, to wash her hair at least once a month, as greasy hair would give the queen even more colds than she was already suffering.[21])

Another little girl in modified adult's dress was the daughter of Sir John and Lady Elizabeth Donne, English Yorkist supporters apparently painted in Bruges by Hans Memlinc (illus. 123).[22] Although at least one of the attendants of Margaret of York, Duchess of Burgundy, was depicted in a gown with a similar wide opening in 1475, it seems to have been also a short-lived fashion for adults, so rarely depicted that its time-span is

123. An English family, that of Sir John Donne, painted in Flanders by Memlinc.

124. The donors of the 'St Hippolytus Triptych', depicted in the skimpy dress of *c.* 1480.

impossible to compute accurately. Apart from Margaret of York's attendant, a lady who appears on a tournament shield in the British Museum wears a cloth-of-gold gown with such an opening, a deep ermine hem and a steeple headdress (therefore after *c.* 1470?), while Memlinc painted Mary Magdalene in a plain grey-blue dress of this variety worn over a red velvet cloth-of-gold under-skirt, making it clear that this rather plain garment is not to be regarded as an underdress which has temporarily escaped to become an outer garment.[23]

125. A detail of the previous illustration, showing how the gown collar stands up on the chest.

Lady Donne's gown has the new V-shaped set to its collar which, combined with the *piece*, gives an almost square shape to the neck area, as does her daughter's dress. Her necklace is the Yorkist livery collar of suns and roses, and is narrower than Maria Portinari's necklace: this may be a reflection of the fashion for increasingly narrow necklaces manifested *c.* 1480 (see illus. 124), although it could equally well be argued that the collar, being more official than a mere necklace, may have retained these dimensions from the past. Her husband's collar is of a similar size and helps to hold down the vestigial lapels of his gown, which has become so narrow that it would close with no room to spare. The urge to split clothes downwards (and hence to appear to elongate them) has also affected his red doublet and his gown sleeves, through which his doublet shows. Sir John is documented as having visited Bruges in 1477,[24] a date not in conflict with the style of his dress: in the background of the Margaret of York scene is a young man in a long, tight gown, open to the waist and slit over the top of the armholes.

In 1480 Pieter Bultync and his wife donated a panel depicting 'The Seven Joys of the Virgin' to the Tanners' Chapel in Bruges:[25] attire similar in outline to theirs, but much more interesting in detail, is worn by Hippolyte de Berthoz and Elisabeth de Keverwyck in their altarpiece of 'The Martyrdom of St Hippolytus', probably begun by Dirk Bouts and finished (including their portraits; illus. 124) by Hugo van der Goes.[26] Husband and wife are dressed in black damask gowns, the husband's purple doublet, visible at neck and sleeves, being echoed by his wife's purple belt. Beneath his open doublet he wears another black garment. The vertical slit in Hippolyte's sleeve has been used to allow his arm to pass out through it, much as in the sleeves of academic gowns today, while the front edges of the gown stand indecisively, neither lying flat to the chest nor turning back to form proper lapels (compare Sir John Donne's gown). Hippolyte's hair is longer than Sir John's, probably both because he is younger and because the picture was painted a few years later; on the ground lies his little hat, still attached to a *cornete*.

Elisabeth de Keverwyck's cap is a truncated version of Lady Donne's, more like that of Maria Hoose (illus. 121), although the veil is folded closer to her head, and the cap itself is quite plain,

126. In the background is the church of Notre Dame du Sablon in Brussels, which stands today.

the black velvet front section having been abandoned. From now on it is the angle of the cap to the head which is important, the angle becoming progressively flatter and the cap less interesting, while necklaces too become less flamboyant and less necessary as the neckline is filled in; both Elisabeth and Hippolyte wear fine chains with a single pendant at the centre. (Compare the dress and jewellery of Barbara van Vlaenderbergh, by Memlinc, and that of a girl, also by Memlinc, dated 1480.[27]) At this point it should be clear that the miniature of 'Mary of Burgundy' (colour illus. 14) presents dress not in keeping with the late 1470s: the gown of the young man in the background, while freed from its belt, is still held out over artificially wide shoulders and 'Mary' has too wide a neckline, too wide a necklace, too tall a hat and too much bosom.

Probably of the early 1480s is the 'Portrait of a Young Man', attributed to the Brussels painter, the Master of the View of Sainte Gudule (illus. 126).[28] On his longish hair the young man wears a brown shrunken acorn cap, and the band crossing his chest is probably the *cornete* of this cap. His black gown, lined in sharply contrasting white, again forms tiny lapels, almost by accident; beneath, he wears a mid-brown doublet, tied shut down the centre front by laces with metal-tipped ends. In his hands he holds a book which is open to form a heart-shape, a less complex version of the book in illustration 113.

Bearing the date 1484 is the triptych commissioned from Memlinc by William Moreel, a burgomaster of Bruges and opponent of the Archduke Maximilian, and his wife Barbara van Vlaenderbergh, depicting themselves and their numerous offspring, the varying ages of the sitters providing an extremely useful indication of the acceptance of shifts in fashion, by different age groups (illus. 127 and 128).[29] William was, at this date, just beginning to be aware of the emergence of lapels (compare their total absence from his probably earlier portrait[30]), but he lagged far behind his sons in this, as he did in the length of his hair. The use of spotted fur for lining men's gowns, so popular in the early sixteenth century, seems to have begun about this time, when there was a sufficient area of dress on which to display a fur interesting in itself. There is a general, though not remarkable, increase in bulk and crumpling in male attire, as well as a move away from pure length reflected in the numerous horizontal folds in the gown sleeves, in the way in which William's gown sleeves have been painted wider, at the last minute, so that five centuries later the original outline shows through the red paint, as its translucency increases with age, and in the lowering of the collars of the doublets, which are also shrinking backwards on the boys' necks.

In the right wing stands St Barbara, clad in cloth-of-gold kirtle with pinned-in false sleeves, one of Memlinc's standard forms of attire for young female saints of the more glamorous variety, complete with a degenerate form of the belt worn by Rogier's

figures in this type of outfit. Before her kneels Barbara van Vlaenderbergh, her headdress positioned more horizontally and more incredibly than in her probably earlier portrait.[30] Although the white fur collar of her black damask gown is scooped rather than pointed, beneath it she has a square-necked under collar, the space between it and the base of her neck being filled in by a round-edged shirt (?). Immediately behind her, in nun's attire, kneels a daughter, behind whom on the right is a girl whose cap is almost non-existent, and more completely horizontal than her mother's.

The dress of the younger daughters is far more interesting, reflecting as it does what will shortly become normal in the dress of adult women: to the right of the saint is a child dressed in one of the gowns with wide centre-front lacing which made rare

127. LEFT: The Bruges burgomaster William Moreel, his patron St William and his sons, in varying degrees of awareness of fashionable developments.

128. ABOVE: Barbara van Vlaenderbergh with St Barbara, who holds a model of the tower in which she was imprisoned, and her daughters.

appearances on adults, and two of her sisters are dressed in gowns with almost square necklines, trimmed with a narrow edge of white fur, which continues down the centre front overlap. Above these necklines the *pieces* continue to rise. From the almost complete acceptance of these square-necked gowns, with their narrow edgings in place of collars, their pronounced vertical centre-front openings, and natural waist levels, we could suppose that innovations were at least occasionally tried out on children's attire first: the lack of general acceptance of the wide open-fronted gown, in spite of its having been around for about a decade, may mean that women, while accepting its practicality for growing children, did not particularly care for it themselves. On the other hand, the almost complete adoption of the vertical, and unconcealed, front opening within half a decade, by about 1490, shows how quickly one idea which was 'right' (i.e. aesthetically acceptable) could supercede another. The deep belt worn by women had probably also accustomed the eye to regarding the body as divided horizontally, not just below the bust, but also near the natural level of the waist. That, coupled with the total absence of wide belts from gowns which opened across the front, would have allowed the introduction of a gown whose waistline was set at approximately natural height. (Compare the way in which Bathsheba's attendant [illus. 20] has no deep belt round her gown, which also has a centre-front, overlapped closure, narrowly edged with its lining.) This new form of bodice, however, should not be taken to show any profound change as yet in the aesthetic standard governing women's dress, since it still contained very strong vertical constricting elements.

One child who may not have enjoyed freer dress than adult women was the three-year-old Margaret of Austria, daughter of Mary of Burgundy, married in 1483 to the thirteen-year-old Dauphin in France. As Mary of Burgundy had died after a hunting accident in 1482, there was always the chance that if Margaret's brother Philip died, all the Burgundian territories north of France would become hers, and eventually her heir's. The toddler arrived in Lille on Saturday, 26 April 1483 wearing a black satin dress, brocaded with gold thread and banded with large pearls and precious stones, and on her head a white linen hood (*beguinet*) under a black velvet cap (*tocque*), perhaps not unlike those in illustration 128. When her father-in-law died later that year, she became Queen of France, and her wardrobe accounts present a bizarre mixture of the realization of what are the main interests and needs of a child at play, such as covers for her dolls and knee pads (*gardegenoulx*) for herself in 1485, and the demands made on her appearance by her rank. Thus, her ladies-in-waiting wore *tocques*, *chapperons* and *gorgeriz* of black velvet, the last-named being some kind of covering for the upper chest, while the child queen had *gorgeriz* of black satin, lined with black taffeta, as well as black satin *brassieres*.[31]

Colour Plate **16.** Here the Master St Giles presents us with several depictions of how men deliberately made their dress appear untidy in the 1490s, mainly by wrapping their gown sleeves round their arms several times and not having the sleeves completely joined to the gown at the armholes.

1498
Das malt Jch nach meiner gestalt
Jch war sex und zwenzig Jor alt
Albrecht Dürer

Olivier de la Marche, apparently writing his '*Le parement et triumphes des dames*' in his old age (he died in February 1502) felt that what he called a '*gorgerette*' should be used to allow the throat and chest to be seen without being naked, and to protect the skin against sunburn and darkening of colour: the fine *gorgerettes* of his youth must have fulfilled the former requirement, while the dark ones here must have fulfilled the latter.[32] In modern French brassières are vests for children, but this is a term which was used occasionally throughout the fifteenth century, for an item worn by adult men and women, as well as children, and in the French royal accounts was often described as '*une (paire de) brasserolles*', and may therefore have meant a jacket whose sleeves covered only the top of the arm (*bras*), much like a bolero jacket. Unfortunately, its complete invisibility (as far as we know) in depictions makes it difficult to decide what it was. One of Margaret's *brassieres* is described as '*unes brassieres de satin noir doubles par le corps de taffetas noir*': it therefore clearly covered some of the torso, and perhaps some of the black neckline fillings we see in the last twenty years of the fifteenth century were *brassieres* and some *gorgeriz*. Other adult aspects of dress show themselves in a black velvet gown, which the queen had in 1485; it was mainly lined with ermine, although thirty bellies of miniver were used in the bodice and sleeves (where they would not be seen), thirty ermines were used in the *get* (outer hem) and cuffs, and it also had a *faulx git* (the underside of the hem?) which required *mouchettes* (spots) and leather. The young Portinari and Donne daughters had dark hems and cuffs on their gowns, which make sense, unlike these white areas in Margaret of Austria's gown, suggesting that we may have here a reflection of the dress of adults.

129. A lady in *robe royal* among fashionably dressed courtiers.

Despite the Moreels' wealth, they were not members of the court circle of the Netherlands, and may have been very slightly out-of-touch with the latest aspects of court dress. The dedication miniature of the French manuscript *Les douze perils d'enfer* (illus. 129)[33] contains male courtiers whose attire would not have been out of keeping with that of the young men in the 1475 Margaret of York miniature referred to above, with their egg-shaped torsoes, and their short caps, while the ladies wear gowns of the types worn by some of the Moreel daughters, with almost completely square necklines, the fur lining showing itself round those necklines and down the front closure of the gowns. The attire of these ladies is more advanced in the filling in of their necklines, with black V-necked insets, which seem to have continued far down their backs, as the gowns plunged into a very low V-neck behind, and in thin little black caps with front lappets swept back over their shoulders. Perhaps a compromise date of *c.* 1480 could be suggested for this scene.

Back in Bruges, in 1486, an anonymous family group, probably mother, son and son's wife, ordered a diptych (illus. 130), attributed to the Master of the Legend of St Ursula.[34] The

Colour Plate **17.** Albrecht Dürer's self portrait of 1498 is the coloured study of a basically only black and white dress in which the shock of the stark contrast is increased by the deliberate untidiness of his dress – even a seam on the cap has not been completed.

mother, aged sixty-two, has done all she can to muffle her head and shoulders without including a neck veil which, we have seen, does not occur in Bruges dress; her headdress is virtually undatable, having nothing remarkable about it, except for the centre front fold popular from *c.* 1480 until *c.* 1510. Her son, aged thirty, is very staid in his dress, having narrow sleeves and no untidiness resulting in lapels in his gown; he has, however, lowered his doublet collar without moving it backwards. His wife, aged twenty-three, is only slightly differently dressed from Barbara van Vlaenderbergh, her gown being pink with a broad white belt partially obscured by the hitching up of her skirt by another narrow gold belt, and with a neckline not as completely filled in.

In the following year, 1487, the twenty-three-year-old Bruges patrician Martin van Nieuwenhove was painted by Memlinc (illus. 131),[35] in a brown woollen gown lined with black fur, over a reddish purple velvet undergarment: at this point we may begin to suspect that, once again, a *piece* is being worn under the doublet, which is worn so far open across the chest that its edge is only just discernible inside the lapels, whence run the ribbons which tie it on across the chest. The doublet is made mainly of black wool, which shows above the elbow, through the front slit in his sleeve which is allowed to trail across the table before him: the lower sleeve, being much more on display, is of the same plum-coloured velvet as the *piece*. (The doublet sleeve constructed in upper and lower sections is by now a useless relic of the puffed shoulders of the 1450s and 1460s.) His doublet has no collar, the otherwise bare neck area being covered by his fluffy, shoulder-length hair.

Probably to be regarded as belonging to the late 1480s is the panel of a family identified by the coats of arms as De Waele, a name common in Ghent, with their patron saints, before the Virgin and St Bernard. It is attributed to an anonymous Brussels painter (illus. 132).[36]

The men of the family lack the sophisticated garments of Martin van Nieuwenhove, their gowns making only the slightest concession to the fashion for lapels, although their shoes have completely lost the pointed toes of earlier years and are moving towards the heavy, round toes which will be part of the new mood for squarer, chunkier outlines in dress. Their hair too is shorter than Martin's. The elderly women (the mother of the family?) wears a gown which would have been acceptable *c.* 1455–60, had it been belted further up the bodice; despite the possibility of the family's being of Ghent origin, there are more reasons for regarding her headdress as the *Brussels* equivalent of that of the mother in illustration 130, being made Bruxellois by the swathing of her neck. The younger woman's hair seems to be encased in a gauzy cap, worn under a transparent veil, to which has been pinned a shorter version of her mother's neck veil. Her gown is as lacking in self-assertion as that of her mother: it is skimpy without being stylishly so, and is typical of the way in which women's dress in the early 1490s seems to have little to say for itself, all the interest and flamboyant changes being confined to men's dress. This square-necked gown with its lowered waistline seems suddenly very different from the more positively outlined V-necked, higher waisted gowns of a few years previously, but it is really a lingering of the old aesthetic standard of tightly fitting gown poured round long slender bodies, lacking the impetus to take the next steps towards the squareness implicit in its structure, and which men's dress absorbed so rapidly in the next decade.

Around 1490, women's dress did try to become more interesting, by incorporating a train usually worn tucked into the belt at the back, to display the pattern of the fur lining and, incidentally, to preserve the train from excess wear as it trailed along the ground: so it is worn by the wife of Jan de Sedano, a Spaniard resident in Bruges (illus. 134),[37] painted by Gerard David. The effect, however, is scarcely one of increased bulk, rather one of emphasized verticality of the skirt. As the cuffs of the sleeves have probably become too inconvenient when worn over the knuckles, they have been drawn back on to the wrists,

130. LEFT: A Bruges family in 1486, showing the conservatism of an older woman.

131. BELOW LEFT: The Bruges patrician Martin van Nieuwenhove in 1487, much more flamboyantly dressed than the man in **130**.

132. ABOVE: The difference in the tastes of two generations appears again in this painting, particularly in the dress of the women.

133. THIS PAGE RIGHT: The Spaniard Jan de Sedano, resident in Bruges, and his son with St John the Baptist in the early 1490s.

134. THIS PAGE FAR RIGHT: The wife of Jan de Sedano. Her bonnet can probably be compared with the understructure of the headdress in **135**.

135. FACING PAGE TOP: Wife beating in the late fifteenth century: a jealous husband and his wife whom he suspects of infidelity. His attire is old-fashioned, but hers belongs to the early 1490s. Her linen veil has fallen off, and with it a tiny black undercap and a black ribbon. (*Roman de la rose*, British Library, Harley ms. 4425, f. 85.)

136. FACING PAGE CENTRE: The Lover of the Rose meets the God of Love.

137. FACING PAGE BOTTOM: The God of Love turns the key of the Lover's heart.

the sleeve itself and its lining being drawn apart and folded. The headdress consists simply of a black damask band and loop binding her auburn hair into a bun, and over all is pinned a transparent shoulder-length veil, with a small centre dip caused by an ironed-in fold. Jan and his son (illus. 133) wear loose gowns with furred lapels over doublets laced across *pieces*, the father's gown being black lined with brown fur and his doublet being red with black laces.

The way in which men put on their clothes *c.* 1490 can be seen in a copy of the *Roman de la rose*: there the narrator, after getting up, has put on a dark red velvet doublet with open lacing, over his baggy shirt, as well as matching red hose, and a red hat, on top of a green bonnet; next he sets off on his journey in his completed outfit, with its rather *recherché* colour scheme of grey gown, lined in red, over a black damask jacket, the main colours being picked up in the hat's grey, red and white feathers. Further on, when the Lover meets the God of Love (illus. 136 and 137), the Lover wears a tawny-coloured coat, lined in black velvet, which shows at the wide lapels, the base of the hanging sleeve, and at the back slit of the gown.[38] The deliberately untidy clutching of the gown across the body is echoed by the bagginess of the hose, both means to increasing the bulk of the dress and making it as lumpy as the shoes.

Dress in various stages of looseness for men and women was portrayed by the Master of Frankfurt in his record of the 'Festival of the Antwerp Archers' (illus. 138), held after 1491 and probably before 1493.[39] Beneath the canopy in the centre sits the master of the feast, his gown draped across his knees, while a girl in a red gown presents him with an apple. Her sleeves are much baggier at the cuffs than those of Jan de Sedano's wife, and they are more advanced than those of the other women at this riotous 'Sunday school picnic': all the other women, with the exception of the smock-clad woman on the right, have straight sleeves, with flared cuffs turned back over the wrists. Rather than being simply square, their necklines actually rise to a point in the centre front. Below the tree on the left sits an aristocratic young couple, the young man as untidily dressed as the lover and the girl in a black headdress similar to those of the ladies in this *Roman de la rose*: the other women have more middle-class headdresses, two with chin cloths such as reappear in the Master's 'Portrait of the Artist and his Wife' of 1496 (illus. 140).[40]

As far as can be determined, the square neckline, once established in women's dress in the Netherlands, remains unaltered throughout the 1490s, but in France there seems to have been a brief excursion in favour of a higher V-neck with centre-front or side-front closing, and the adoption of a curiously uncomfortable sway-back stance by which the whole spine was thrown into a concave curve. The Master of Moulins' portrait of a lady, said to be Madeleine de Bourgogne, one of the last of Philip the Good's bastards (illus. 139), who lived in France, shows very clearly this posture in which the body seems to be encased in a gown which forces it into this shape:[41] beside her, the woman outside the gate at the Archers' Feast is standing almost upright. This gown has an off-centre closing, although that of Anne de Beaujeu (illus. 142), the daughter of Louis XI and Regent for Charles VIII, has a centre-front closing. Anne's cuffs are slightly baggier, although the lining and the sleeve are still pulled apart at the wrist. The increasing size of the sleeve and the sudden appearance of a crimped gold edge on the linen under-cap, a feature which continues into the 1530s, suggests that this picture is a few years later than that of 'Madeleine de Bourgogne': the original inclusion of a portrait of Anne's daughter Suzanne de Bourbon, now separated from the main panel, suggests that Anne was painted *c.* 1493, when Suzanne was two. The child in her

138. FACING PAGE: The Antwerp Archers' Feast. The dress of the woman beside the throne is more advanced than that of the woman at the gate, as it has wider sleeves.

139. LEFT: Madeleine de Bourgogne and St Mary Magdalene. The saint's face matches the type of beauty described in *La nef des dames vertueuses*, first published in 1503, with her rather long, sharply chiselled nose and greenish eyes.

140. ABOVE: In a self-congratulatory display of skill, the Master of Frankfurt has painted two life-size flies on the surface of the panel, as though the flies were attracted by his realistic painting of the food.

white damask cap and gown has echoes of her mother's attire in her V-neckline and drawn-back cuffs, but some common sense has gone into covering the front of the bodice with a bib tied under the arm. The baby's father, Pierre, Duke of Bourbon (illus. 141), was considerably older than his wife, and was probably going bald when this portrait was painted, as the current fashion for long fluffy hair for men is rather beyond him, although his dark red velvet gown is probably quite as untidy and bulky as fashion could demand.[42] To echo the square edge of the gown's enormous lapels, the under-arm seam of the sleeve has been left incomplete where it would normally have joined the armhole, and that section of the armhole seam has also not been sewn up, resulting in the protrusion of a corner of the sleeve on the extreme left. Other 'corners' are added to men's dress by the cutting of the

141. FACING PAGE: Pierre de Bourbon with his patron St Peter, in the untidy attire introduced *c.* 1490.

142. LEFT: Anne de Beaujeu with St John the Evangelist. The chunky jewellery is a feature of the dress of both Anne de Beaujeu and Madeleine de Bourgogne.

143. ABOVE: The baby Suzanne de Bourbon, dressed in white damask as befitted her rank.

144, 145. These portraits show very clearly the differing speeds at which men's and women's dress was gaining bulk and untidiness.

brim of the hat into flaps which have to be tied up, as here; presumably as the acorn cap of the late 1460s shrank, its lower edge was turned over, as in the 'Portrait of a Man' by the Master of the View of Sainte Gudule (illus. 126), until the turned-over edge became a feature for development in its own right. (James IV of Scotland acquired one of these 'luggit' bonnets, as his Treasurer called them, in 1489.[43]) Looking at this family group, it is easy to believe contemporary reports that Pierre was rather Anne's devoted slave than her husband, that Louis XI called his sharp-faced daughter the least stupid woman in France, that she terrified her brother the king, and it is easy to see the irony of her writing an instruction manual for her daughter, telling her to be humble and meek in her dealings with everyone, of whatever rank.[44]

Commonly, but probably wrongly, identified as Charles VIII and his second wife Anne, Duchess of Brittany, are the couple in illustrations 144 and 145, both dressed mainly in pink and black.[45] The untidiness of the man's dress is extreme, his 'luggit cap' sitting low over his head, his hair reaching his shoulders, his pink gown sporting great black damask lapels and sleeves slit vertically to reveal the floppy yellow upper part of his doublet sleeve, the lower part being striped and appearing at his wrist and failing to contain his white shirt at that point. Even the doublet is worn open, showing its panné velvet lining as further lapels, over an open-necked shirt tied shut only at its smocked neckband. Beside him, the woman's first tentative steps at cutting the surface of her dress appear quite tidy: Anne de Beaujeu's black head-cloth has grown downwards so far that this lady has had to slit it vertically to allow it to fall over her shoulders, and it is slipping backwards very slightly on top of her head to reveal the crimped edge of her undercap, which in turn has moved back to show a little of her hair, a fairly revolutionary step for a married woman to take after forty years of the almost total covering of women's hair. The edging of the black cap is a series of gold thistles, and it is probably to this fashion which Olivier de la Marche referred in his '*Le parement et triumphes des dames*', when he commented favourably on the current fashion at court for hoods of velvet or satin for ladies, and of black or red cloth for *bourgeoises*, the court ladies decorating their hoods with golden chains and spangles.[46] Beneath the hood's front flaps, the gown's neckline seems to be squaring off, and moving back the neckline of the *gorgeriz/brassieres* as it goes; nevertheless, any increase in chunkiness in this outfit is almost incidental, and not nearly as contrived as in her husband's.

Headdresses of the type we have just seen—velvet cloth over crimped under-cap—tend to remain an upper-class prerogative for the next half century of their existence, and women who do not wear them are presumably, more often than not, middle or working class. A French manuscript of the Dance of Death, which the dress suggests was illustrated *c.* 1500, depicts hideously cheerful corpses dragging away women of various classes and occupations: in illustration 146 Death summons a *marchande* and in illustration 147, a *nouvelle mariée*.[47] The merchant's wife wears a lumpy black hood, with a turned-back front resembling the front section of the steeple headdress, and a V-necked gown with an off-centre fastening. Although the cuffs of her sleeves have belled outwards quite considerably, the upper part of the sleeve is still quite closely fitting. The new bride, however, is probably slightly classier, as her sleeves are wider and more deeply cuffed, the lining being what looks like bands of miniver. The horizontal thrust of her neckline has continued, bringing the outer edges

146, 147. Death seizes a merchant's wife and a more fashionably dressed bride.

near the shoulder socket, followed fairly closely by the black under-garment. Although the torso remains tightly encased within its centre-front closing bodice, there are many more broken and lumpy areas in the dress, like the sleeves, the folding over of the back section of the hood on to the top of the head and the introduction of pleats into the back of the skirt.

Most of these devices for widening the female silhouette appear, and succeed, in the portrait of Jeanne de Bourbon-Vendôme (illus. 149), datable between her marriage to Jean de la Tour, comte d'Auvergne (illus. 148) in 1495 and Jean's receipt in 1498 of the Order of Saint Michel, whose collar he would assuredly have worn for his portrait, had he been entitled to do so.[48] The countess wears the, by now, usual upper-class headdress of black velvet cloth over an under-cap edged with a crêped band. Although her black under-collar and gauze scarf have not moved particularly far back towards her shoulders, she has abandoned the centre-front closing to achieve an unbroken area across the front of the bodice, choosing instead to close her gown at her left (our right) side, still forcing her body into the curious French lurch as it narrows sharply towards her waist. There are deliberately set vertical folds in the back of her skirt, and less contrived folds and puckers in her sleeves which are turned back to reveal their ermine lining, while retaining a curious reminder of the earlier way of drawing sleeves back, in the way in which equal areas of sleeve and lining are displayed on the upper-most fold, on our right. Although rather effectively hidden from our scrutiny by his *prie-dieu*, the count seems quite fashionably, if rather tidily, dressed, with his long fluffy hair, his large lapelled cloak in which slits have been made to accommodate his arms and to provide a square-cornered flap-back, the baggy upper sleeve on his doublet, and his bizarre hose, apparently pale stockings slashed to show a darker lining; this fashion more normally resembles patchwork, as worn by a sinner in a strange panel of the 'Seven Deadly Sins and the Seven Works of Mercy', painted in Antwerp, in which the painter has happily mixed historical dress with the more bizarre aspects of fashionable dress for maximum theatricality.[49] Even the count's shoes have become squarer at the toes than reason would have thought possible.

In these two portraits we have all the elements which will go towards creating the popular concept of early sixteenth century dress, deriving mainly from vague memories of portraits by Holbein. Men are set on the road towards bulk in their gowns and doublets, their shoes are stubby, and slashing of an outer layer of clothing to reveal a lining has appeared. Women have committed themselves to accepting as square and bulky an outline as their menfolk, and are incorporating the features necessary to achieve this, by changing their necklines, their sleeves and the width of their skirts, although Gothic constraints remain on the shape of the torso.

148, 149. The aristocrats Jean de la Tour and Jeanne de Bourbon-Vendôme in cloth of gold, shortly after their marriage in 1495.

8 The Last Refuge of the Gothic World

No book which purported to examine late Gothic dress could justifiably ignore dress in that most Gothick of all regions, Germany. Such an examination, however, is fraught with difficulties more complex and finally more unrewarding than those which beset the examination of French or Netherlandish dress. The problems stem partly from the geographical and political structure of fifteenth-century Germany, and partly, and more seriously, from the use of dress itself.

The Germany of the fifteenth century was completely fragmented: there were local rulers, of varying powers and independence, governing areas ranging in size from towns to provinces, and there were 'free' cities in the midst of these small territories, owing allegiance directly to the German Emperors, the successors of Charlemagne as Holy Roman Emperors in the west. The 'Empire' spread from Brussels in the west to near Cracow in the east and from Hamburg in the north to Siena in the south, with each region, not unnaturally, being more concerned with its own neighbourhood than in contributing to something as intellectually amorphous as a German state. Areas open to French or Flemish influence expressed this influence in their art and dress, and areas open to influences from eastern Europe incorporated increasingly bizarre (by western standards) eastern European elements in their dress. Stephan Lochner, the chief Cologne painter from *c.* 1430 to 1451, introduced the Netherlandish technique of translucent painting to Cologne; Hans Memlinc came from the Middle Rhine to work in Bruges. The Limbourg brothers had come from border territories to Paris and, ultimately, the service of Jean de Berry; Jan van Eyck probably came from near Maastricht, on the eastern borders of modern Belgium with Germany. As Dutchwomen's dress departs from the norm of Flanders and Brabant, incorporating a few aspects of the type of dress worn in southern Germany, so Cologne dress departs from southern German dress towards the dress of Flanders and Brabant. The trading possible along the Rhine and the Scheldt helped make for the cultural entanglement of Holland and north-western Germany at this date, and the valley of the Danube, running almost due west to east, seems to have

150. A self-portrait by Albrecht Dürer in 1493, displaying all the casualness typical of south German dress at the end of the fifteenth century. This is sometimes said to have been a betrothal portrait because of the flower in his hand. (Paris, Louvre.)

produced roughly the same types of dress within its sphere. When such evidence becomes available, the best a dress historian can hope to do is to sift out the various elements and attribute them to their respective areas, on a sliding scale of 'slightly Flemish' to 'completely southern German'.

Were these geographical, and hence cultural, problems not sufficient, we have also the problem of a lack of visual evidence of dress: paintings there are in plenty, but not enough showing women's clothing without an all-enveloping cloak. What had been an occasionally middle- or lower-class phenomenon in the southern Netherlands, the wearing of a cloak by a woman in church, becomes common in portraits of middle-class donatrices in Holland;[1] by the time this idea reaches German lands, married women are nearly always encased in dark, enshrouding cloaks. Since the majority of portraits, for most of the century, occur in conjunction with religious scenes, the effect of this behaviour is disastrous for anyone seeking a comprehensive view of the fashions of men and women: had we been forced to rely solely on Dürer's drawing of a Nuremberg housewife going to church (illus. 166), we should never have guessed at the bizarre and elaborate dresses sometimes worn underneath (illus. 165).

With these reservations in mind, let us proceed as far as we can with an unavoidably cursory look at dress in northern and southern Germany, mainly around Cologne and Nuremberg, with occasional departures to other regions where the material offers itself, on the understanding that when I refer to 'Germany' I mean an area including modern East and West Germany, and that when I refer to things as 'Teutonic' I mean that they come from German-speaking lands. Since these varying forms of dress are being considered as items corresponding to a departure from Franco-Burgundian standards, with which we have by now come to grips, I make no further apology for referring to items, where necessary, under their French names.

The International Gothic style had an impact on aristocratic dress in Bohemia and north-western Germany, around Cologne, although there is little evidence extant to suggest that married women in southern Germany paid much attention to it. Further east the *Willehalm* of the Emperor Wenzel, probably from the 1380s, depicts International dress as worn in Prague,[2] with bearded courtiers in hip-length outer garments with extremely wide sleeves, and the same short-legged, long-toed appearance which we saw in contemporary France (illus. 16 and 34). The women display more regional peculiarities, in the princess's undisguised front lacing on her gown and her enveloping cuffs, and in the queen's headdress composed of layers of frilled veils, a form of head decoration evolved sooner in Teutonic regions than further west.

Between 1403 and 1404 Konrad von Soest produced an altarpiece for Bad Wildungen, near Cassel in Hesse: one of the witnesses of the 'Crucifixion' is dressed very splendidly in a shell pink hip-length, unbelted *houppelande*, with matching long-toed hose. From the back sleeve seam hangs a double layer of short oblong white strips, which are repeated as white fringing on the *pate* of his pink hood: the sleeve's decoration can be compared to that in illustration 38. A similarly elegant witness, in blue and silver, appears at the Crucifixion in the 'Golden Altar' (originally from Lüneburg, south-east of Hamburg), which was painted before 1418, and betrays the influence of Konrad von Soest.[3]

Austrian aristocratic dress of the same time contained many normal aspects of International dress, as far as can be judged from Duke William of Austria's copy of Gulielmus Durandus's *Rationale*, in which he appears with his Duchess Joanna of Durazzo, during the two years (1404–6) in which William held the title.[4] His blue *houppelande* has wide, square-dagged sleeves, while his attendant's shorter blue gown has closed *bombarde* sleeves, striped, as livery, blue and white on one side, matching his blue and white hose. The duchess has a red *houppelande* with a strange close-fitting white cap, which reappears in the dress of her lady-in-waiting who is otherwise muffled up in her cloak, one of many exasperatingly well-hidden Teutonic women.

In southern Germany, in Nuremberg, the epitaph painting of Paul Stromer, who died in 1406, presents a middle-class family, in which the mother is enveloped in a cloak and a linen headscarf closed under her chin and pulled up into a peak above her forehead, over an under-cap. Her unmarried daughter has bound her hair round her head in a plait, and wears a gown with closed *bombarde* sleeves, like her father's and brothers'.[5] Women in this area of Germany continue to appear dressed thus, both mothers and daughters, into the 1430s, although their menfolk follow Netherlandish trends, as in the Master of the Hiltpoltstein Altarpiece's 'Flagellation' which bears the epitaph of Katherina Rümmel (died 1435), the third wife of Hans Löffelholz, who is depicted in a carefully gathered *heuque* type of garment, very like that of Giovanni Arnolfini in 1434 (illus. 59), except for its closing at the hem at the side.[6]

The coats-of-arms on a 'Crucifixion and Donors' (illus. 151) apparently point to the area between Koblenz and Mainz as the source of the painting and to the knight Konrad Beier of Boppard, who died in 1421, or to the family of the Schenk of Liebenstein, which died out in 1423.[7] The donor, whoever he was, wears a shortish dagged gown over his armour, complete with dagging at the hem and the outer sleeve; both the dagging and the flared lower sleeve are carefully outlined, suggesting a comparison with the increasing tendency to outline dagging in France and the Netherlands towards 1420. Although his hair is longer than that of men farther west, it does not necessarily invalidate the painting's being *c.* 1420, as young and aristocratic

151. OVERLEAF: Dress in the Rhine Valley *c.* 1420, by Master Berthold of Nördlingen.

south-German men wore their hair longer and wilder throughout the century. The donatrix wears a mixture of Netherlandish and Teutonic features in her outfit: her hair is dressed into horns at the sides of her head, but her frilled veils are stacked so deeply that her headdress seems to consist not of veils, but of a roll on top of her head and another round her shoulders. Her gown is of the *houppelande* type, but the cape-like sleeves, with their dagging, are unlike normal dress for Frenchwomen in the 1410s, the dagging alone being enough to mark its departure from these norms, as do the 'purse' sleeves on the gowns of German girls. Likewise, married women in Aachen (and probably also Cologne) wore layers of veils on their heads, pulled into three ridges across their foreheads, two ridges covering their 'horns' of hair and the third ridge sitting in the middle, as on the women of the family of Count Werner of Palant, the count's mother also covering her neck very closely.[8]

The curious scale-like dagging which appeared on the *heuque* of one of Yolande Belle's sons (illus. 46) in 1420 and on Charles VII's *heuque* (p. 107), makes an appearance in Cologne on the leaf-green *heuque* worn by the son of the von Esch von dem Wasservass family, and his hair is short enough to meet the requirements of his western neighbours. His wife wears a leaf-green *houppelande* with *bombarde* sleeves lined in white, to match his green-and-white outfit, and has a veil draped casually over her 'horns' and her shoulders. The daughter, having been added on to the painting's dark surface, now appears to be dressed in a much darker green, green pigment tending to turn brown with time. Her gown has the standard closed *bombarde* sleeves of German girls.[9]

The hysterical disapproval which women's 'horns' occasioned in Flanders and Paris in 1428 and 1429, finds a much paler reflection in contemporary Cologne in Stephan Lochner's 'Last Judgement': there, some of the Damned wear their hair netted into conveniently diabolical sharp horns, while the Saved enter heaven, virtuous in their simply plaited hair, which with hind-sight looks like a non-German caricature of German female hairstyles.[10]

Between Stuttgart and the Rhine lies the village of Tiefen-bronn, where the parish church still contains the altarpiece painted for it by Lucas Moser, bearing the sometimes disputed date of 1432.[11] Below it, is a predella panel showing 'The Wise and Foolish Virgins', some of the girls wearing varieties of the lower Rhenish headdresses we have seen already, in the 'Palant Altarpiece' and in the 'Wasservass Altarpiece'. The most interest-ing headdress of all is on the right, the brown hood with *bourrelet* and *pate* slashed and dagged, worn over a linen veil and plaits of hair coiled into horns on the temples, a compromize between the offending horns and respectable *hausfrau* hairdressing. The hood is of the type worn by the women inspecting building work in

152. Upper class dress in south Germany *c.* 1450.

illustration 63, and to the left is a cape-sleeved gown like that of Catherine of Cleves (illus. 52), showing again how ideas in dress must have travelled up and down the Rhine, and not in accordance with our ideas of national boundaries.

Back in Cologne, there seems to have evolved *c.* 1440 an alternative way of wearing a number of layers of fluted veiling. A lady, probably called Katherine von Merode, appears in a stained-glass window,[12] wearing a fluted headdress where the usually unbroken upper edge has been moved round to the back of her head, instead of running straight across her head and her shoulders. The crinkly selvedges and the straight edges of the cloth's folds are joined at the centre front and probably down the back of her head: the result is a set of 'horns' such as can be produced if a paper bag is stretched open half way between its side folds. Her pale purple damask gown has the tight sleeves which were usual under cape-sleeved gowns, and her undershirt shows at her ermine cuffs. This outfit has nothing Netherlandish in it, except for the outline of the headdress; the high neckline, its loop-fastenings and the gathering of the gown's bulk into folds under the bust, resulting in conspicuously flat side areas on the shirt, as in Franco-Burgundian male dress, are all thoroughly Teutonic, even to the use of aspects which another civilization would have considered purely male. This particular headdress probably explains the 'paper-bag' outline of other Cologne women's heads when they are enveloped in cloaks, as in the case of Bela Hirsch, as she witnesses the 'Vision of St John'.[13]

Other male influences occurring in female dress are doublet-like collars standing above the round necks of gowns, as worn by Agnes von Werdenberg (illus. 152) where she appears with her second husband Wilhelm IV Schenk of Schenkenstein, whom she married sometime after being widowed in 1441:[14] this is perhaps a marriage portrait. As the couple lived in southern Germany, near Lake Constance, not only is Agnes's attire completely lacking in links with Franco-Burgundian fashions, but Wilhelm's is also becoming rather eccentric by these standards. Agnes's doublet collar is laced shut, her gown is clasped shut and her upper torso is quite different from those of Netherlandish women in the 1440s, with its almost natural waistline and its closer resemblance to the female form of the early 1950s. Wilhelm's straw hat resembles Flemish furry ones, as worn by Giovanni Arnolfini (illus. 59), but his hair is too long and too curly, and his doublet collar is too straight, which doublet collars remain in deepest Germany. Across his chest he wears the sash of the Order of the Jar, whose device was a jar holding white lilies, referring to the pot of lilies usually depicted in scenes of the Annunciation of the Virgin, as a symbol of her purity. The order's sash could be worn only on Saturdays, not as silly as it sounds at first, as Saturdays were days particularly given over to veneration of the Virgin.

When Olivier de la Marche saw the Emperor Frederick III in Besançon in 1442, Frederick was an impressive figure, about twenty-six years old, dressed in a doublet '*à gros cul, à la guise de Behaigne*' and a blue-brown cloth gown:[15] the doublet was presumably of the type commonly seen on Teutonic youths, and used by Jean Fouquet in illustration 91, where sometimes a separate gathered vertical section was set into the back of the garment below the shoulder blades and continuing to the hips. On his head, the Emperor wore a small grey hat and the imperial crown, while round his neck was a hood whose *pate* reached his saddle, and was slashed '*à grans lambeaulx*' (*lambeaux* are the heraldic device for differentiating the coat of arms of the eldest son from his father's, being a horizontal band from which depend short strips of the same colour). Dagging on a hood was quite usual at this date, but southern-German dress retained this, by now, increasingly strange fashion until the end of the century.

The eccentric nature of truly Teutonic dress for both sexes shows itself around the late 1440s in the illustrations by 'Martinus Opifex' for a *Historia destructionis Troiae*, probably produced in Vienna.[16] On folio 69 Paris marries Helen, in the presence of King Priam, Queen Hecuba and various courtiers. The two older Trojan men and the priest, with their beards, are probably in the 'oriental and historical' tradition, but Paris and one of the witnesses have the large fluffy heads of hair, exaggerated like every other aspect of these figures, which tend to be flaunted by young dandies in the more untainted areas of Teutonic culture: indeed, these hairstyles surpass those of the women, whose hair seems quite restrained in comparison. Paris's gown is belted at natural waist height, as in contemporary Burgundian circles (compare illus. 74), but its length and its stiffly vertical folds are not Burgundian. The women's gowns are belted at levels between the bust and almost natural waist height, with old-fashioned (by Burgundian standards) gathering on the bodices, continuing down the skirts; yet again, the gown sleeves are cut off at the shoulders, forming cape-sleeves and displaying elaborately patterned under-sleeves.

In 1447 in Cologne Stephan Lochner painted a charming 'Presentation in the Temple', with a number of coy female attendants.[17] Holding a tall candle is a girl in a high-waisted, hanging-sleeved green gown, and behind her stand two muffled-up women. The woman immediately behind the girl seems simply to have continued under her chin the four layers of frilled veil, having first tucked the frilled edge underneath, while her companion has kept the frills on top of her horned plaits, and strapped a single cloth over her chin and on to the sides of her head; both women have covered not just their necks, but also their chins. To the right back is a woman in a plum velvet cap with a strand of pearls across her forehead between her jewelled 'horns'; the horns are outlined by a plum-coloured plait, typical of German headdresses' tendency to incorporate patently false hair as plaits or fringes, which may in the latter case be only a 'frozen' vestige of dagging, and which today's interpretations may cause us to regard as hair.

The use of one long cloth covering the head and strapping up the jaw becomes increasingly popular, particularly in south-eastern Germany, around Nuremberg and Ulm, after the abandoning of the centre-front gable-like peak of the early years: its initial stage appears on the tiny figure of the wife of Heinrich von Haunstetten, in a panel depicting the 'Man of Sorrows'

153, 154. OVERLEAF: The men of the Nördlingen family of Fuchshart are boringly dressed by Netherlandish standards, while their womenfolk have done their best to conceal what interest their clothes might have held.

155. A south German youth painted in 1460.

which the couple presented to an Ulm convent in 1457.[18] There, the cloaked donatrix wears a rectangular linen head cloth, pulled down on to her forehead, tucked in at her temples and its corners joined under her chin, much as some Turkish women wear scarves today. Her husband is much more international in his dress, with his *heuque* covering a knee-length gown, and a furry bowler hat lying on the ground before him.

Further north and east, in Nördlingen, Friedrich Herlin painted the 'St George Altarpiece' for the family of Jakob Fuchshart, between 1462 and 1465.[19] There, the men (illus. 153) wear cloaks open down one side, which would cause a certain untidiness and difficulty if the left arm had to be used, and with these cloaks, very softly rolled hoods, one of which has a fringed edge (La Marche's *lambeaux*?), or else very old-fashioned, by Burgundian standards, knee-length gowns with slits up the sides and obvious vertical front closings: only the shaggy hat and lengthening hair could have passed unnoticed in Flanders. Thus, although their hairstyles are not noticeably Germanic, everything else about them is, particularly the latent possibilities for untidiness and assymmetry in the cloaks. Opposite them (illus. 154) are Jakob's two wives Katharina and Agnes, and in front his daughters, Barbara and Agnes. The wives wear probably square veils folded diagonally over thick 'chin-strap' veils, as worn by the Ulm donatrix above, while the daughters wear several layers of veiling, set increasingly farther back on their heads, like rows of tiles on a roof, under a bulky upper veil whose selvedges appear across the top of their heads but are tucked away under their chins, as on the headdress of one of the Lochner 'Presentation' women.

An extravagantly Germanic young man was one Heinrich Blarer, painted in 1460 in the Lake Constance region (illus. 155).[20] On his long, probably artificially curly hair he wears a two-toned furry cap, quite un-Burgundian, as is his high square-edged doublet collar, rising above a round-necked gown which bears not a trace of wide Burgundian shoulders. In 1462 a middle-aged ambassador from Frederick III came to Philip the Good, resplendent in a trailing green cloth-of-gold gown, unbelted and with a wide Bohemian collar, whatever that was, furred with something like long-haired black beaver; his hair, despite his age, was long and held back ('*à grands cheveux retournés en arrière*').[21]

The mountains south of Salzburg and Vienna must have provided good brigand hideouts, and the appearance of Jörg von Pottendorf in armour in 1467 (illus. 156) is probably not an example of a traditional conceit for portraying aristocrats, of whatever degree of lethargy, in full armour: Jörg *was* a notorious gang leader.[22] His armour and his bizarrely decorated helmet are as Gothick as Hollywood could have desired, while his wives are as non-Netherlandish as could be found. The first and second wives, kneeling behind Jörg, wear high, aggressively laced

156. FACING PAGE: The bandit Jörg von Pottendorf and his wives with an assembly of fairly obscure saints in a panel in which the figures have been 'stacked up' the picture space in a very Teutonic way.

157, 158. ABOVE: St Clare in her worldly attire before the Bishop of Assisi, and RIGHT: discarding such vanities before St Francis.

doublet collars under loose gowns with wide collars and sleeves, and 'turbans' with an outer roll (over their plaited hair?) strapped under their chins. (Very similar gowns are worn in the Tyrol by the donors, the Jöchl brothers of Friedrich Pacher's 'Peter and Paul Altarpiece', probably *c.* 1475,[23] a further indication of the androgynous nature of southern-German dress.) The third wife, Elspeth von Liechtenstein, wears a similar headdress and 'doublet' collar, and her over-gown is of the more usual high-waisted type with centre-front pleats below the bust and fur-trimmed hanging sleeves. The wide trumpet-shaped under-sleeve is perhaps attached to the 'doublet' collar, or else to the innermost sleeve, peeping out from under the trumpet sleeve.

In the same year died Barbara Vetzer of Nördlingen and the panel in which she appears with her daughter may commemorate her.[24] Barbara's attire, not surprisingly, resembles that of the women in the 'St George Altarpiece' (illus. 154) while her unmarried daughter can be seen to be dressed more like Elspeth von Liechtenstein, complete with a sway-back stance which she manages to maintain although she is kneeling. Her hair is bound in plaits, with what looks like an artificial fringe at the back of her head.

The structure of these hairstyles, and their artificiality, is shown in pictures from Bamberg, forty miles north of Nuremberg down a branch of the River Main (illus. 158).[25] On the left, St Clare kneels, dressed in her worldly finery, which includes broad plaits on her head under a fancy band with a fringe at the back. On the right, St Francis shears off her own hair, and her headdress lies, undone, on the altar; the broad plaits have been undone to remove the headdress, suggesting that her own hair was worked into the false hair which is caught in two strands on to the centre front of the headband, and the fringe is a separate item, bound on by narrow laces. Her gown is, by comparison, disappointingly uninformative about its structure, being of a standard pattern for her age group.

Around 1475, Friedrich Pacher's 'Peter and Paul Altarpiece', referred to above, presents us with some interesting information on the cut of men's doublets, at least in the Tyrol, as does the sub-Michael Pacher 'Stoning of St Stephen', now in Moulins in France.[26] The doublets retain the deeply inset armhole of the early years of the century, and some have an inserted section of radiating pleats below the shoulder blades, while less impressive examples simply gather the excess material of the doublet back into folds in this area.

Much further north, in Guelders, Sophia van Bylant was depicted, with her late husband Reynalt von Homoet, in a Book of Hours bearing the date 1475.[27] Reynalt's clothes are difficult to date, partly because of his having died in 1458 or 1459 and partly because the short side-slit gown which he is shown wearing on f. 150 would have been twenty years out of date in the southern

Netherlands and yet was still being worn in Nördlingen in the early 1460s (illus. 154). It is much easier to see contemporary Flemish influence in Sophia's outfit, for although the gown has a Teutonic open neck and under-bust pleats, her headdress is clearly related to the steeple headdresses of France and Flanders, even if it lacks a black velvet front section as worn in the *City of God* (illus. 114) by Maria Portinari.

Probably dating from the early 1480s is the Cologne Master of the Holy Kindred's 'Altarpiece of the Family of Gumprecht von Neuenahr' which depicts an aristocratic family, dressed in Netherlandish modes which tend towards the Teutonic.[28] The men who are not in splendid late-Gothic armour wear gowns with the narrowish sleeves we should expect in contemporary Flanders, or what look like vestments edged at their V-necks with red velvet, over plum-red under-garments, and their hair is generally of Flemish length. The mother's cloth-of-gold gown is round necked, as are some of her daughters' plum velvet gowns, with their baggy sleeves and pleats below their busts: in this aspect of their dress, they are as Teutonic as Sophia van Bylant, and like her, they conform to contemporary Flemish taste in their headdresses, which consist of very shrunken 'steeples', like those of the Moreel women in 1484 (illus. 128).

Further south a fairly rapid increase in deliberate untidiness seems to have taken place, particularly in the dress of young men, although it also affected women's dress, sometimes in the same way. Michael Wolgemut's portrait of Ursula Harsdorfer (which bears her married name of Tucher and the date of her marriage, 1481, to confuse the issue) originally bore a date before her marriage, 1478.[29] It shows that although Nuremberg women were continuing to wear a beehive-like turban of 'tiled' veils, strapped on under the chin, the high standing doublet collar has slipped down flat on to her shoulders and almost disappeared round the back of her neck. Likewise, the centre bodice V-shaped closing of Elspeth von Liechtenstein has opened slightly, to display a fairly aggressive lacing across the shirt.

The Middle Rhenish (Mainz?) painter, the Master of the Housebook, produced a charming betrothal portrait, probably a few years later,[30] in which the outward and downward movement of women's necklines has proceeded with remarkable rapidity. The doublet collar now seems no more than an addition to the gown's neckline, with what had once been a series of individual rings for the lacing having evolved into a piece of gold jewellery. Since the shirt has such an obvious, indeed essential, part to play, it has been decorated far more lavishly than will occur to Western Europe to do for another forty years, being composed of finely gathered sections of linen between gold ribbons. The 'turban' is extremely elaborate, with its gold star-and-net embroidery, and her plaited hair has somehow been decorated with spangles: this may well be a 'special occasion' headdress.

Her intended's neckline is as wide-set as hers, and a lot deeper, but basically the same influences can work towards the same effect, as the dress of men and women seem to have had so much in common to start with. A shocking degree of informality appears in his displaying his bare forearm, while his doublet (for such we must assume the low-necked garment to be) has an excuse for a sleeve, incapable of covering his shirt sleeve or of reaching to his wrist. The heavy cord knotted on his chest is attached to his cloak, slung sideways, as the Fuchshart sons had done (illus. 153). In the centre, each of the couple holds one end of his fringed hood, the fringes being a continuation from the wider dagging above it: the structure of this hood is quite baffling. Much play is made in the dress of both sexes with narrow lines, mainly vertical, as in the gathering of the shirts and the fringing on the hood, and lacing, in whatever direction it runs, has a share in this linearity.

159. FACING PAGE: A young couple sit on a garden seat, chaperoned by the girl's lapdog, by the Master of the Housebook.

160. ABOVE: Friedrich Herlin's altarpiece for an unknown Nördlingen family in 1488.

161. FACING PAGE: The date of Dürer's monogram on this drawing may not be original but the dress is still that of the 1490s, as worn in the area of Nuremberg (Berlin, Kupferstichkabinett, Kat. Nr. KdZ.3.)

In Nördlingen in 1488 Friedrich Herlin produced an altarpiece for an unidentified family, the resulting work being referred to quite logically as the 'Family Altarpiece' (illus. 160), the family kneeling in a menagerie of an owl (on a ledge on the left), on the throne a tiny winged bull (of St Luke, the patron saint of painters and bookbinders, hence the saint's holding the book with which the child plays), a dragon (of St Margaret) and a curious dog (behind the mother).[31] On the left kneels the conservatively attired father, wearing a loosish, closed gown with wide sleeves over a doublet with a curved collar, such as was going out of fashion in the Netherlands: compare illustrations 127 and 131. His hair is neatly cut and lacks both the length and frizziness of his sons' and of Martin van Nieuwenhove's. Behind him kneels a son in the skimpy hose and doublet outfit with untidy baggy sleeves and cloak frequently depicted by the Master of the Housebook, as in his full-length drawing of a young couple (illus. 159).[32] The son's doublet sleeve has not been properly attached to the body of his doublet, instead allowing his shirt to protrude in the curve taken by the Pachers' deeply set armholes of the 1470s. Beneath the mother's enveloping headscarves and cloak it is still possible to see that she is the owner of a gown with central folds and rather immodestly bare wrists, an effect carried to just below the elbows in a portrait of *c.* 1500 from Ulm by Bartholomäus Zeitblom of 'Ursula Greck', who wore an otherwise elaborate gown embroidered on one half of the bodice with oak branches.[33] The two elder daughters wear only slightly less concealing versions of the front-clasped gown of Agnes von Werdenberg (illus. 152), and their hair is bound into plaits so thick that they call to mind St Clare's false plaits (illus. 158).

The obsession with lacing to close openings which were quite unnecessary in the first place is splendidly recorded in a 'Portrait of a Woman' by the Nördlingen painter Sebald Bopp, probably from the 1490s.[34] Her collar has one set of fine lacing, which gives way to a much more obvious lacing down the gown front; if the lacing was done upwards, the laces would have zigzagged across the opening, down through the *top* of each clasp, before being turned up into the next clasp on the opposite side, resulting in their looped appearance at the clasps. The same procedure was used in lacing up the sleeves which are too skimpy in themselves to meet round the arms. The headdress is an unusual variant on the 'tiled turban', and has a clearly visible row of pinheads marking the points at which the layers of veiling are held together.

Cologne in the 1490s produced many altarpieces, remarkable only for the ordinariness of the dress of the donors when compared to the fashions further south. In general, men continued to wear garments displaying various degrees of awareness of contemporary Netherlandish fashion, while women dressed, as usual, to incorporate aspects of western and southern

162. A sobering return to the unimaginative dress of Cologne.

influences on their tastes. Hermann Rinck, donor of the 'Aachen Altarpiece' (between 1489–96) and mayor of Cologne, and his wife Gertrud von Ballem (illus. 162)[35] exemplify well this provincialism in dress in Cologne, with Hermann's out-moded gown and Gertrud's clinging to a fairly large, diagonally set cap under her veil. Cologne women in their preference for Teutonic round necks on their gowns were in a perfect position to adopt, with a minimum of fuss, the increasingly popular square neckline of France and the Netherlands. Instead they clung to their own type of neckline, even, as in the case of Christina Hackeney (1500–3), drawing the neckline down into a V over an infill.[36] The only aspect of Franco-Netherlandish dress which Cologne women followed consistently in the next ten or twenty years was the fashion for lengthening and widening sleeves, which in fact had already been an element of their gowns from their Teutonic heritage (compare illus. 159).

In Nuremberg in 1498 Albrecht Dürer produced a 'Self Portrait' at the age of 27,[37] showing the artist in thoroughly Teutonic attire, self-consciously elegant and untidy at the same time (illus. 163). His dark cloak is, typically, worn on one shoulder only, and underneath, his black and white doublet is scooped back to provide only a shoulder strap to which the sleeves can be attached, and enough material to fasten the garment at the waist. The front section of the shirt has been very finely pleated, and presumably stitched, for a couple of inches before it is allowed to billow out. The upper edge of the gathering has a gold ribbon as decoration.

The aggressive linearity of the black-and-white contrasts in the doublet serve to break up visually an already physically broken structure, with its slashes at the back of the sleeve and the elbow, both ideas of stark colouring and of broken structure continuing into the cap with its unfinished seam at the start of the brim, and into the tassels, only partly bound into a clump. His hair does not seem to have been subjected to a good barber for many years, probably instead having been bound in rags or plaits to produce these corkscrew curls: one of Dürer's own drawings, of 'The Men's Bath',[38] shows a number of men with their hair bound up on their heads into small lumpy 'headscarves' which have approximately the same rolled effect at the back of their heads as do women's much larger 'turbans', implying perhaps that Nuremberg men were in the habit of doing the fifteenth-century equivalent of appearing in public in rollers. The final touches of 'untidiness' are provided by the shirt's being too loose to lie neatly across the chest, and the doublet sleeve and the glove gauntlet's being both too long to meet neatly: the gauntlet has therefore been forced to turn back over on to the glove, showing the zigzag stitching and the zigzag edging cut on the leather 'hem'.

To conclude, we shall consider four illustrations of women,

1498

163. FACING PAGE: Probably the most famous of Dürer's self-portraits and certainly the one which shows most clearly his obsessive interest in himself and in clothes.

164. LEFT: A Nuremberg housewife, one of the series of drawings which Dürer did of women's dress in 1500. His wife Agnes Frey may have been his model.

three of which are dated 1500 and the fourth of which must be of a similar date: let us look first at the portrait of Barbara Ungelter (née Wespach) of Ulm, whose husband's portrait bears the date 1500.[39] There are many general points of similarity between her attire and that of Ursula Greck, also of Ulm, mentioned above: both women have elaborate, one-sided embroidery on their gowns and bands of embroidery on the veils which cover their 'turbans', the patterns being so eccentric as to be rather *farouche*. Barbara's veil is decorated with flowers, leaves and letters worked in small pearls, which are also used to create the pattern on the left sleeve, the intertwining branches all round her neckline and the studs on her belt. The most bizarre, if not surreal, effect in this dress is the appearance of a wickerwork fence along the top of her undergarment; below this point the potentially wide and deep gown neckline of the Housebook Master's 'fiancée' (see p. 223) has been drawn together somewhat by two double strands of fine chain. Generally, this outfit does not differ markedly from those worn by two women of the Tucher family whom Dürer painted in 1499,[40] except that these Nuremberg women lacked lop-sided embroidery on their gowns.

In 1500 Dürer did three costume drawings of Nuremberg women, dressed for different occasions.[41] The woman in indoor dress (illus. 164) wears the usual south-German turban and a curious adaptation of the fashion for under-bust pleats: an apron which follows their pattern, hanging in a narrow band from strings which disappear behind her shoulder cape, and then departing from that outline by radiating round her hips. A wide, open neckline could not always have been pleasant to wear, particularly in a cold house, and in this case it has been covered over by a pinkish shoulder cape. The green gown has tight, but too-long sleeves which because of their presumably archaic tailoring bunch and 'bind' under the arms.

A much more formal outfit is depicted on the 'Nuremberg woman going to a dance' (illus. 165), and it also reveals something of the posture which south-German women's dress was forcing them to adopt. Balancing on her head an enormous 'tiled turban', complete with rows of pin heads on the topmost veil, which also serves to strap the edifice over her chin, the lady stands in a green velvet gown trimmed with fur, gathering round her, not her trailing skirt, but her hanging sleeves, which are continuations of the bodice front. Once again, the armhole looks distinctly uncomfortable as the back of the gown puckers into it: it is cut too far on to the arm at the back, adding to the impression of extended shoulder blades at the back. Once again we are encountering women whose dresses threaten to obey the laws of gravity, and once again the solution is found in drawing forward the points of the shoulders and hunching the back; although the result is not the extremely sway-backed stance of the early years of the century in France, the woman still has a pronounced stomach

165. A Nuremberg woman going to a dance, as the inscription informs us. Dürer's drawings of dress include Venetian women and costumes of the Imperial court, as well as a drawing of his wife in Netherlandish dress when they visited Flanders in 1521.

over which the centre-front pleats of her gown cascade like a waterfall. The woodcuts to an edition of Le Chevalier de La Tour Landry's book produced in 1493 in Basel (although the women wear Nuremberg dress), and attributed to Dürer, show that at least some of these wide-necked gowns were V-necked at the back, which may have increased the tendency of the shoulders to slip, although the tightness of the upper sleeves may have counteracted this tendency, by simply refusing to allow the shoulders of the gown to slip very far.[42]

166. The root of the problem in discussing German women's dress, particularly in south Germany: the tendency to conceal everything beneath a large cloak, as does this Nuremberg woman dressed to go to church.

Our final illustration shows a Nuremberg woman dressed to go to church (illus. 166), and she returns us to one of our main problems in dealing with German women's dress, that of the swathing of the body in a cloak when in the presence of anything connected with religion: that the dress below a cloak could still be quite elaborate is hinted at by the watered silk and fur hem of the small area of the gown visible at the front. In the case of this woman's attire, the urge for elaboration, firmly confined to southern Germany at this time, finds expression in the strange, box-shaped headdress and in the careful 'sun-ray' pleating of the cloak, in which the pleats grow deeper as they descend towards the ground. The lining of this cloak, where it is visible, shows itself to be free of pleating; this peculiar double layering of conflicting uses of textiles is repeated in the dress of the donatrix and her married daughter in Dürer's 'Paumgartner Nativity' of 1500–3, as is the box headdress.[43]

The main points to emerge from this brief tour of German-speaking lands seem to be that the area around Cologne suffered, as far as imaginative tailoring was concerned, from being a frontier land where two differing approaches to Gothic design met, often with subdued results: once the International Gothic phase had passed, men and women in Cologne seem, on the whole, to have dressed conservatively and without much inspiration.

In the heart of 'the Empire', the Gothic spirit flourished in an entirely Teutonic way, with an obsessive incorporation of linearity into every aspect of dress, and on any scale. Although France and the Netherlands had abandoned Gothic's love of slender linearity,[45] in Germany in the early sixteenth century lines swirled and twisted their way through people, their clothes and the landscapes they inhabited, particularly in the work of Matthias Grünewald, where the potential life of an inanimate object threatens the viewer in a most disconcerting manner. In the final analysis, 'disconcerting' is probably the best description that can be applied to much late-Gothic dress in southern Germany, with its strange surface decorations and its continuing distortion of the female body.

167. OVERLEAF: A thoroughly untidy and disconcerting German with disconcertingly linear trees: Dürer's friend Oswold Krel, painted in 1499. (Munich, Alte Pinakothek.)

·1499·

Notes

Chapter One

1. F. M. Graves, *Deux inventaires de la maison d'Orléans (1389 et 1408)*, Paris, 1926. E.g., p. 119, no. 560 'Nuef chemises de Lombardie'; no. 562 three Lombard kerchiefs without embroidery.

2. Paris, Archives Nationales, KK 43, f. 47r, 'Hans . . . du pays dalemaigne tailleur de robes', in 1403.

3. L. Douët-d'Arcq, *La chronique d'Engueran de Monstrelet en deux livres avec pièces justificatives 1400–1444*, 6 vols., Société de l'histoire de France, Paris, 1857–62; I, pp. 168, 267.

4. J. Guiffrey, *Inventaries de Jean duc de Berry (1401–1416)*, 2 vols., Paris, 1894–6.

5. *ibid.*, p. 59, no. 149.

6. *The Bedford Hours*, London, British Library, Add. ms. 18850; *The Salisbury Breviary*, Paris, Bibliothèque Nationale, ms. lat. 17294; and perhaps the *Sobieski Hours*, Windsor, Royal Collection.

7. New York, Metropolitan Museum of Art, The Cloisters: M. Meiss, *French Painting in the Time of Jean de Berry: The Limbourgs and Their Contemporaries*, Thames and Hudson, 1974, p. 331.

8. *Heures de Turin* (destroyed), formerly Royal Library, Turin, and *Heures de Milan*, now in Turin, Museo Civico. See A. Chatelet, *Heures de Turin. Quarante-cinq feuillets à peintures provenant des Très Belles Heures de Jean de France, duc de Berry*, Turin, 1967.

9. J. Calmette and G. Durville, *Philippe de Commynes Mémoires*, 3 vols., Les classiques de l'histoire de France au moyen âge, fasc. 3, 5 and 6. Paris, 1924–5; 3, pp. 13–4.

10. M. le baron Kervyn de Lettenhove, *Oeuvres de Georges Chastellain*, 8 vols., Académie Royale de Belgique, Brussels, 1863–6; IV, pp. 365–6.

11. Calmette and Durville, *op. cit.*, 5, p. 326.

12. Brussels, Musées Royaux des Beaux-Arts: see M. J. Friedländer, *Early Netherlandish Painting*, 14 vols., Leyden and Brussels, 1967–76; II, no. 93, pl. 109.

13. 'The Passion of Christ', Turin, Galleria Sabauda: see Friedländer, *op. cit.*, VIa, pls. 86–7.

14. Melbourne, National Gallery of Victoria: see *Anonieme Vlaamse Primitieven*, Bruges, 1969, no. 45.

Chapter Two

1. Left wing of 'Resurrection Triptych', Paris, Musée du Louvre: see M. J. Friedländer, *Early Netherlandish Painting*, 14 vols., Leyden and Brussels, 1967–76; VIa, pl. 24.

2. Paris, Musée du Louvre: see C. Sterling and H. Adhémar, *Peintures Ecole Française XIVe, XVe et XVIe siècles*, Editions des Musées Nationaux, Paris, 1965, no. 11, pls. 28–38; Paris, Musée du Louvre: Sterling and Adhémar, *op. cit.*, no. 14, pl. 49: on loan to Musée des Beaux-Arts, Dijon since 1968.

3. K. Clark, *The Nude, A Study of Ideal Art*, Penguin Books, 1976, p. 19.

4. M. Roy, *Oeuvres poétiques de Christine de Pisan*, 3 vols., Société des anciens textes français, Paris, 1886–96: II, pp. 192–5.

5. *ibid.*, pp. 204–7.

6. Marquis de Queux de Saint-Hilaire and G. Raynaud, *Oeuvres complètes de Eustache Deschamps publiées d'après le manuscrit de la Bibliothèque Nationale*, 11 vols., Sociéte des anciens textes français, Paris, 1878–1903: III, pp. 220, 244, 373; IV, p. 8; V, pp. 186–7.

7. *ibid.*, IV, p. 318.

8. *ibid.*, pp. 273–4.

9. J. Huizinga, *The Waning of the Middle Ages*, Penguin Books, 1976, p. 299.

10. Paris, Bibliothèque Nationale, ms. fr. 1586, f. D; see F. Avril, *Manuscript Painting at the Court of France. The Fourteenth Century (1310–1380)*, Chatto and Windus, 1978, no. XIII.

11. Turin, Museo Civico and Paris, Bibliothèque Royale, ms. nouv. acq. lat. 3093; ill. comes from the latter, f. 162.

12. Queux de Saint Hilaire and Raynaud, *op. cit.*, VIII, pp. 169–70.

13. *ibid.*, IX, p. 49.

14. M. Meiss and E. H. Beatson, *Les Belles Heures de Jean Duc de Berry*, Thames and Hudson, 1974.

15. Chantilly, Musée Condé, ms. 65, f. 25v.

16. Paris, Bibliothèque de l'Arsenal, ms. 664, f. 137v. See M. Meiss, *French Painting in the Time of Jean de Berry: The Limbourgs and Their Contemporaries,* Thames and Hudson, 1974, p. 336.

17. Paris, Bibliothèque Nationale, ms. fr. 2810, f. 98v. See M. Meiss, *French Painting in the Time of Jean de Berry: The Late Fourteenth Century and the Patronage of the Duke*, Phaidon, 1967, p. 49.

18. Ghent, St.-Baafskathedraal. See L. B. Philip, *The Ghent Altarpiece and the Art of Jan van Eyck*, Princeton University Press, Princeton, 1971, pl. 171.

19. Friedländer, *op. cit.*, I, pl. 5.

20. *ibid.*, II, pls. 24–8.

21. Lille, Palais des Beaux-Arts. See Friedländer, *op. cit.*, III, no. 31, pl. 47 and p. 63.

22. Danzig, Museum Pomorskie. See Friedländer, *op. cit.*, VIa, pl. 27.

23. Washington, D.C., National Gallery of Art, Rosenwald Collection. See C. Eisler, *Drawings of the Masters Flemish and Dutch Drawings From the 15th to the 18th Century*, Little, Brown and Company, Boston, Toronto, 1963, pl. 3.

24. Brussels, Musées Royaux des Beaux-Arts. See Friedländer, *op. cit.*, IV, no. 82, pl. 74.

25. Berlin (East), Staatliche Museen zu Berlin (Bode-Museum). See Friedländer, *op. cit.*, VIII, pl. 41.

26. Vienna, Kunsthistorisches Museum. See Friedländer, *op. cit.*, VIa, pl. 33.

27. Stuttgart, Staatsgalerie: See Friedländer, *loc. cit.*, p. 49.

28. Huizinga, *op. cit.*, p. 300.

29. Friedländer, *op. cit.*, VIa, pl. 35.

30. Bruges, Groeninge Museum. See Friedländer, *op. cit.*, VIb, p. 100, pls. 168–9.

31. Brussels, Musées Royaux des Beaux-Arts. See Friedländer, *op. cit.*, VIII, pl. 82 and p. 70.

32. Antwerp, Koninklijk Museum voor Schone Kunsten. See *Anonieme Vlaamse Primitieven*, Bruges, 1969, colour pl. facing p. 158.

Chapter Three

1. A. de Courde de Montaiglon, *Le Livre du chevalier de La Tour Landry pour l'enseigement de ses filles*, Paris, 1854, pp. 104; 46–8.

2. Marquis de Queux de Saint-Hilaire and G. Raynaud, *Oeuvres complètes de Eustache Deschamps*, 11 vols., Société des anciens textes français, Paris, 1878–1903; VI, p. 202.

3. J. Pichon, *Le Ménagier de Paris, Traité de morale et d'économie domestique composé vers 1393, par un bourgeois parisien*, 2 vols., Société des bibliophiles françois, Paris, 1846: I, pp. 13–5. de Courde de Montaiglon, *op. cit.*, pp. 105–111; 59.

4. de Queux de Saint-Hilaire, *op. cit.*, IX, no. MCCCCXCVIII. J. Crow, *Les Quinze Joyes de Mariage*, Blackwell's French Texts, Oxford, 1969, pp. 6–9.

5. A. Tuetey, *Journal d'un bourgeois de Paris 1405–1449*, Société de l'histoire de Paris et de l'Ile-de-France, Paris, 1881, p. 6. A. Tuetey, *Journal de Nicolas de Baye Greffier du Parlement de Paris 1400–1417*, 2 vols., Société de l'Histoire de France, Paris, 1885–8: I, p. 292.

6. Mlle. Dupont, *Mémoires de Pierre de Fenin, comprenant le récit des événements qui se sont passés en France et en Bourgogne sous les règnes de Charles VI et Charles VII (1407–27)*, Société de l'histoire de France, Paris, 1837, p. 147. Baron Kervyn de Lettenhove, *Oeuvres de Georges Chastellain*, 8 vols., Académie Royale de Belgique, Brussels, 1863–6: I, pp. 178–9.

7. J. A. Buchon, *Collection des chroniques nationales françaises*, 47 vols., Paris, 1826–8: vol. 38, pp. 113–14, 120.

8. Tuetey, *Bourgeois*, p. 382 and note 2, pp. 382–3. L. Douët-d'Arcq, *La Chronique d'Enguerran de Monstrelet en deux livres avec pièces justificatives 1400–1444*, 6 vols., Société de l'histoire de France, Paris, 1857–62: IV, pp. 303–5. Kervyn de Lettenhove, *op. cit.*, IV, pp. 365–6. Buchon, *op. cit.*, vol. 39, p. 132. B. de Mandrot, *Chronique de Jean de Roye connu sous le nom de Chronique Scandaleuse 1460–1483*, 2 vols., Société de l'Histoire de France, Paris, 1894–6: I, p. 111. Buchon, *op. cit.*, vol. 37, p. lxxx.

9. A. A. Hentsch, *De la Litterature Didactique du moyen âge s'adressant specialement aux femmes*, Cahors, 1903, p. 165.

10. J. Calmette and G. Durville, *Philippe de Commynes. Mémoires*, Les classiques de l'histoire de France au Moyen Age, fasc. 3, 5 and 6, Paris, 1924–5: 3, pp. 137–8.

11. Buchon, *op. cit.*, vol. 39, p. 161. Calmette and Durville, *op. cit.*, fasc. 3, p. 140.

12. Paris, Archives Nationales, KK 43, f. 57v.

13. Comte de Laborde, *Les ducs de Bourgogne*, Seconde partie, *Preuves*, 3 vols., Paris, 1849–52; III, p. 157, no. 5825, p. 190, no. 5979; I, p. 203, no. 696, pp. 252–3, no. 868.

14. London, Collection of Count Antoine Seilern: Friedländer, *op. cit.*, II, p. 91; Madrid, Museo del Prado: Friedländer, *ibid.*, p. 42 as *c.* 1428.

15. A. Jubinal, *Recherches sur l'usage et l'origine des tapisseries à personnages dites historiées, depuis l'antiquité jusqu'au 16e siècle inclusivement*, Paris 1840, pp. 65ff.

16. J. Porcher, *Jean Lebègue Les histoires que l'on peut raisonnablement faire sur les livres de Salluste*, Société des Bibliophiles François, Paris, 1962.

17. Granada, Capilla Real: see Friedländer, *op. cit.*, VIA, pl. 50; Lübeck, St. Annen Museum: Friedländer, *loc. cit.*, pls. 10–11.

18. A. Lecoy de La Marche, *Extraits des comptes et mémoriaux du roi René pour servir à l'histoire des arts au XVe siècle*, Société de l'école des chartes, Paris, 1873, pp. 243–4, 258–9; p. 231; p. 331.

19. M. Mollat, *Les affaires de Jacques Coeur. Journal du Procureur Dauvet*, 2 vols., Ecole pratique des Hautes Etudes—VIe section Centre de Recherches Historiques, Paris, 1952–3, p. 637.

20. H. Beaune and J. D'Arbaumont, *Mémoires d'Olivier de La Marche, maître d'hôtel et capitaine des gardes de Charles le Téméraire*, 4 vols., Société de l'Histoire de France, Paris, 1883–8; I, p. 362.

21. E.g., 'Altarpiece of the Adoration of the Magi', Madrid, Museo del Prado: see Friedländer, *op. cit.*, V, pl. 48, where the youngest Magus wears a purse-shaped sleeve with long fringing.

22. Laborde, *op. cit.*, I, p. 301, no. 1057; pp. 277–8, no. 981 *et passim*; p. 298, no. 1052; p. 303, no. 1062.

23. M. de Laurière et al., *Ordonnances des Roys de France de la troisième Race, recueillies par ordre chronologique*, 23 vols., Paris, 1733–1847: vol. 13, pp. 79, 74.

24. de Lauriere, *loc. cit.*, p. 78, Evreux, p. 74, Bernay. E.g., in 1494, James IV of Scotland acquired knee-length hose which required as much as 1¼ ells of white cloth: see *Compota Thesaurariorum Regum Scotorum Accounts of the Lord High Treasurer of Scotland*, ed. T. Dickson, I, Edinburgh, 1877, p. 225.

25. de Laurière, *loc. cit.*, pp. 381, 338.

26. C. Couderc, 'Les comptes d'un grand couturier parisien au XVe siècle', *Bulletin de la société de l'histoire de Paris et de l'Ile-de-France*, XXXVIII, Paris, 1911, pp. 118ff.

27. Paris, Archives Nationales, KK 44, p. 4.

28. Couderc, *op. cit.*, p. 155.

29. Laborde, *op. cit.*, I, p. 278, no. 981.

30. Couderc, *op. cit.*, pp. 126, 165.

31. A. Tuetey, *Journal de Clément de Fauquembergue greffier du Parlement de Paris, 1417–1435*, 3 vols., Société de l'Histoire de France, 1903–15: III, p. lxxiv.

32. Tuetey, *Nicolas de Baye*, I, pp. 281–2 and note p. 281.

33. Tuetey, *Bourgeois*, pp. 137–9.

34. Tuetey, *Fauquembergue*, II, pp. 233, 302–4 for goldsmiths. A. Longnon, *Paris pendant la domination anglaise (1420–1436)*, Société de l'Histoire de Paris et de l'Ile-de-France, Paris, 1878, pp. 311–13 for wares of sellers of '*tissuz de soye*' and pp. 46ff and pp. 200–2 for activities of weavers.

Chapter Four

1. The Hague, Museum Meermanno-Westreenianum, ms. 10 B. 23, f. 2. See F. Avril, *Manuscript Painting at the Court of France. The Fourteenth Century (1310–1380)*, Chatto and Windus, 1978, p. 110.

2. Paris, Bibliothèque Nationale, ms. fr. 12420, f. 134. See M. Meiss, *French Painting in the Time of Jean de Berry: The Late Fourteenth Century and the Patronage of the Duke*, Phaidon, 1967, p. 47.

3. A. de Courde de Montaiglon, *Le Livre du chevalier de La Tour Landry pour l'enseignement de ses filles*, Paris, 1854, pp. 236–9 for tale of girl who insisted on wearing unlined clothes in winter to impress prospective suitor by her slenderness and lost him to sensibly dressed sister who looked rosy-cheeked and warm, even if slightly muffled up, while she herself turned black with cold.

4. J. A. Buchon, *Collections des chroniques nationales françaises*, 47 vols., Paris, 1826–8: 39, p. 13.

5. J. Pichon, *Le Ménagier de Paris, traité de morale et d'économie domestique composé vers 1393, par un bourgeois parisien*, 2 vols., Société des bibliophiles françois, Paris, 1846: II, pp. 64–7.

6. Paris, Musée du Louvre.

7. Chantilly, Musée Condé, ms. 65, f. 161v.

8. Comte de Laborde, *Les ducs de Bourgogne*, seconde partie, *Preuves*, 3 vols., Paris, 1849–52: III, pp. 41–2, no. 5448; *ibid.*, p. 52, nos. 5498–9; M. Roy, *Oeuvres poétiques de Christine de Pisan*, 3 vols., Société des anciens textes français, Paris, 1886–96: II, p. 239; J. B. de La Curne de Sainte-Palaye, *Mémoires sur l'ancienne chevalerie*, 2 vols., Paris, 1826: I, p. 469.

9. Turin, Museo Civico, f. 87.

10. Marquis de Queux de Saint-Hilaire and G. Raynaud, *Oeuvres complètes de Eustache Deschamps*, 11 vols., Société des anciens textes français, Paris, 1878–1903: VI, p. 201.

11. London, British Library, Roy. ms. 20 B VI, f. 2.

12. de Queux de Saint-Hilaire and Raynaud, *op. cit.*, III, p. 195.

13. Baron Kervyn de Lettenhove, *Chroniques relatives à l'histoire de la Belgique sous la domination des ducs de Bourgogne*, 3 vols., Commission Royale d'Histoire, Brussels, 1870–6: I, p. 115.

14. de Courde de Montaiglon, *op. cit.*, pp. 98–100.

15. de Queux de Saint-Hilaire and Raynaud, *op. cit.*, VI, pp. 199–201.

16. Paris, Archives Nationales, KK 43, ff. 36–7.

17. *ibid.*, f. 14.

18. *ibid.*, f. 46v.

19. Paris, Bibliothèque Nationale, ms. fr. 12595, f. 1.

20. Paris, Bibliothèque Nationale, ms. fr. 12420, f. 93: Meiss, *op. cit.*, p. 47.

21. [A.]Vallet de Viriville, *Chronique de Charles VII roi de France par Jean Chartier*, 3 vols., Paris, 1858: III, pp. 266–7.

22. C. de La Trémoille, *Les La Trémoille pendant cinq siècles*, 5 vols., Nantes, 1890–6: I, p. 63; de Laborde, *op. cit.*, III, p. 41, no. 5445; de Queux de Saint-Hilaire and Raynaud, I, note pp. 371–2; de Laborde, *op. cit.*, I, p. 123, no. 361, pp. 126–7, no. 385.

23. Paris, Bibliothèque Nationale, mss. fr. 606, 835–6. See M. Meiss, *French Painting in the Time of Jean de Berry The Limbourgs and Their Contemporaries*, Thames and Hudson, 1974, p. 292. Illustrated is ms. fr. 606, f. 32.

24. Paris, Bibliothèque Nationale, mss. fr. 607 and fr. 1178–9; Brussels, Bibliothèque Royale, ms. 9393. See Meiss, *Limbourgs*, p. 290 and figs. 35–7, 39–41, 43–4.

25. New York, Metropolitan Museum of Art, The Cloisters Collection, 1954. Folio 191. See M. Meiss and E. H. Beatson, *Les Belles Heures de Jean Duc de Berry*, Thames and Hudson, 1974, p. 19.

26. Paris, Archives Nationales, KK 43, f. 29 *'viij espingles dargent'*.

27. Paris, Bibliothèque Nationale, ms. lat. 1161. See M. Meiss, *French Painting in the Time of Jean de Berry: The Boucicaut Master*, Phaidon, 1968, p. 126 for dating.

28. London, British Library, Roy. ms. 19 E VI, ff. 78 and 10. See Meiss, *Late Fourteenth Century*, p. 405, note 106, for purchase.

29. Paris, Bibliothèque Nationale, ms. fr. 23279, f. 53. Meiss, *Boucicaut Master*, p. 124.

30. A. Tuetey, *Journal d'un bourgeois de Paris 1405–1449*, Société de l'histoire de Paris, Paris, 1881, p. 6.

31. J. Longnon and M. Meiss, *Les Très Riches Heures du Duc de Berry*, Thames and Hudson, 1969, pl. 2.

32. de Laborde, *op. cit.*, p. 118, no. 340; p. 119, no. 345; p. 141, no. 440.

33. See Meiss, *Boucicaut Master*, fig. 70.

34. Antwerp, Koninklijk Museum voor Schone Kunsten.

35. Paris, Musée du Louvre. See E. Michel, *Catalogue raisonné des peintures du Moyen-Age, de la Renaissance et des temps modernes. Peintures flamandes du XVe et du XVIe siècle*, Editions des Musées Nationaux, Paris, 1953, fig. 71 and pp. 111–3.

36. Paris, Bibliothèque Nationale, ms. fr. 2810, f. 226. See Meiss, *Late Fourteenth Century*, p. 49.

37. Paris, Bibliothèque de l'Arsenal, ms. 664, f. 137v. See Meiss, *Limbourgs*, p. 336.

38. Chantilly, Musée Condé, ms. 65, f. 5v. See Longnon and Meiss, *op. cit.*, p. 20 for dating.

39. London, British Library, Harley ms. 4431, f. 376.

40. de Laborde, *op. cit.*, I, p. 67, no. 216.

41. Tuetey, *op. cit.*, p. 44.

42. de Laborde, *op. cit.*, III, p. 262, nos. 6229–30.

43. Meiss, *Limbourgs*, pp. 191–2.

44. Munich, Alte Pinakothek. See M. J. Friedländer, *Early Netherlandish Painting*, 14 vols., Leyden and Brussels, 1967–76: II, pl. 71.

45. de Laborde, *op. cit.*, I, p. 87, no. 251.

46. *ibid.*, III, p. 267, no. 6241.

47. *ibid.*, p. 76, no. 5577.

48. London, British Library, Harley ms. 4431, f. 3. See Meiss, *Limbourgs*, pp. 17, 39, 290.

49. Paris, Archives Nationales, KK 43, f. 57v.

50. *ibid.*, ff. 13, 13v; F. M. Graves, *Deux inventaires de la maison d'Orléans (1389 et 1408)*, Paris, 1926, p. 111, no. 495.

51. *ibid.*, p. 131, no. 695.

Chapter Five

1. Rotterdam, Museum Boymans-van Beuningen. For connexion of this drawing with tomb of Louis de Mâle in Lille, see M. Sonkes, *Les primitifs flamands, III. Contributions à l'étude des primitifs flamands. Dessins du XVe siècle: groupe Van der Weyden*, Brussels, 1969, pp. 245–8.

2. Comte de Laborde, *Les ducs de Bourgogne*, Seconde partie, *Preuves*, 3 vols., Paris, 1849–52: I, p. 139, no. 429; p. 140, no. 432.

3. Ypres, Hôtel de Ville.

4. [A.]Vallet de Viriville (ed.), *Chronique de Charles VII roi de France par Jean Chartier*, 3 vols., Paris, 1858: III, p. 303.

5. A. Longnon, *Paris pendant la domination anglaise (1420–1436)*, Société de l'Histoire de Paris et de l'Ile-de-France, Paris, 1878, pp. 7–9.

6. A. Tuetey, *Journal d'un bourgeois de Paris 1405–1449*, Société de l'Histoire de Paris et de l'Ile-de-France, Paris, 1881, pp. 382–3, note 2. Hereafter called 'Teutey, *Bourgeois*'. A. Tuetey, *Journal de Clément de Fauquembergue greffier du Parlement de Paris, 1417–1435*, 3 vols., Société de l'Histoire de France, Paris, 1903–15: II, p. 163.

7. London, British Library, Add. ms. 18850, f. 288v.

8. L. Douët d'Arcq, *La chronique d'Enguerran de Monstrelet en deux livres avec pièces justificatives 1400–1444*, 6 vols., Société de l'Histoire de France, 1857–62: IV, pp. 303–5.

9. Tuetey, *Bourgeois*, p. 235.

10. Paris, Bibliothèque Nationale, ms. lat. 1156B, f. 163. Marguerite was daughter to murdered Louis of Orléans; 1426 married Richard, comte d'Etampes, 1438 widowed.

11. Paris, Bibliothèque Nationale, ms. lat. 1158, ff. 34v, 27v. Compare headdresses in M. Clayton, *Catalogue of Rubbings of Brasses and Incised Slabs*, 2nd. ed., Her Majesty's Stationery Office, 1968, pl. 16 and p. 23; pls. 18, 20.

12. Amsterdam, Rijksmuseum: *All the paintings of the Rijksmuseum in Amsterdam A completely illustrated catalogue*, Amsterdam Maarsen, 1976, p. 651.

13. New York, Pierpont Morgan Library, M 917 and M 945. Facsimile: J. Plummer, *The Hours of Catherine of Cleves*, Barrie and Rockliff, 1966. Dating: *La miniature hollandaise. Le grand siècle de l'enluminure du livre dans les Pays-Bas septentrionaux*, Bibliothèque Royale Albert Ier, Brussels, 1971, pp. 40–1.

14. de Laborde, *op. cit.*, I, pp. 309–10, 317–8.

15. Ternant, Eglise Notre-Dame. For discussion outlined see R. Didier, 'Les Retables de Ternant', in *Congrès archéologique du Nivernais*, Paris, 1967, pp. 258–76.

16. London, National Gallery.

17. New York, Metropolitan Museum of Art, Cloisters Collection. Purchase. For summary of peculiarities of this altarpiece see L. Campbell, 'Robert Campin, the Master of Flémalle and the Master of Mérode', *The Burlington Magazine*, no. 860, CXVI, 1974, pp. 643–5.

18. London, National Gallery. Reproduced in M. J. Friedländer, *Early Netherlandish Painting*, 14 vols., Leyden and Brussels, 1967–76, I, pl. 18.

19. de Laborde, *op. cit.*, I, p. 309, no. 1071.

20. Ghent, St Baafskathedral.

21. J. Pichon, *Le Ménagier de Paris, Traité de morale et d'économie domestique composé vers 1393, par un bourgeois parisien*, 2 vols., Société des bibliophiles françois, Paris, 1846; I, p. 13.

22. London, National Gallery.

23. H. Cocheris, *Le Blason des couleurs en armes, livrées et devises par Sicile Herault d'Alphonse V, roi d'Aragon*, Paris, 1860, pp. 57, 88.

24. Berlin–Dahlem, Gemäldegalerie der Staatlichen Museen. See M. Davies, *Rogier van der Weyden. An essay, with a critical catalogue of paintings assigned to him and to Robert Campin*, Phaidon, 1972, pp. 200–1.

25. Vienna, Kunsthistorisches Museum. Friedländer, *op. cit.*, II, no. 11, *p. 62 and pls. 18–19.*

26. Frankfurt, Staedelsches Kunstinstitut: compare Friedländer, *op. cit.*, I, p. 66 and pl. 61 E, F, G.

27. J. A. Buchon, *Mémoires de Jacques du Clerq (1448–1467)*, vols. 37–40 of *Collection des chroniques nationales françaises*, 47 vols., Paris 1826–8; vol. 38, pp. 211–12. H. Beaune and J. D. Arbaumont, *Mémoires d'Olivier de La Marche, maître d'hôtel et capitaine des gardes de Charles le Téméraire*, 4 vols., Société de l'Histoire de France, Paris, 1883–8; II, p. 54.

28. London, British Library, Yates Thompson ms. 3, f. 172v. At least some of it postdates Van Eyck's 'Madonna of Chancellor Rolin', *c.* 1435, because of the reliance of f. 162 on Van Eyck's composition.

29. Antwerp, Koninklijk Museum voor Schone Kunsten.

30. de Laborde, *op. cit.*, II, p. 422, nos. 5174, 5178.

31. *ibid.*, II, pp. 420–1.

32. Bruges, Groeninge Museum.

33. London, National Gallery. Friedländer, *op. cit.*, II, p. 63; M. Davies, *National Gallery Catalogues: Early Netherlandish School*, 3rd ed., Trustees of the National Gallery, 1967, pp. 173–6.

34. de Laborde, *op. cit.*, I, p. 308, no. 1070

35. *ibid.*, p. 317, no. 1075.

36. *ibid.*, p. 282, no. 997.

37. *ibid.*, p. 298, no. 1052.

38. Madrid, Museo del Prado. Friedländer, *op. cit.*, II, p. 14.

39. Davies, *Rogier van der Weyden*, p. 14.

40. Florence, Galleria degli Uffizi.

41. Friedländer, *op. cit.*, II, pl. 34.

42. Berlin-Dahlem, Gemäldegalerie der Staatlichen Museen. See Friedländer, *op. cit.*, II, pl. 95.

43. Munich, Alte Pinakothek. See Friedländer, *op. cit.*, II, pls. 71–2.

Chapter Six

1. Antwerp, Koninklijk Museum voor Schone Kunsten. See E. Panofsky, 'Two Roger Problems: the Donor of The Hague *Lamentation* and the Date of the Altarpiece of the Seven Sacraments', *Art Bulletin*, XXXIII, New York, 1951, pp. 33–40; *Beschrijvende Catalogus Oude Meesters*, Antwerp, 1959, p. 263; M. J. Friedländer, *Early Netherlandish Painting*, 14 vols, Leyden and Brussels, 1967–76: II, pls. 34–5.

2. A. Lecoy de La Marche, *Extraits des comptes et mémoriaux du roi René pour servir à l'histoire des arts au XVe siècle*, Société de l'école des chartes, Paris, 1873, p. 228, no. 611.

3. M. G. A. Vale, *Charles VII*, Eyre Methuen, 1974, p. 94, quoting Bibliothèque Nationale, ms. fr. 2701, ff. 55v and 99.

4. A. Tuetey, *Journal d'un bourgeois de Paris 1405–1449*, Société de l'Histoire de Paris et de l'Ile-de-France, 1881, p. 382.

5. Paris, Musée du Louvre: C. Sterling and H. Adhémar, *Peintures école Française XIVe, XVe et XVIe siècles*, Editions des Musées Nationaux, Paris, 1965, p. 7. no. 15.

6. J. A. Buchon, *Collection des chroniques nationales françaises*, 47 vols., Paris, 1826–8: 37, p. 47; [A.]Vallet de Viriville, *Chronique de Charles VII roi de France par Jean Chartier*, 3 vols., Paris, 1858: II, p. 162.

7. Vienna, Österreichische Nationalbibliothek, Cod. 2549, f. 80. See F. Unterkircher, *European Illuminated Maunuscripts in the Austrian National Library*, Thames and Hudson, 1967, p. 225.

8. Brussels, Bibliothèque Royale, ms. 9242, f. 1. See M. Davies, *Rogier van der Weyden. An essay, with a critical catalogue of paintings assigned to him and to Robert Campin*, Phaidon, 1972, p. 208.

9. New York, Metropolitan Museum of Art, Robert Lehman Collection, 1975.

10. Ghent, Groot Vleeshuis. See drawing before restoration and photograph afterwards in *Gent Duizend Jaar Kunst en Cultur*, I, Museum voor Schone Kunsten, Ghent, 1975, p. 65 and pl. 9 respectively. M. Sonkes, *Les primitifs flamands, III. Contributions a l'étude des primitifs flamands. Dessins du XVe siecle: Groupe Van der Weyden*, Brussels, 1969, p. 110 and pl. XXIIIb.

11. Paris, Archives Nationales, KK 51, ff. 10v, 12, 18v, 19, 41.

12. Each horn has a pin in H. Clifford Smith, *The Goldsmith and the Young Couple or the Legend of S. Eloy and S. Godeberta by Petrus Christus*, privately printed, 1915, frontispiece: compare Friedländer, *op. cit.*, I, pl. 75.

13. Compare illus. 85 and 'The Presentation in the Temple', in Musée des Beaux-Arts de Dijon, *Catalogue des peintures françaises*, Dijon 1968, p. 12 and pl. II.

14. G. de Beaucourt, 'Roles de dépenses du temps de Charles VII (1450–1451)', *Annuaire-Bulletin de la Société de l'Histoire de France*, tome II, seconde partie, Paris, 1864, pp. 123–53.

15. Brussels, Bibliothèque Royale, ms. 9278–80, ff. 1, 16.

16. Paris, Musée du Louvre. See Davies, *op. cit.*, p. 21.

17. Berlin-Dahlem, Gemäldegalerie der Staatlichen Museen. Antwerp, Koninklijk Museum voor Schone Kunsten: see *Beschrijvende Catalogus . . .*, Antwerp, pp. 88–9 for opinions.

18. Munich, Alte Pinakothek. See Friedländer, *op. cit.*, II, pl. 72 and III, pl. 39.

19. Berlin-Dahlem, Gemäldegalerie der Staatlichen Museen. See L. Campbell, *Van der Weyden*, Jupiter, 1979, p. 51 for donor.

20. Riggisberg, near Bern, Abegg-Stiftung: Friedländer, *op. cit.*, II, pl. 134; Brussels, Musées Royaux des Beaux-Arts: Friedländer, *op. cit.*, I, pl. 93.

21. H. Cocheris, *Le Blason des couleurs en armes, livrées et devises par Sicile Herault d'Alphonse V, roi d'Aragon*, Paris, 1860, pp. 108–9.

22. Tuetey, *op. cit.*, p. 282; Vallet de Viriville, *op. cit.*, II, p. 34.

23. H. Beaune and J. D'Arbaumont, *Mémoires d'Olivier de La Marche, maître d'hôtel et capitaine des gardes de Charles le Téméraire*, 4 vols., Société de l'Histoire de France, Paris, 1883–8: II, p. 372; G. Du Fresne de Beaucourt, *Chronique de M. d'Escouchy*, 3 vols., Société de l'Histoire de France, Paris, 1863–4: II, p. 227.

24. Paris, Musée du Louvre: see Sterling and Adhémar, *op. cit.*, no. 40, p. 16 and pl. 113.

25. Beaune, Hôtel-Dieu. See Davies, *op. cit.*, p. 19.

26. New York, Metropolitan Museum of Art, Michael Friedsam Collection. See Friedländer, *op. cit.*, II, no. 103, pl. 115.

27. Vienna, Österreichische Nationalbibliothek, Cod. 2583, f. 13. See Unterkircher, *op. cit.*, pp. 220–1.

28. Paris, Archives Nationales, KK 51ff. 38, 38v.

29. Paris, Bibliothèque Nationale, ms. fr. 1051, f. 23v.

30. Paris, Musée du Louvre. See Sterling and Adhémar, *op. cit.*, no. 43, p. 407.

31. Rotterdam, Museum Boymans-van Beuningen. See Sonkes, *op. cit.*, no. E15, pp. 242, 247.

32. Collection of the Earl of Verulam: on loan to the National Gallery, London. See Friedländer, *op. cit.*, I, pl. 73.

33. Comte de Laborde, *Les ducs de Bourgogne*, Seconde partie, *Preuves*, 3 vols., Paris, 1849–52: I, p. 449, no. 1681; Paris, Archives Nationales, KK 51, f. 40v; other gowns *passim*.

34. Paris, Musée du Louvre.

35. Paris, Musée du Louvre. The inscription 'LE TRES VICTORIEVX ROY DE FRANCE. . .' is said to refer most probably to his victory at Formigny (1450): see J. Wescher, *Jean Fouquet and His Time*, Pleiades Books, 1947, p. 52.

36. Paris, Archives Nationales, KK 51ff. 23v, 45.

37. Vaduz, Liechtenstein, Sammlungen des regierenden Fürsten von Liechtenstein.

38. Munich, Bayerische Staatsbibliothek, Cod. Gall. 6, f. 2v.

39. Buchon, *op. cit.*, vol. 38, p. 261.

40. Cocheris, *op. cit.*, p. 114; p. 113.

41. Paris, Bibliothèque Nationale, ms. fr. 9198, f. 91.

42. J. B. de La Curne de Sainte-Palaye, *Mémoires sur l'ancienne chevalerie*, 2 vols., Paris, 1826: II, pp. 184–5.

43. Baron Kervyn de Lettenhove, *Oeuvres de Georges Chastellain*, 8 vols., Académie Royale de Belgique, Brussels, 1863–66: IV, p. 218.

44. Washington, D.C., National Gallery of Art, Andrew Mellon Collection 1937.

45. Cocheris, *op. cit.*, pp. 102–3.

46. O. de la Marche, *Le parement et triumphes des dames*, Paris, 1554, no pagination.

47. M. Mollat, *Les affaires de Jacques Coeur. Journal du Procureur Dauvet*, 2 vols., Ecole pratique des Hautes Etudes—VIe section Centre de Recherches Historiques, Paris, 1952–3: I, p. 36.

48. Washington, D.C., National Gallery of Art, Samuel H. Kress Collection 1961.

49. Brussels, Bibliothèque Royale, ms. 9232, f. 423.

50. Berlin-Dahlem, Gemäldegalerie der Staatlichen Museen.

51. Brussels, Bibliothèque Royale, ms. 9026, f. 425.

52. Buchan, *op. cit.*, 39, p. 95.

53. T. Tzara and J. Dufournet, *François Villon Poésies*, Gallimard, Paris, 1973, 'Le Testament', stanza XXXIX, p. 68, ll. 309–11.

54. Brussels, Musées Royaux des Beaux-Arts. See L. Campbell, 'Rogier van der Weyden's "Portrait of a Knight of the Golden Fleece": The Identity of the Sitter', *Bulletin des Musées royaux des Beaux-Arts*, XXI, Brussels, 1972, pp. 7–14.

55. Brussels, Bibliothèque Royale, ms. 9631, f. 2v.

Chapter Seven

1. Paris, Archives Nationales, KK 51, f. 29.

2. Paris, Bibliothèque Nationale, ms. fr. 2695. I am dating the manuscript on the dress in spite of the exhaustive study by O. Pächt, 'René d'Anjou—Studien 'I' and 'II', in *Jahrbuch der Kunsthistorischen Sammlungen in Wien*, 69, Vienna 1974, pp. 85–126; 73, Vienna, 1977, pp. 7–106, in which he attempts to show that all the *Tournois* manuscripts belong in the mid or late 1460s.

3. O. de la Marche, *Le parement et triumphes des dames*, Paris, 1554, not paginated.

4. Berlin-Dahlem, Gemäldegalerie der Staatlichen Museen.

5. Paris, Bibliothèque Nationale, ms. Roth. 2534, ff. 20v, 130v.

6. Brussels, Bibliothèque Royale, ms. 9510, f. 1. Note in card catalogue in Bibliothèque Royale.

7. Vienna, Österreichische Nationalbibliothek, Cod. 2617, ff. 14, J. Wescher, *Jean Fouquet and His Time*, Pleiades Books, 1974, p. 102.

8. J. A. Buchon, *Collection des chroniques nationales françaises*, 47 vols., Paris, 1826–8: 40, pp. 139–40; *ibid.*, 37, p. lxxviij.

9. Vienna, Österreichische Nationalbibliothek, Cod. 1857, f. 14v. This illustration is one of several on single folios and therefore not necessarily of same date as rest of ms. See F. Unterkircher and A. de Schryver, *Gebetbuch Karls des Kuhnen vel potius Stundenbuch der Maria von Burgund Codex Vindobonensis 1857 der Österreichischen Nationalbibliothek*, Akademische Druck-u. Verlagsanstalt, Graz, 1969, p. 7 on gathering of folios and pp. 158–9 for attempt to date ms. to 1474.

10. Oxford, Bodleian Library, Laud Misc. ms. 751, f. 127: see O. Pächt and J. J. G. Alexander, *Illuminated Manuscripts in the Bodleian Library Oxford. 1. German, Dutch, Flemish, French and Spanish Schools,* Oxford at the Clarendon Press, no. 357, p. 27.

11. Banbury, Upton House. See M. J. Friedländer, *Early Netherlandish Painting*, 14 vols., 1967–76, Leyden and Brussels; IV, Supp. 115.

12. Brussels, Bibliothèque Royale, mss. 6–9: ms. 7, f. 387v. Note in Bibliothèque's card catalogue.

13. Paris, Bibliothèque Nationale, ms. Roth. 2973, f. 1. See J. Porcher, *French Miniatures from Illuminated Manuscripts*, Collins, 1960, p. 79.

14. Paris, Bibliothèque Nationale, ms. fr. 18, f. 3v. See M. Manion, *The Wharncliffe Hours: A Study of a Fifteenth-Century Prayerbook*, Sydney University Press for the Australian Academy of the Humanities, Art Monograph 1, Sydney, 1972, pp. 8–13.

15. New York, Metropolitan Museum of Art, Bequest of Benjamin Altman, 1913.

16. Brussels, Musées Royaux des Beaux-Arts: Friedländer, *op. cit.*, III, p. 87, note 41.

17. H. Cocheris, *Le Blason des couleurs en armes, livrées et devises par Sicile Herault d'Alphonse V, roi d'Aragon*, Paris, 1860, p. 126.

18. Brussels, Musées Royaux des Beaux-Arts.

19. Paris, Musée du Louvre: C. Sterling and H. Adhémar, *Peintures Ecole Francaise, XIVe, XVe et XVIe siècles,* Editions des Musées Nationaux, Paris, 1965, no. 36, pp. 14–15.

20. Florence, Galleria degli Uffizi. See C. Thompson and L. Campbell, *Hugo van der Goes and the Trinity Panels in Edinburgh*, Trustees of the National Gallery of Scotland, Edinburgh, 1974, pp. 103–4, note 3.

21. Boccaccio, *The Decameron*, (trans. G. H. McWilliam), Penguin Books, 1972, p. 228; M. Wood, *Foreign Correspondence with Marie de Lorraine Queen of Scotland. From the originals in the Balcarres Papers 1537–1548*, 3rd series, vol. 4, Scottish History Society, Edinburgh, 1923, p. 228.

22. London, National Gallery.

23. Oxford, Bodleian Library, Douce 365, f. 115: see Pächt and Alexander, *op. cit.*, no. 351, pl. XXVIII; London, British Museum, Bruges Bequest; Bruges, Sint Janshospitaal, 'Altarpiece of the Lamentation': Friedländer, *op. cit.*, VIA, pl. 19, p. 45 for dating.

24. M. Davies, *National Gallery Catalogues: Early Netherlandish School*; 3rd ed., Trustees of the National Gallery, 1967, p. 125.

25. Munich, Alte Pinakothek: see Friedländer, *op. cit.*, VIA, no. 33, pl. 82 and p. 50.

26. Bruges, St Salvatorskathedraal: see Friedländer, *op. cit.*, IV, pp. 27, 70.

27. Brussels, Musées Royaux des Beaux-Arts: see Friedländer, *op. cit.*, VIA, pl. 111; Bruges, Sint Janshospitaal: Friedländer, *loc. cit.*, pl. 123.

28. London, National Gallery: see Davies, *op. cit.*, pp. 113–15.

29. Bruges, Groeninge Museum.

30. Brussels, Musées Royaux des Beaux-Arts: see Friedländer, *loc. cit.*, pl. 110.

31. M. Bruchet, *Marguerite d'Autriche Duchesse de Savoie*, Lille, 1927, pp. 9, 309–11.

32. de la Marche, *op. cit.*

33. Paris, Bibliothèque Nationale, ms. fr. 449, f. 1. The arms on this folio are of France and Savoy: the book therefore must have belonged to Charlotte of Savoy, Queen of France, who died in 1483.

34. Antwerp, Koninklijk Museum voor Schone Kunsten: Friedländer, *op. cit.*, VIA, no. 116.

35. Memlingmuseum O.C.M.W., Sint Janshospitaal, Bruges.

36. Antwerp, Koninklijk Museum voor Schone Kunsten; *Beschrijvende Catalogus Oude Meesters*, Antwerp, 1959, p. 139 as from Brussels; J. Van Roey, 'Het wapen op "De lactatio van de H. Bernardus" van het Koninklijk Museum voor Schone Kunsten te Antwerpen', *Jaarboek Koninklijk Museum voor Schone Kunsten*, Antwerp, 1954–60, pp. 21–3, on coats of arms.

37. Paris, Musée du Louvre. See H. Adhémar, *Les primitifs flamands, I. Corpus de la peinture des anciens Pays-Bas méridionaux au quinzième siècle. La musée nationale du Louvre, Paris,* I, Brussels, 1962, pp. 106–7 for variety of dates suggested. Compare the dress of the women in the following reference.

38. London, British Library, Harley ms. 4425, ff. 7, 24, 24v.

39. Antwerp, Koninklijk Museum voor Schone Kunsten. Dating a verbal communication from Dr Lorne Campbell.

40. Antwerp, Koninklijk Museum voor Schone Kunsten.

41. Paris, Musée du Louvre. See C. Sterling and H. Adhémar, *op. cit.*, no. 29, p. 12.

42. Paris, Musée du Louvre. See Sterling and Adhémar, *op. cit.*, nos. 26–8, pp. 11–12.

43. T. Dickson (ed.), *Compota Thesaurariorum Regum Scotorum. Accounts of the Lord High Treasurer of Scotland*, I, Edinburgh, 1877, p. 146.

44. A. A. Hentsch, *De la Litterature Didactique du moyen âge s'adressant spécialement aux femmes*, Cahors, 1903, p. 201.

45. Paris, Bibliothèque Nationale, ms. lat. 1190.

46. de la Marche, *op. cit.*

47. Paris, Bibliothèque Nationale, ms. fr. 995, ff. 30, 32.

48. Raleigh, North Carolina, North Carolina Museum of Art, Gift of Samuel H. Kress Foundation. See C. Eisler, *Paintings from the Samuel H. Kress Foundation. European Schools Excluding Italian*, Phaidon, Oxford, 1977, pp. 249–50.

49. Antwerp, Koninklijk Museum voor Schone Kunsten. See *Beschrijvende Catalogus, etc.*, pp. 141–2.

Chapter Eight

1. Compare Brussels, Bibliothèque Royale, ms. 9232, f. 269 and the 'Christ and Donor Family', Utrecht, Centraal Museum, in M. J. Friedländer, *Early Netherlandish Painting*, 14 vols., Leyden and Brussels, 1967–76; III, no. 41, pl. 58.

2. Vienna, Kunsthistorisches Museum: see A. Stange, *Deutsche Malerei der Gotik*, 11 vols., Kraus Reprint, Nendeln/Liechtenstein, 1969; II, no. 46, pp. 47–8.

3. Bad Wildungen, near Cassel, Town Church: reproduced in colour in H. Landolt, *German Painting: The Late Middle Ages (1350–1500)*, Skira, Geneva, 1968, p. 48. Hannover, Niedersächsisches Landesmuseum: see *Vor Stefan Lochner Die Kölner Maler von 1300 bis 1430*, Wallraf-Richartz-Museum, Cologne, 1974, no. 52, pp. 112, 180.

4. Vienna, Österreichische Nationalbibliothek, Cod. 2765, f. 274v. See F. Unterkircher, *European Illuminated Manuscripts in the Austrian National Library*, Thames and Hudson, 1967, pp. 94–5.

5. Nuremberg, St Lorenz-Kirche: Stange, *op. cit.*, IX, no. 5, p. 8.

6. Nuremberg, St Sebaldus-Kirche: Stange, *loc. cit.*, no. 34, p. 22.

7. Bonn, Rheinisches Landesmuseum: Stange, *op. cit.*, III, no. 184, p. 135.

8. Aachen, Suermondt Museum: *Vor Stefan Lochner*, etc., no. 49, pp. 109–10.

9. Cologne, Wallraf-Richartz-Museum: *Vor Stefan Lochner*, etc., no. 45, pp. 107–8, 175.

10. Cologne, Wallraf-Richartz-Museum: Stange, *op. cit.*, III, no. 113, p. 100 as mid-1430s.

11. Tiefenbronn, near Pforzheim, Parish Church.

12. Darmstadt, Hessisches Landesmuseum: *Herbst des Mittelalters Spätgotik in Köln und am Niederrhein*, Kunsthalle, Cologne, 1970, no. 49, p. 59 and Taf. VIII.

13. Cologne, Wallraf-Richartz-Museum: Stange, *op. cit.*, v, no. 13, p. 14.

14. Donaueschingen, Sammlungen Fürst Furstenberg: Stange, *op. cit.*, iv, no. 34, p. 31.

15. H. Beaune and J. D'Arbaumont, *Mémoires d'Olivier de La Marche, maître d'hôtel et capitaine des gardes de Charles le Téméraire*, 4 vols., Société de l'Histoire de France, Paris, 1883–8; i, p. 276.

16. Vienna, Österreichische Nationalbibliothek, Cod. 2663, f. 69: Unterkircher, *op. cit.*, pp. 102–3.

17. Darmstadt, Hessisches Landesmuseum.

18. Munich, Alte Pinakothek: see E. Buchner, *German Late Gothic Painting*, Hirmer Verlag, Munich, 1960, p. 22 and illus. 48.

19. Nördlingen, Städtisches Museum: see Stange, *op. cit.*, viii, nos. 186–7, p. 89.

20. Konstanz, Rosgartenmuseum: see Stange, *op. cit.*, vii, no. 91, pp. 43–4.

21. Baron Kervyn de Lettenhove, *Oeuvres de Georges Chastellain*, 8 vols., Académie Royale de Belgique, Brussels, 1863–6: iv, p. 424.

22. Vaduz, Liechtenstein, Sammlungen des regierenden Fürsten von Liechtenstein: O. Benesch, *Collected Writings Volume III German and Austrian Art of the 15th and 16th Centuries*, Phaidon, 1972, p. 177 and Stange, *op. cit.*, xi, no. 148, p. 67.

23. A. Ronen, *The Peter and Paul Altarpiece and Friedrich Pacher,* Weidenfeld and Nicholson, Jerusalem, for Tel Aviv University Faculty of Fine Arts, 1974, p. 8 and pl. 5.

24. Bern, Historisches Museum: Stange, *op. cit.*, viii, no. 204, p. 95.

25. Bamberg, Historisches Museum: Stange, *op. cit.*, xi, no. 191, pp. 89–90.

26. Ronen, *op. cit.*, pls. 15–16, 20; Moulins, Musée d'Art et d'Archéologie.

27. Cologne, Wallraf-Richartz-Museum: Stange, *op. cit.*, v, nos. 148–9 and p. 71, where portraits not yet identified, and *Late Gothic Art from Cologne*, Trustees of the National Gallery, London, 1977, no. 31, pp. 90–3.

28. Cologne, Wallraf-Richartz-Museum: *Herbst* etc., no. 22, p. 44.

29. Cassel, Staatliche Kunstsammlungen: *Albrecht Dürer 1471–1971* (exhibition at Germanisches Nationalmuseum, Nuremberg), Munich, 1971, no. 97, p. 64; Stange, *op. cit.*, ix, no. 108.

30. Gotha, Castle Museum: Stange, *op. cit.*, vii, no. 226, p. 103.

31. Nördlingen, Städtisches Museum.

32. Coburg, Kunstsammlungen der Veste Coburg.

33. See Stange, *op. cit.*, viii, no. 58, p. 30.

34. Munich, Bayerische Nationalmuseum: Stange, *op. cit.*, viii, no. 210, p. 99.

35. Liverpool, Walker Art Gallery: *Late Gothic Art from Cologne*, etc., no. 39, p. 108.

36. Cologne, Wallraf-Richartz-Museum: *Late Gothic Art from Cologne*, etc., no. 19, p. 65.

37. Madrid, Museo del Prado.

38. Schweinfurt, Sammlung Otto Schäfer: *Albrecht Dürer 1471–1971*, etc., no. 462, pp. 232–3.

39. Stuttgart, Gemäldegalerie: Stange, *op. cit.*, viii, no. 64, p. 33.

40. Portrait of Felicitas Tucher in Weimar, Schlossmuseum; portrait of Elspet Tucher in Cassel, Gemaldegalerie. See A. Ottino della Chiesa, *The Complete Paintings of Dürer*, Weidenfeld and Nicolson, London, 1971, no. 55 and p. 95; pl. xv and p. 95.

41. Vienna, Albertina.

42. R. Kautzsch, *Die Holzschnitte zum Ritter vom Turn (Basel 1493)*, no. 44 of *Studien zur Deutschen Kunstgeschichte*, J. H. Ed. Heitz (Heitz & Mündell), Strassbourg, 1903, fig. 13.

43. Munich, Alte Pinakothek: reproduced in A. Ottino della Chiesa, *op. cit.*, pl. xxv and p. 102.

Bibliography

ADHÉMAR, H., *Les primitifs flamands, I. Corpus de la peinture des anciens Pays-Bas méridionaux au quinzième siècle. La musée nationale du Louvre, Paris*, I, Brussels, 1962.

AMSTERDAM, Rijksmuseum, *All the paintings of the Rijksmuseum in Amsterdam. A completely illustrated catalogue*, Amsterdam, Maarsen, 1976.

ANTWERP, Koninklijk Museum voor Schone Kunsten, *Beschrijvende Catalogus Oude Meesters*, Antwerp, 1959.

AVRIL, F., *Manuscript Painting at the Court of France. The Fourteenth Century (1310–1380)*, Chatto and Windus, 1978.

de BEAUCOURT, G., 'Roles de dépenses du temps de Charles VII (1450–51)', in *Annuaire-Bulletin de la Société de l'Histoire de France*, II, seconde partie, Paris, 1864.

BEAUNE, H. and J. D'ARBAUMONT, *Mémoires d'Olivier de La Marche, maître d'hotel et capitaine des gardes de Charles le Téméraire*, 4 vols., Société de l'Histoire de France, 1883–8.

BENESCH, O., *Collected Writings Volume III: German and Austrian Art of the 15th and 16th Centuries*, Phaidon, 1972.

BRUCHET, M., *Marguerite d'Autriche Duchesse de Savoie*, Lille, 1927.

BRUGES, Groeninge Museum, *Anonieme Vlaamse Primitieven*, Bruges, 1969.

BRUSSELS, Bibliothèque Royale, *La miniature hollandaise. Le grand siècle de l'enluminure du livre dans les Pays-Bas septentrionaux*, Brussels, 1971.

BUCHNER, E., *German Late Gothic Painting*, Hirmer Verlag, Munich, 1960.

BUCHON, J. A., *Collections des chroniques nationales françaises écrites en langue vulgaire du treizième au quinzième siècle*, 47 vols., Paris, 1826–8.

CALMETTE, J. and G. DURVILLE, *Philippe de Commynes. Mémoires*, Les classiques de l'histoire de France au Moyen Age, fasc. 3, 5 and 6, Paris, 1924–5.

CAMPBELL, L., 'Rogier van der Weyden's "Portrait of a Knight of the Golden Fleece": The Identity of the Sitter', *Bulletin des Musées royaux des Beaux-Arts*, XXI, Brussels, 1972, pp. 7–14.

CAMPBELL, L., 'Robert Campin, the Master of Flémalle and the Master of Mérode', *The Burlington Magazine*, CXVI, 1974, pp. 634–46.

CAMPBELL, L., *Van der Weyden*, Jupiter, 1979.

CHATELET, A., *Heures de Turin quarante-cinq feuillets à peintures provenant des Très Belles Heures de Jean de France, duc de Berry*, Turin, 1967.

CLARK, K., *The Nude, A Study of Ideal Art*, Penguin Books, 1976.

CLAYTON, M., *Catalogue of Rubbings of Brasses and Incised Slabs*, 2nd ed., Her Majesty's Stationery Office, 1968.

COCHERIS, H., *Le Blason des couleurs en armes, livrées et devises par Sicile Herault d'Alphonse V, roi d'Aragon*, Paris, 1860.

COLOGNE, Kunsthalle, *Herbst des Mittelalters Spätgotik in Köln und am Niederrhein*, Cologne, 1970.

COLOGNE, Wallraf-Richartz-Museum, *Vor Stefan Lochner Die Kölner Maler von 1300 bis 1430*, Cologne, 1974.

COUDERC, C., 'Les comptes d'un grand couturier parisien au XVe siècle', *Bulletin de la société de l'histoire de Paris et de l'Ile-de-France*, XXXVIII, Paris, 1911, pp. 118ff.

de COURDE DE MONTAIGLON, A., *Le livre du chevalier de La Tour Landry pour l'enseignement de ses filles*, Paris, 1854.

CROW, J., *Les Quinze Joyes de Mariage*, Blackwell's French Texts, Oxford, 1969.

DAVIES, M., *National Gallery Catalogues: Early Netherlandish School*, 3rd ed., Trustees of the National Gallery, 1967.

DAVIES, M., *Rogier van der Weyden. An essay, with a critical catalogue of paintings assigned to him and to Robert Campin*, Phaidon, 1972.

DICKSON, T., et al., *Compota Thesaurariorum Regum Scotorum. Accounts of the Lord High Treasurer of Scotland*, Edinburgh, 1877 (in progress).

DIDIER, R., 'Les retables de Ternant', *Congrès archéologique du Nivernais*, Paris, 1967, pp. 258–76.

DIJON, Musée des Beaux-Arts, *Catalogue des peintures françaises*, Dijon, 1968.

DOUËT-D'ARCQ, L., *La chronique d'Enguerran de Monstrelet en deux livres avec pièces justificatives 1400–1444*, 6 vols., Société de l'histoire de France, Paris, 1857–62.

DU FRESNE DE BEAUCOURT, G., *Chronique de M. d'Escouchy*, 3 vols., Société de l'Histoire de France, Paris, 1863–4.

DUPONT, MLLE., *Mémoires de Pierre de Fenin, comprenant le récit des événements qui se sont passés en France et en Bourgogne sous les règnes de Charles VI et Charles VII (1407–27)*, Société de l'histoire de France, Paris, 1837.

C. T. EISLER, *Drawings of the Masters. Flemish and Dutch Drawings From the 15th to the 18th Century*, Little, Brown and Company, Boston, Toronto, 1963.

EISLER, C., *Paintings from the Samuel H. Kress Collection. European Schools Excluding Italian*, Phaidon for Samuel H. Kress Foundation, Oxford, 1977.

FRIEDLÄNDER, M. J., *Early Netherlandish Paintings*, 14 vols., Leyden and Brussels, 1967–76.

GHENT, Museum voor Schone Kunsten, *Gent Duizend Jaar Kunst en Cultur*, Ghent, 1975.

GRAVES, F. M., *Deux inventaires de la maison d'Orléans (1389 et 1408)*, Paris, 1926.

GUIFFREY, J., *Inventaires de Jean Duc de Berry (1401–1416)*, 2 vols., Paris, 1894–6.

HENTSCH, A. A., *De la Litterature Didactique du moyen âge s'adressant specialement aux femmes*, Cahors, 1903.

HUIZINGA, J., *The Waning of the Middle Ages*, Penguin Books, 1976.

JUBINAL, A., *Recherches sur l'usage et l'origine des tapisseries à personnages dites historiées, depuis l'antiquité jusqu'au 16e siècle inclusivement*, Paris, 1840.

KAUTZSCH, R., *Die Holzschnitte zum Ritter vom Turn (Basel 1493)*, no. 44 of *Studien zur Deutschen Kunstgeschichte*, J. H. Ed. Heitz (Heitz & Mündell), Strassbourg, 1903.

KERVYN DE LETTENHOVE, Baron, *Oeuvres de Georges Chastellain*, 8 vols., Académie Royale de Belgique, Brussels, 1863–6.

KERVYN DE LETTENHOVE, Baron, *Chroniques relatives à l'histoire de la Belgique sous la domination des ducs de Bourgogne*, 3 vols., Commission Royale d'Histoire, Brussels, 1870–6.

de LABORDE, Comte, *Les Ducs de Bourgogne*, Seconde partie, *Preuves*, 3 vols., Paris, 1849–52.

de LA CURNE DE SAINTE-PALAYE, *Mémoires sur l'ancienne chevalerie*, 2 vols., nouvelle édition, Paris, 1826.

de LA MARCHE, O., *Le parement et triumphes des dames*, Paris, 1554.

LANDOLT, H., *German Painting The Late Middle Ages (1350–1500)*, Skira, Geneva, 1968.

de LA TRÉMOILLE, C., *Les La Trémoille pendant cinq siècles*, 5 vols., Nantes, 1890–6.

de LAURIÈRE, M., *et al.*, *Ordonnances des Roys de France de la troisième Race, recueillies par ordre chronologique*, 23 vols., Paris, 1733–1847.

LECOY DE LA MARCHE, A., *Extraits des comptes et memoriaux du roi René pour servir à l'histoire des arts au XVe siècle*, Société de l'école des chartes, Paris, 1873.

LE GLAY, M. A., *et al.*, *Inventaire-sommaire des archives départmentales antérieures à 1790 . . . Nord, Repertoire numerique*, Lille, 1863, etc.

LONDON, National Gallery, *Late Gothic Art from Cologne*, Trustees of the National Gallery, London, 1977.

LONGNON, A., *Paris pendant la domination anglaise (1420–1436)*, Société de l'Histoire de Paris, 1878.

LONGON, J., and MEISS, M., *Les Très Riches Heures du Duc de Berry*, Thames and Hudson, 1969.

DE MANDROT, B. *Journal de Jean de Roye connu sous le nom de Chronique Scandaleuse 1460–1483*, 2 vols., Société de l'histoire de France, Paris, 1894–6.

MANION, M., *The Wharncliffe Hours: A Study of a Fifteenth-Century Prayerbook*, Sydney University Press for the Australian Academy of the Humanities, Art Monograph 1, Sydney, 1972.

MEISS, M., *French Painting in the Time of Jean de Berry: The Late Fourteenth Century and the Patronage of the Duke*, Phaidon, 1967.

MEISS, M., *French Painting in the Time of Jean de Berry: The Boucicaut Master*, Phaidon, 1968.

MEISS, M., *French Painting in the Time of Jean de Berry: The Limbourgs and Their Contemporaries*, Thames and Hudson, 1974.

MEISS, M., and BEATSON, E. H., *Les Belles heures de Jean duc de Berry*, Thames and Hudson, 1974.

MICHEL, E., *Catalogue raissoné des peintures du Moyen-Age, de la Renaissance et des temps modernes. Peintures flamandes du XVe et du XVIe siècle*, Editions des Musées Nationaux, Paris, 1953.

MOLLAT, M., *Les affaires de Jacques Coeur. Journal du Procureur Dauvet*, 2 vols., Ecole pratique des Hautes Etudes—VIE section Centre de Recherches Historiques, Paris, 1952–3.

NUREMBERG, Germanisches Nationalmuseum, *Albrecht Dürer 1471–1971*, Munich, 1971.

OTTINO DELLA CHIESA, A., *The complete paintings of Dürer*, Weidenfeld and Nicolson, London, 1971.

PÄCHT, O., 'Rene d'Anjou—Studien I' and 'II' in *Jahrbuch der Kunsthistorischen Sammlungen in Wien*, 69, Vienna, 1974, pp. 85–126, and vol. 73, Vienna, 1977, pp. 7–106.

PÄCHT, O., and ALEXANDER, J. J. G., *Illuminated Manuscripts in the Bodleian Library Oxford*, 2nd ed., 1, Clarendon Press, Oxford, 1969.

PANOFSKY, E., 'Two Roger Problems: The Donor of The Hague *Lamentation* and the Date of the Altarpiece of the Seven Sacraments', *Art Bulletin,* XXXIII, New York, 1951, pp. 33–40.

PHILIP, L. B., *The Ghent Altarpiece and the Art of Jan van Eyck*, Princeton University Press, Princeton, 1971.

PICHON, J., *Le Ménagier de Paris, Traité de morale et d'économie domestique composé vers 1393, par un bourgeois parisien*, 2 vols., Sociéte des Bibliophiles Français, Paris, 1846.

PLUMMER, J., *The Hours of Catherine of Cleves*, Barrie and Rockliff, 1966.

PORCHER, J., *French Miniatures from Illuminated Manuscripts*, Collins, 1960.

PORCHER, J., *Jean Lebègue. Les histoires que l'on peut raisonnablement faire sur les livres de Salluste*, Société des Bibliophiles Français, Paris, 1962.

DE QUEUX DE SAINT-HILAIRE, Marquis, and RAYNAUD, G., *Ouvres complètes de Eustache Deschamps publiées d'après le manuscrit de la Bibliothèque Nationale*, 11 vols., Société des anciens textes Français, Paris, 1873–1903.

VAN ROEY, J., 'Het wapen op "De lactatio van de H. Bernardus" van het Koninklijk Museum voor Schone Kunsten te Antwerpen', *Jaarboek Koninklijk Museum voor Schone Kunsten, Antwerpen, 1954–60*, Antwerp.

RONEN, A., *The Peter and Paul Altarpiece and Friedrich Pacher*, Weidenfeld and Nicolson, Jerusalem, for Tel Aviv University Faculty of Fine Arts, 1974.

ROY, M., *Oeuvres poétiques de Christine de Pisan*, 3 vols., Société des anciens textes Français, Paris, 1886–96.

SMITH, H. C., *The Goldsmith and the Young Couple or the Legend of S. Eloy and S. Godeberta by Petrus Christus*, privately printed, 1915.

SONKES, M., *Les primitifs flamands, III. Contributions à l'étude des primitifs flamands. Dessins du XVe siècle: Groupe Van der Weyden*, Brussels, 1969.

STANGE, A., *Deutsche Malerei der Gotik*, 11 vols., Kraus Reprint, Nendeln/Liechtenstein, 1969.

STERLING, C., and ADHÉMAR, H., *Peintures Ecole Française, XIVe, XVe et XVIe siècles,* Editions des Musées Nationaux, Paris, 1965.

THOMPSON, C., and CAMPBELL, L., *Hugo van der Goes and the Trinity Panels in Edinburgh*, Trustees of the National Gallery of Scotland, Edinburgh, 1974.

TUETEY, A., *Journal d'un bourgeois de Paris 1405–1449*, Société de l'histoire de Paris et de l'Ile-de-France, 1881.

TUETEY, A., *Journal de Nicolas de Baye Greffier du Parlement de Paris 1400–1417*, 2 vols., Société de l'histoire de France, Paris, 1885–8.

TUETEY, A., *Journal de Clément de Fauquembergue greffier du Parlement de Paris, 1417–1435*, 3 vols., Société de l'histoire de France, Paris, 1903–15.

TZARA, T., and DUFOURNET, J., *François Villon Poésies*, Gallimard, Paris, 1973.

UNTERKIRCHER, F., *European Illuminated Manuscripts in the Austrian National Library*, Thames and Hudson, 1967.

UNTERKIRCHER, F., and DE SCHRYVER, A., *Gebetbuch Karls des Kühnen vel potius Stundenbuch der Maria von Burgund Codex Vindobonensis 1857 der Österreichischen Nationalbibliothek*, Akademische Drucku. Verlagsanstalt, Graz, 1969.

VALE, M. G. A., *Charles VII,* Eyre Methuen, 1974.

VALLET DE VIRIVLLE, [A.], *Chronique de Charles VII roi de France par Jean Chartier*, 3 vols., Paris, 1858.

WESCHER, P., *Jean Fouquet and His Time*, Pleiades Books, 1947.

Glossary

This glossary provides an explanation of some of the terms used in the text, as well as offering some contemporary references.

Abbreviations used in Glossary

AN
Archives Nationales, Paris

Bourgeois
A. Tuetey, *Journal d'un bourgeois de Paris 1405–1449,* Société de l'histoire de Paris et de l'Ile-de-France, Paris, 1881.

Chronique Charles VII
[A.] Vallet de Viriville, *Chronique de Charles VII roi de France par Jean Chartier*, 3 vols., Paris, 1858.

Inventaire . . . Nord
M. A. Le Glay et al., *Inventaire-sommaire des archives départementales antérieures à 1790 . . . Nord, Répertoire numerique*, Lille, 1863, etc., vol. VII.

de Laborde
comte de Laborde, *Les Ducs de Bourgogne*, Seconde partie, *Preuves*, 3 vols., Paris, 1849–52.

Lebègue
J. Porcher, *Jean Lebègue Les histoires que l'on peut raisonnablement faire sur les livres de Salluste*, Société des Bibliophiles François, Paris, 1962.

Les La Trémoille
C. de La Trémoille, *Les La Trémoille pendant cinq siècles*, 5 vols., Nantes, 1890–6.

Nicolas de Baye
A. Tuetey, *Journal de Nicolas de Baye Greffier du Parlement de Paris 1400–1417*, 2 vols., Sociéte de l'histoire de France, Paris, 1885–8.

Orléans Inventory
F. M. Graves, *Deux inventaires de la maison d'Orléans (1389 et 1408)*, Paris, 1926.

Villon
T. Tzara and J. Dufournet, *François Villon Poésies*, Gallimard, Paris, 1973.

Glossary

Bombarde sleeves
The most common type of sleeve in accounts in the International period: the most popular sleeve in illustrations is of a very full trumpet shape, open at the wrist. *Bombardes* (cannons) had open mouths, much like the ends of trumpet-shaped sleeves. 1403: a *houppelande* (q.v.) with *grandes manches a bombardes*, *AN*, KK 43, f. 50. 1408: a *houppelande* with *manches closes et grands bombardes* (trumpet-shaped sleeves sewn shut at the wrist?) *Orléans Inventory*, p. 146.

Bourrelet
The padded brim of a man's hood or the padded rolls used to make women's headdresses. From 'bourrer', to stuff (?) 1403: $2\frac{1}{4}$ ells black satin for the queen's *bourrelet AN*, KK 43, f. 14. 1432–3: 28 hoods for the archers of the Duke of Burgundy, with *bourrelets* and *thoile . . . dessoubz* (as padding?) de Laborde, I, p. 278.

Brassieres/brasserolles
In modern French, a child's vest, but apparently a type of bolero jacket in the fifteenth century, worn as an undergarment, partially visible at the end of the century in women's dress. 1402/3: for Isabella of Bavaria *unes braserolles* made from 1 ell of fine white linen. *AN*, KK 43, f. 5. 1408: with nearly-new *linge: treze chemises et une brasserolle, Orléans Inventory*, p. 133, no. 734. 1419: *unes braceroles de blanchet, fourrées de gris*, i.e., a bolero of *blanchet* (a blanket-like cloth), furred with grey squirrel; owned by man. *Nicolas de Baye*, II, p. lxxj, no. 295.

168. A detail of Memlinc's portrait of Barbara van Vlaenderbergh (**128**), showing her damask belt and the elaborate metalwork on it.

Cornette
A part of the hoods of men and women, which required little material but was often lavishly decorated. By process of elimination (see *pate*), must be tail at back of hood. In slang, used to mean hangman's noose. 1389: *cornette en quatre, décopée en franges*, de Laborde, III, p. 41, no. 5445. 1403: $\frac{1}{4}$ ell green satin to line *cornette* for lady, *AN*, KK 43, f. 13v. 1396: Women in the La Trémoille household had silver-gilt spangles (*pailletes*) hanging from their hoods with six silver double-links per spangle. *Les La Trémoille*, I, p. 48, 1461–2: Villon leaves to enemies '*A chacun une grande cornette . . . Pour pendre . . . à leurs chapeaux de fautres*' i.e., to each of them, a big cord to hang . . . on their felt hats. *Villon*, p. 109.

Cote (or *Cotte*)
Used inconsistently to mean two separate garments, united only by their being tightly-fitting. Apparently, a *cote* could be a lined, partially lined or unlined dress with short sleeves, or no sleeves at all, worn under a more formal outer garment. One version acted as a corset, laced up the bodice front, and had short sleeves to which fancier false sleeves could be attached, to show at the wrists. The other main use was as a closely-fitting outer-dress, worn throughout the century as a street dress by working-class women and perhaps as 'occupational dress' by prostitutes (*Villon*). The dress proper seems to have been called a *cote hardie*, a daring *cote*. English version at this date seems to have been called a kirtle. Useful references: 1403: a *cotte simple* (unlined?) with a *cote hardie*, *AN*, KK 43, ff. 11, 11v. 1408: a *cote simple* of velvet in grain, embroidered with pearls in Vs and mulberries, the sleeves decorated likewise, as part of a *robe* (q.v.) of four garments for the Duchess of Orléans, *Orléans Inventory*, pp. 99–100. *C.* 1417 a *cote* seems to be nothing more than a closely fitting outer-dress, *Lebègue* (not paginated: story of Fulvia). 1369: a *cote hardie* for the Duchess of Bar, with a fur lining of 320 stomachs of miniver, *Inventaire . . .Nord*, p. 65. 1403: a *cote hardie* '*brodee pour la royne*'. *AN*, KK 43, f. 52v. 1408: '*une fourreure d'une cote hardie de cendal vermeil où il fault une manche*', *Orléans Inventory*, p. 145. 1461–2: '. . . . *filles mignottes Portans surcots et justes* [tight-fitting] *cottes*', *Villon*, p. 156.

Damask
A form of satin weave, which uses the free-floating threads on the surface of satin, alternating the 'floating' threads along the length of the textile and across its width. The different ways in which light travels along the floating threads creates the impression of a fabric made from two tones of the one colour, when it is in fact normally made from threads of the one tone and colour.

Decopeures or dagging
A series of slashes on the edge of a garment, or a piece of slashed cloth, applied to a garment. Some patterns cut by special die. 1389: a hood for the Duke of Touraine with a tail (*cornete*) '*decoppé en franges*' (fringes), *de Laborde*, III, p. 41. 1416: '*decopeures faictes d'un fer dentelé*', '*faictes d'un menu fer en manière de quareaulx*', *ibid.*, I, pp. 123 and 126.

Ell
A measurement of length, more or less equivalent to a yard or a metre, but varying in length from country to country and town to town.

Heuque
Apparently a sleeveless overgarment, worn almost exclusively by men. Often connected with liveries and worked with the badges or mottos of the nobility: probably a type of cloak. 1412: '*une paire de manches ouvertes pour mettre soux une heuque*' of black satin with brocaded design of green leaves and gold baskets, *de Laborde*, I, p. 67. 1414: for knights and squires—twenty heuques to be made from thirty-nine ells vermilion cloth, and twelve ells white cloth to make badges on them: all lined in white (forty-four ells), *Les La Trémoille*, I, pp. 126–7. 1426: Inventory of Margaret Duchess of Bavaria (living in Holland) a black double '*heuke*' of cloth, for riding. A sable furring, cut on the sides, *Inventaire . . . Nord*, p. 201.

Houppelande (and various spellings)
Garment of varying lengths for men and always full-length for women. Fashionable *c.* 1380–*c.* 1420. Had open or closed sleeves with various names. Was often elaborately embroidered and/or slashed. Had collar, turned down by 1416, by which time it was also cut in gores (*girons*). Presumably an outer garment because of its expensive decoration. Useful references: 1384: '*. . . pour avoir brodé une courte hopelande de vert que nous vestimes le premier jour de may, où il a fait un arbre peuple de feulles, tout au bout de la manche senestre et se rent d'une part en l'espaule par derrière et par devant en la poitrine . . .*', *Inventaire . . . Nord*, p. 10. 1403: '*a grans decoppeures*', *AN*, KK 43, f. 10, '*a manches closes et grans poignetz*', *ibid.*, f. 46v, '*a grandes manches a bombardes*', *ibid.*, f. 50. 1408: '*. . . quatre houppelandes . . . une bastarde, une courte, une longue . . .*', *Chronique Charles VII*, III, pp. 264–5. 1412: '*à my jambe*', *de Laborde*, I, pp. 67, 70, 73. 1416: '*colet assis*' *ibid.*, pp. 118, 138–9, '*faicte à girons*' *ibid.*, p. 139. 1426: '*dechicquetée*' (slashed), *Bourgeois*, p. 382, note 2.

Pate
Apparently the shoulder-cape section of the Balaclava-like hood. Often slashed at its edges. *c.* 1417: Sempronia depicted with the shoulder-cape section of her hood standing out over her face: instructions to illustrator reads '*ung chapperon la pate devant*' *Lebègue*, not paginated.

Robe royale
The name given to a set of garments worn by the royal family and the aristocracy, presumably on formal occasions. Incorporates many elements of dress 'frozen' from the fourteenth century. Male *robes royales*: 1405/6 for the princes: four garments of scarlet, *mantel, seurcot clos, seurcot ouvert, cotte simple*, with hoods and hose, *AN*, KK 43, f. 142. Female *robes royales*: 1405/6 for the princesses: five '*garnemens*', each of scarlet, *chappe, mantel aparer* (sic), *seurcot clos, seurcot ouvert* and *cotte simple*, *AN*, KK 43, f. 142. Compare the *robe à quatre garnemens* of the Duchess of Orléans in 1408 *le manteau à parer . . . fais de veluau en grainne brodé de perles, à ronces et à Vs. Une chappe de mesmes ouvrée de perles et brodée comme le dit manteau, laquelle est en deux pièces, et le chaperon d'icelle chappe. Ung surcot ouvert en deux pièces ouvré de perles, et brodé comme ladite chappe. Une cote simple du mesmes, ouvrée de perles, et brodé comme dessus, garnie de manches pareillement ouvrées, Orléans Inventory*, pp. 99–100. It is impossible to sort out the layers of the male *robe royale*, but it clearly involves a cloak and a tunic beneath it, sometimes having a hood draped over one shoulder. With the female *robe royale*, it is a little easier: there is sometimes a cloak over all, while underneath there is a gown open at the sides to reveal an under-dress. The 1405/6 outfits suggest that the innermost layer was the *cotte simple* (unlined kirtle?), over which was worn the *seurcot clos* (closed over-dress?) and then the *seurcot ouvert* (open-sided over-dress?), with the cloak (*mantel à parer*). To complete the outfit, the *chappe* may have been a shoulder-cape.

169. BELOW: A *robe royale* which can be studied in three dimensions on the statue of Jeanne de Bourbon in Jean de Berry's palace at Poitiers (1384–6), and with greater ease in a cast in the Musée des Monuments Français in Paris.

Acknowledgements

While I was writing this book, and even before, I received invaluable help from many people, which I acknowledge here. Dr Fedja Anzelewski of the Berlin Kupferstichkabinett tracked down an illustration for me; Dr Lorne Campbell of the Courtauld Institute of Art offered to read the Franco-Netherlandish section of my manuscript, and any errors which may remain after his thorough criticism are mine alone. Madame Micheline Comblen-Sonkes of the Centre de Recherches 'Primitifs Flamands' in Brussels gave me much assistance and tea when I consulted the photographs in her care. Jane Gingell of Leicester Polytechnic spent hours discussing the possible structure of garments with me, and Peter Martin and Joe Newton allowed themselves to be inveigled into cinemas when I needed brain-rest. At the Groeninge Museum in Bruges Vincent Molhamt and Francine Huys, of the conservation department, very kindly and enthusiastically showed me the Van der Goes 'St Hippolytus' panels when they were under their care, and discussed the X-rays and the discoveries they had made. My sister Carol Scott acted as uncomplaining porter through the cathedrals and museums of France. My editor Michael Stephenson showed unfailing interest and enthusiasm in the progress of the book. Mrs Mary Stewart, my head of school at Leicester Polytechnic, and Mrs Ruth Winter took too-great pains to acquire photographs for me in Paris during their summer holiday, and I apologize here for the trouble it caused them.

The staff of various libraries also helped: of the Archives Nationales and of the Bibliothèque Nationale in Paris; of the Bibliothèque Royale in Brussels and of the British Library in London, both in the department of printed books and the department of manuscripts.

Moira Knox, after more generously, perhaps, than wisely, offering to transform my unspeakable manuscript into typescript, then had to watch me cut up and re-assemble her work, as my initial enthusiasm led me to write too much; I am most grateful for the silent way in which she handed me the necessary scissors and glue.

Illustration Acknowledgements

Illustration 36 is reproduced by gracious permission of Her Majesty the Queen. The author and publishers would also like to thank the following for providing photographs and giving permission to reproduce them: A.C.L., Brussels; Albertina, Vienna; Alte Pinakothek, Munich; Bayerische Staatsbibliothek, Munich; Bibliothèque Nationale, Paris; Bibliotheque Royale, Brussels; Bildarchiv Preussischer Kulturbesitz, Berlin; Bodleian Library, Oxford; British Library, London; Centre Hospitalier de Beaune, Beaune; Courtauld Institute of Art, London; Eglise Notre-Dame, Ternant, Nièvre; Giraudon, Paris; Groeninge Museum, Bruges; Historisches Museum, Bamberg; Hôtel de Ville, Ypres; Koninklijk Museum voor Schone Kunsten, Antwerp; Kunstsammlungen der Veste Coburg, Coburg; Memlingmuseum O.C.M.W., Bruges; Metropolitan Museum of Art, New York; Musée Condé, Chantilly; Musée du Louvre, Paris; Musées Royaux des Beaux-Arts, Brussels; Museo Civico, Turin; Museo del Prado, Madrid; Museum Boymans-van Beuningen, Rotterdam; Museum Meermanno-Westreenainum, The Hague; National Gallery, London; National Gallery of Art, Washington; National Trust, Upton House; North Carolina Museum of Art, Raleigh, N.C.; Österreichische Nationalbibliothek, Vienna; Palais des Beaux-Arts, Lille; Pierpont Morgan Library, New York; M. Platteeuw, Bruges; Réunion des musées nationaux, Paris; Rheinisches Landesmuseum, Bonn; Rijksmuseum, Amsterdam; Rosgartenmuseum, Konstanz; St Baafskathedraal, Ghent; St Salvatorskathedraal, Bruges; Sammlungen Fürst Furstenberg, Donaueschingen; Sammlungen des Regierenden Fürsten von Liechtenstein, Vaduz; Executors of the late Count Seilern, London; Staatliche Museen Preussischer Kulturbesitz, Gemäldegalerie, Berlin (West); Staatsbibliothek, Stiftung Preussischer Kulturbesitz, Berlin; Staatsgalerie, Stuttgart; Staedelsches Kunstinstitut, Frankfurt; Städtisches Museum, Nördlingen; Uffizi, Florence; Walker Art Gallery, Liverpool.

Index